THE
MONEY DOCTOR
FINANCE ANNUAL

2011

Gill & Macmillan

Gill & Macmillan Ltd
Hume Avenue, Park West, Dublin 12
with associated companies throughout the world
www.gillmacmillan.ie

978 0 7171 4821 9

Print origination O'K Graphic Design, Dublin
Printed by Brunswick Press Ltd, Dublin
Index compiled by Cover to Cover

The paper used in this book is made from the wood pulp of managed forests. For every tree felled, at least one tree is planted, thereby renewing natural resources.

A catalogue record is available for this book from the British Library.

1 3 5 4 2

The publisher would like to acknowledge the following for the use of their logos: Life Insurance Association, The Irish Brokers Association, Professional Insurance Brokers Association, Financial Services Ombudsman, AIB, Bank of Ireland, Permanent TSB, National Irish Bank, Ulster Bank, the Credit Union, VHI Healthcare, Hibernian Aviva Health and Quinn Healthcare.

Photographs © Alamy and Getty.

Whilst every effort has been made to ensure accuracy, no legal or other liability on the part of the author or publishers can be accepted for any information or advice given.

CONTENTS

PART 2 YOUR FINANCIAL RIGHTS

PART 7 PLANNING FOR A RICHER RETIREMENT

PREFACE

Welcome to the 2011 edition of Ireland's most comprehensive finance guide and thank you for making last year's edition the bestselling financial reference guide in Ireland.

2010 will for some have been the calm before the storm but by the time you have read through this book, you will 'feel glowy, warm and hopeful' (*The Money Doctor Finance Annual 2010* as reviewed by Claire O'Mahony in the *Sunday Tribune T2*, 27 June 2010).

While there was stability in ECB interest rates in 2010 (the European Central Bank rate remains at 1% and will in every likelihood stay at this level until at least the last quarter of 2011 – good news for *tracker mortgage* borrowers) some lenders chose to raise *standard variable* interest rates in an effort to compensate for the loss-making *tracker* rates that the fortunate majority of borrowers enjoy.

Borrowings on an interest-only basis when the interest-only term had expired were, in most cases, begrudgingly extended for between six and 12 months in proven cases of hardship. For some of these borrowers, though, being forced to repay capital in cases where one or both borrowers are out of work can lead to bankruptcy and repossession.

I have included a special appendix in this issue, *The quick and easy way to fix your finances* (Appendix 9), which deals with all aspects of debt and how to cope with it – no matter how bleak the picture may be. The number one consideration is addressing the debt, communicating with your lender at all times and not putting your head in the sand.

For the younger reader (aged five to ten years) there is an eight-page supplement (Appendix 10: *Money – it's child's play*) to start them on their way to understanding money and appreciate what a good job Mum and Dad do! All you have to do is cut it out, staple the pages and give them to your children.

2010 saw the introduction of the *National Asset Management Agency* (NAMA) in a bid to corral the *toxic debts* or *impaired loans* of some of the Irish financial institutions – all €77 billion of them. And there's more, to borrow one comedian's catchphrase: Bank of Ireland had a successful rights issue which further strengthened the notion that investing in banks may still be a good idea.

Borrowing, however, became a contentious issue for the SME (small business) and private sectors. The continuing lack of liquidity, primarily in the mainstream banks, along with the resulting increasing cost of funding put paid to earlier generosity towards these sectors, despite protestations that applications were being approved. In fairness to some of these lenders, it may have been difficult to justify further facilities with some businesses.

The government also introduced a number of fiscal and structural reforms in banking, including the appointments of a new *Central Bank* governor (Professor Patrick Honahan) and a *Financial Regulator* (Mr Matthew Elderfield). Already their positive effects have been felt. In October, the functions carried out by the Financial Regulator were merged with those of the *Central Bank* to form a new *Central Bank of Ireland*.

Some reports alluded to lenders' *gross negligence* and *reckless lending*. Heads rolled – but not wealth – and there are now numerous solicitors, barristers, management consultants, accountants and other professional entities eagerly anticipating juicy litigation and tribunal contracts over the coming years.

The Irish stock market continued to improve, albeit from a very low base, following the world's worst performances in 2007 and 2008. *Doom* and *gloom* are still the buzz words, **but** don't panic – there are still some of us who beat a more positive drum.

In this 2011 edition, all the changes from Budget 2010 have been made, and I have also summarised Budget 2011 – described as the harshest ever – in Appendix 11, but don't despair; by reading this book you *can* save and make money, and you *will* survive.

My new revamped website – www.moneydoctor.ie – now houses a revised *100 Top Tax Tips* and the *Money Doctor's Jargon Buster*. Follow us on Twitter, Facebook, LinkedIn and Plaxo and you can also subscribe to our newsletter at no cost.

I have included a section in this year's *Annual* for those wanting to press the flesh when it comes to financial advice. In *Money Doctor Services* (Appendix 6) I have highlighted two main services – *Money Doctor Seminars* (aimed at company owners, employers, CEOs and HR departments) and *Money Doctor Personal Financial Reviews*. The reviews are aimed at anyone who wishes to regularise, optimise and structure their finances – or better manage their money. There are TWO types of review: in-depth or prescriptive. You can avail of these through the *Money Doctor* office or the offices of self-employed financial advisers, having their own authorisation from the Central Bank of Ireland and their appointment letter from *Money Doctor*.

Therefore if you do need a **personal, one-to-one financial review**, someone to give you solid independent and authorised advice, you should consider the advantages of a consultation with a **Money Doctor**. Go directly to our website (www.moneydoctor.ie) or email me directly (jlowe@moneydoctor.ie). You can also contact the **Administration Manager** (+353 1 278 5555 or administrator@moneydoctor.ie) to organise an appointment with myself or your own preferred **Money Doctor adviser**.

I often use the following analogy to explain why financial planning is so important:

If you were driving from, say, Cork to Belfast you wouldn't choose a road at random and hope that it would take you where you wanted to get. Rather, you would plan your journey in advance. If, as you travelled, you encountered diversions, you'd get out the road map and decide on the new route. Throughout the journey you'd check your progress.

This book will act then as both a planner and a map on your journey to sound finances.

For many years I have felt that Ireland lacked an annual finance guide that offered genuinely helpful, accurate and independent money advice in language that anyone could understand. I believe that this book fills the gap. Why?

- It is **comprehensive**. Every possible subject has been covered – from getting the best deal on your mortgage to saving for retirement and from slashing your tax bill to working overseas.
- No less importantly, it is packed with **practical** advice. Whatever your circumstances, whatever questions you need answered, whatever your financial goals – you'll find the answers in the following pages.
- All the information here is presented in **plain, jargon-free English** and accompanied by **action-oriented** tips. You'll find real-life examples, checklists and a comprehensive index, too.

The book has also been written for 2011 – and so it is 'bang up to date'.

MORE THAN A BOOK

Actually, I am referring to this as a 'book' – but really it is more of a 'service', because there is also a website with lots of extra information. So if you need personalised advice you can always email me additional questions at: jlowe@moneydoctor.ie.

THE BIGGER PICTURE

Another advantage that this book has over anything else available in Ireland is that it provides lots of guidance on financial planning. So you can use this book to resolve specific issues (such as paying off all your loans or cutting the cost of your insurance) or to create your own money plan.

WHY THE MONEY DOCTOR?

The short answer is that I aim to do for your wealth what a medical doctor will do for your health. That is to say, I will show you how to overcome any financial 'illnesses' you may be suffering from and also how to improve your financial fitness dramatically. I don't want to stretch the analogy too far but you can rely on me – as you would rely on a good doctor – to be honest, trustworthy and professional. I'm qualified and I'm experienced.

That's the short answer. Now let me give you the slightly longer answer.

In 1999, at the age of 47, I resigned from my job as senior manager of an Irish bank and turned my back on 27 years of working for mainstream financial institutions. I gave up job security, a pension, a company car and five weeks a year paid holiday. This wasn't the act of a mad man, but the act of someone who had had enough of 'selling' and wanted to start 'telling'.

There is a lot that's still right with our financial services sector. It is now relatively well regulated and offers both choice and value. But it has one major flaw: it is sales driven, not *solution* driven. Banks, building societies and insurance companies always promote their own products rather than someone else's – even if their products are less appropriate and/or more expensive. This has led to a great deal of consumer cynicism and – quite frankly – suspicion. The reason why I gave up my job and changed direction was because I wanted to be above such suspicion. I wanted to be independent – free to do what was best for the 'patient'.

With my first book and this, my sixth finance annual – together with the revamped www.moneydoctor.ie website – I aim to fill what I perceive to be a real gap in the market. That is to say:
- reliable, up-to-date and accurate personal finance information
- unbiased, easy-to-understand and relevant financial advice.

In particular, I cover both the principles of better financial management and the practical aspects of taking financial decisions. *The Money Doctor* will answer all your questions about how to make the most of your money. If there is something you feel I have left out please let me know so that I can include it in future editions.

ONE FINAL POINT

Dealing with money shouldn't be a chore, but a pleasure. Whether you read this book from cover to cover or dip in and out, I hope it will inspire you in all your future financial dealings. It's not about waiting for the storm to pass, it's about learning to dance in the rain.

John Lowe
Dublin, December 2010

IS THIS BOOK FOR YOU?

This book is for everyone living in Ireland who wants to better manage and structure their personal finances.

- You will find this book relevant, regardless of your financial position, age or gender.
- One of the most important aspects of the guide is that it concentrates on 'how to' information, as in: how to cut the cost of your mortgage, how to get rid of your debts, how to build up savings, how to save tax and how to protect your family.
- If there is a particular subject you want to learn about, then check the detailed contents page or the index.
- The book is written in plain English and contains plenty of:
    - case histories
    - real-life examples
    - checklists
    - action-orientated advice.
- The book is divided into nine sections covering every aspect of personal finance. It is an annual handbook so the information it contains will be up to date, and include the latest budgetary and legislative changes.
- Each chapter begins with a summary and ends with a list of action points.
- Decision trees (Appendix 2) are designed to help you make a decision by setting out the logic process graphically and allowing you to easily retrace the steps made in coming to that decision. While they are not a substitute for proper research, they can enhance the user's ability to implement what they know.

Look out for the symbols used throughout the book:

Money Doctor Wealth Warning This symbol is used to warn you about something that may have an adverse affect on your financial wealth!

Money Doctor Wealth Check This symbol is used to highlight something that could really improve your financial fitness.

GETTING THE MOST OUT OF THIS BOOK

The Money Doctor says this book will be of relevance to you if you
- have money questions and don't know to whom to turn for an honest, accurate, unbiased answer
- want the latest financial information
- want to reduce your tax bill
- worry about money
- have, or plan to get, a mortgage
- have credit cards, store cards, hire purchase agreements, an overdraft, personal loans, a mortgage or any other borrowings, because it will show you how it is possible to pay all these debts off in a matter of years simply by following a simple, proven, logical plan
- have money on deposit or save money on a regular basis
- want to build up your capital worth and guarantee yourself a comfortable (and possibly an early) retirement
- have capital and don't know how to invest it
- have dependants and you are worried about their well-being
- have (or think you should have) any sort of life or critical illness cover
- worry about the quality of financial advice you are receiving
- are separating, or thinking of it.

THE MONEY DOCTOR WEBSITE

The Money Doctor is not just a book: it is a complete service. Visit the free Money Doctor website at www.moneydoctor.ie. The Money Doctor website offers you:
- extra articles and checklists covering a huge range of personal finance topics
- the latest personal finance tips, advice and information
- 100 top tax tips (updated regularly)
- jargon buster
- up-to-the-minute mortgage and investment rates
- special calculators allowing you to see (at the press of a button) what your mortgage or other loan will cost you – as well as how much your savings will earn you
- an online interactive budget planner

- timely information such as the current tax rates and allowances
- the chance to arrange a consultation with the Money Doctor or one of the Money Doctor advisers
- podcasts on a variety of financial subjects
- an opportunity to receive the Money Doctor's free monthly newsletter or e-zine, join on Facebook, Twitter, LinkedIn, plus read the weekly Money Doctor blog.

The website is updated daily and all the information it contains is available *free* – without charge and without obligation.

You should only deal with an Authorised Advisor to provide insurance, investment and pension advice and deal with a Mortgage Intermediary who has formal authorised agencies with lenders to provide credit services. This will mean that they are legally obliged to provide you with the best possible or most appropriate advice.

You can be certain that any individual or firm who is authorised will not only have had to pass a stringent series of tests to qualify, but that their performance will be strictly monitored on an ongoing basis.

Extra consumer protection

You should be aware that there are a number of professional bodies covering the financial services industry. My own belief is that you should only deal with members of these bodies. These are:

Irish Brokers association

- The Irish Brokers Association (IBA).

- Professional Insurance Brokers Association (PIBA).

PIBA

- Life Insurance Association (LIA).

The professional association for those who give and support financial advice

Your financial adviser should ideally be a QFA (Qualified Financial Adviser) as well as having substantial financial experience. Individual membership of other professional bodies, such as the Institute of Bankers in Ireland, is also desirable.

Finally, if you are looking for advice on buying company shares then you should deal with intermediaries who are members of (or affiliated members of) the Irish Stock Exchange or an Authorised Advisor.

Don't allow yourself to be talked into accepting advice from someone who isn't both independent and qualified. If in doubt visit my website – www.moneydoctor.ie.

ACKNOWLEDGMENTS

There are many people who deserve a clap on the back for their personal help and support to me and who have guided me throughout my career. Included are family, friends, mentors and colleagues. Special mention and special thanks go to the following for their great assistance in the production of this my sixth book:

My family who continue to support and love me. Jonathan Self (writer, novelist and mentor). George Butler (Money Doctor). John P. Carlin (friend, accountant and Co. Tyrone supporter). Simon Carty (Solicitor). Monica McInerney (best-selling novelist) for her introduction to my publishers Gill & Macmillan. Nora Mahony (proofreader), Aoife O'Kelly (Managing Editor) and all the talented team at G&M – every one a gem. Fergal Tobin (Gill & Macmillan) for his fantastic help and for giving me the excuse to tell my friends I was having lunch with my publisher! Special thanks to RTÉ, Newstalk 106FM, Today FM, 4 FM, East Coast Radio, Sunshine Radio, Q 102, FM 104, LMFM, Clare FM and the myriad of radio stations around the country for their great support.

PART 1

HOW TO BECOME FINANCIALLY FIT IN 2011

IT ALL COMES DOWN TO BELIEF PATTERNS

I am far too practical a person to be taken in by 'psycho-babble'. However, I do believe that *if you want to be financially better off than you are at the moment then you simply must come to grips with your own belief patterns as they relate to money.* One method of explaining what I mean is to quote some of the different things people have said to me about money:

> 'I would always shop around for a better deal on most things – but not on financial products.'
>
> 'I hate talking about money. I find it embarrassing.'
>
> 'Money seems to slip through my fingers.'
>
> 'I worry about money all the time but I don't do anything about it, because I am not sure what to do.'
>
> 'Money is boring. We have enough. Why think about it?'

In my experience almost everyone has deeply held beliefs in relation to money – usually negative beliefs. Most can be attributed to one or more of the following factors:

Formative experiences. Take, for instance, the case of someone whose family suffered financial hardship when they were growing up. Naturally, it would influence their attitude to money.

Parental influence. Some parents talk about money, others don't – but either way, children can end up being worried about there not being enough. By the same token, some parents are spendthrift while others are positively tight-fisted – again influencing their children's beliefs.

Lack of education. Though there have been recent moves to change the national curriculum, 'personal finance' is still not really taught properly in our schools.

The mystification of money. Financial institutions seem to conspire to make money as mysterious a subject as possible.

Lack of trust in personal finance professionals. Bank managers are viewed as 'fair-weather friends' and the institutions they work for as impersonal and greedy. Insurance and pensions salespeople are hardly revered in society. People are suspicious of the experts they rely on to give them advice.

Society's attitude to money. There are some societies where money is discussed openly. In Ireland, however, it is considered rude to talk about money and crass to spend too much time managing it.

THE LINK BETWEEN BELIEF AND BEHAVIOUR

There is no doubt in my mind that there is a direct link between (a) what you believe about money, (b) your behaviour in relation to money and (c) how much money you end up having. The fact is that if you view money in a negative way, you are reducing your chances of a financially stable life. You aren't giving yourself a proper chance.

What's more, if you think that sorting out your personal finances will take more time and effort than *not* sorting them out, think again. Not paying attention to money is likely to result in you:

- wasting a vast amount of energy worrying
- wasting a vast amount of cash
- putting yourself and your dependants at risk
- reducing your standard of living
- increasing the number of years you have to work
- suffering a shortfall in your pension fund when you reach retirement age.

If you start to *think* positively about money, I guarantee that you will begin to *behave* more positively about money. And if you behave more positively about money, I guarantee that you will find yourself able to build up much greater wealth.

What are your financial dreams?

- To own your own home without a mortgage?
- To have enough money to retire early?
- To be wealthy enough to pay for all the things you want – such as an education for your children or a second home – without going into debt?

Whatever your dreams, unless you are very, very lucky, the only way to make them come true is to make a proper plan. Such a plan – a financial plan – will help ensure that you get from where you are to where you want to be. Creating one is a lot simpler and quicker than you may imagine, as I explain in this section of the book. Furthermore, I guarantee that the process of writing a plan will – in itself – make you substantially better off. Why? Read on and you'll find out.

MONEY DOCTOR WEALTH CHECK

The section on financial planning explains:

- what a financial plan is
- why you need a financial plan
- the different stages involved in writing a financial plan
- practical tips on writing your own plan
- where to get professional financial planning help you can trust
- sample financial plans.

And more besides. Everything, in fact, you need to make financial planning easy.

1
ALL IT TAKES IS A LITTLE PLANNING

HOW YOUR FINANCIAL PLAN WILL MAKE YOU BETTER OFF

Many people are under the impression that financial planning is a complex process requiring great expertise. In fact, creating a financial plan is a remarkably straightforward activity involving three easy steps:

1 Decide what your financial or money objectives are, and prioritise them.

2 Assess what resources you have available to you now, and consider what resources you may have in the future.

3 Work out what actions you need to take to make your financial (or your 'money') objectives come true.

This short chapter explains the 'ins and outs' of writing a first-class financial plan. The next chapter explains, in greater detail, how to write your own.

WHY YOU NEED A FINANCIAL PLAN

Your financial plan should have the same qualities as the road map analogy as described in the introduction. That is to say, it should help you reach your destination; make your journey as fast as possible; and prevent you wasting time or energy.

MONEY DOCTOR WEALTH CHECK

A little planning brings big rewards

Having a financial plan will bring both *material* and *emotional* rewards. From a **material** perspective a financial plan will make it possible for you to meet your financial objectives. These might include some or all of the following:

- wiping out all your personal debts
- paying off your mortgage years earlier
- never having to borrow again

- having enough money to afford the things that are important to you, such as an education for your children or a second home
- having enough money to retire early
- knowing that you and your dependants are protected against financial hardships
- being wealthy enough never to have to worry about the future – whatever it may bring.

And the **emotional** benefits? You'll feel a tangible peace of mind once you have your financial affairs in order. In addition, a well-considered financial plan guarantees that you will never need to waste energy worrying about money again.

Some people's circumstances, of course, may be such that they will not manage to achieve any or all of these objectives. For these people, financial planning is crucial to getting the maximum advantage from limited resources.

SUPPOSING YOU DON'T PLAN?

Suppose you don't bother with a financial plan at all? Leaving something as important as your financial future to chance is risky. True, we live in a country with a relatively generous state benefit system. But would you really want to rely on it? You probably wouldn't starve, but you wouldn't have an easy time of it.

Incidentally, many people assume that the worst thing anyone can do is ignore financial planning completely. In fact, in my experience the people who are worst off are those who *compartmentalise* their money decisions. Let me give you just three examples:

1 When you want to buy a home, you look for a mortgage.
2 When you begin to think about retirement, you start a pension.
3 When you have a young family, you take out life insurance.

The trouble with a compartmentalised approach to money is that it is both wasteful and risky because you may:

- end up spending more than you have to on borrowing money
- by default, pay more tax than you need to
- end up with inferior and expensive financial products

- risk your capital, your income, and the standard of living of you and your dependants
- miss opportunities and
- make yourself unhappy worrying about your financial security.

A symptom of this approach is responding to ad hoc situations in a knee-jerk manner, for example, subscribing for newly issued shares on a whim, or paying for education fees when you hadn't expected to do so.

INSTANT SAVINGS AND MORE

Incidentally, one of the key benefits of creating a financial plan is that it will involve a review of your existing financial products. Such a review is bound to result in all sorts of savings as you identify products that are either over-priced or unnecessary. Let me give you just one real-life example:

> One of the Money Doctor's 'patients', Tony, an ex-banker, told me that he'd spent more time choosing his last car than choosing his mortgage. As a result he was, without realising it, paying 1% above the home loan market rate. He'd also allowed himself to be sold a very expensive life insurance plan. I calculated that, over the 25-year term of Tony's €210,000 mortgage, these two products alone would cost him a staggering additional €38,000 in unnecessary loan and insurance payments.

Frankly, because people pay less attention to their finances than to other areas of their lives, they tend to get 'ripped off'. With a financial plan in place, you'll know that you aren't:

- accepting lower rates of return on your savings
- paying more tax than you have to
- paying more to borrow than you have to
- taking out insurance policies that you don't need, or that don't provide you with the protection that you want, and that may well be over-priced
- making poor investment decisions
- failing to plan properly for your retirement or
- putting your money at risk.

WHAT DOES A FINANCIAL PLAN LOOK LIKE?

Your financial plan may be no more than a single piece of paper on which you've jotted down appropriate notes. You might think of it in the same way that you think of a career plan or any other sort of life plan. It is to guide you, save you time, and ensure that none of your effort is wasted. Or, if you are comfortable using spreadsheet software, you could also do it electronically. Whatever way you choose to complete a financial plan, remember it is essential for giving you a map for your financial road to the future.

HOW LONG SHOULD A FINANCIAL PLAN LAST FOR?

Obviously, there is no set period for a financial plan. My general advice is to write it so that it covers the **current** and **next phase** of your life. For instance, if you've just left university and you're starting your first job, then you might write a financial plan designed to take you through to when you own your home. Bear in mind that financial plans need to be *flexible*. You may change your own ideas about what you want or circumstances may intervene and require a change of direction.

A financial plan that only covers a specific, short-term requirement (for instance, saving for your retirement) isn't going to bring you lasting financial success.

IF YOU THINK YOU NEED HELP

You will find everything you need to write your own financial plan in this book. However, you may decide you'd like some professional help. There are any number of people who would like to help you with your personal finances, from bank managers to life insurance salespeople, from credit brokers to pension specialists.

> **The golden rule is: the fewer options the 'experts' can offer you, the less you should trust them.**

Let me give you one pertinent example. If you go to your bank and express an interest in taking out a pension, whoever you speak to is duty bound to offer you something from the bank's own range of products, if they have their own tied agency, even if he or she knows that you would get a better deal elsewhere. If, on the other hand, you go to an independent financial adviser (an Authorised Advisor for insurance and investments or a mortgage intermediary who has access to agencies with *all* the lenders) he or she will recommend the best and most competitively priced product for your needs. For more tips on getting professional help, see p. 29.

THE MONEY DOCTOR SAYS...

- There is nothing in the least bit complicated about writing a financial plan. It is simply a matter of working out what your money ambitions are, how far you have got to date, and what action you need to take to get to where you want to go.

- Unless you are very, very lucky, the only way you are going to make your financial dreams come true is by planning.

- Your plan may be a single piece of paper with a few notes.

- The process of writing a plan is likely to bring big savings as you identify financial products you have already bought that are either (a) over-priced or (b) not really necessary.

- Everything you need to write a financial plan is in this book. But if you want help, use an Authorised Advisor or mortgage intermediary who has authorised agencies with all the lenders. Their assistance could well be free.

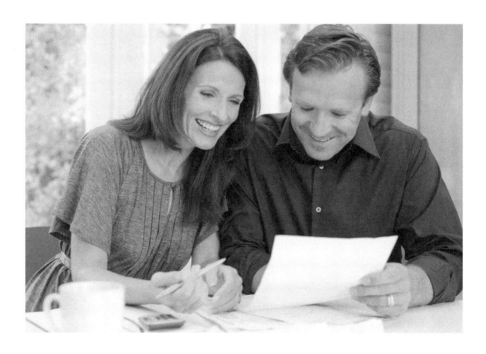

2
WRITING A FINANCIAL PLAN

EVERYTHING YOU NEED TO KNOW TO WRITE YOUR OWN FINANCIAL PLAN (OR TO GET SOMEONE ELSE TO DO IT FOR YOU)

If you've put off writing a financial plan because you thought it would be both time consuming and tedious, then this chapter will reassure you. Not only is it possible to produce a detailed financial plan in a matter of hours but as you get involved in the process you may find it considerably more interesting than you ever imagined.

MONEY DOCTOR WEALTH CHECK

First things first

Many people begin the whole financial planning process because they want to resolve a particular financial question. But you shouldn't look at financial needs in isolation. Every financial decision you make should be part of an overall plan. Thus, a particular product – such as a mortgage, loan, insurance policy or investment – should not just be judged on its own particular merits but also in terms of how it moves you closer to your financial objectives. For this reason, no financial plan can be created until you have set and prioritised your **financial objectives**.

HOW DO YOU DECIDE WHAT YOUR FINANCIAL OBJECTIVES SHOULD BE?

My advice is to start by **dreaming**. Consider what you'd like to be doing in, say, five years' time, ten years' time, and twenty years' time. Consider what work (if any) you'll be doing, where you'll be living, and how you'll be spending your leisure time. What will your family situation be? Once you have a clear picture of the future life you'd like to have, start expressing it in financial terms.

Your possible financial objectives might include:

- owning your own home, outright, without a mortgage

- making sure you have sufficient income to retire (possibly early) and live in comfort
- ensuring that you and your dependants will not suffer financial hardship regardless of any misfortunes that may befall you
- having sufficient wealth to pay for things that you consider important, whether it's charitable donations, an education for your children, or some other item such as a second home or a caravan
- having sufficient wealth to allow you to spend your time as you wish, for instance, having the money to start your own business.

PRIORITISING YOUR FINANCIAL OBJECTIVES

Having produced a list of financial objectives, your next task should be to put them in **order of priority**.

What you consider important will be determined to a great extent by your personal circumstances. For instance, if you're in third-level education, you'll have a very different view of money to someone five years away from retirement. Someone with a lot of debts will have different concerns to someone with a lump sum to invest.

Nevertheless, regardless of your age, existing wealth, health, number of dependants, or – for that matter – any other factor, I would recommend that you keep the following principles in mind when deciding what your financial priorities should be:

1   For most people, their greatest asset is their **income**. Unless you are fortunate enough to receive a windfall, it is almost certainly your income which you will use to achieve your financial objectives. Under the circumstances you don't want to risk it and you don't want to waste it. There are all sorts of inexpensive insurance policies designed to protect your income. And by making sure that you don't waste a single cent (especially when buying financial services) you can ensure that it's used to optimum purpose.
2   **Personal debt** – by which I mean everything from store cards to mortgages – will be the biggest drain on your income. If you've borrowed money (and, obviously there are many circumstances under which this makes excellent sense) then you should make it a priority to repay your loans as quickly as possible. This is easily achievable as I explain in Part 3.
3   It's vital to have a safety net or **emergency fund** to deal with those little

trials, tribulations and extra expenses that life often throws our way. In Part 6, I suggest how much this fund should be, and the best way to build it up.

4 If you've got a good, secure income, it doesn't actually matter what other assets you own. Emotionally, it's nice to have the security of owning your own home. Financially, it certainly makes sense. But, actually, the best investment that most people could ever make is in a really decent **pension plan**. With a good pension plan you can leave work early and – if you live to 100 or more – never have to worry about money again. One of the best things about modern pension plans is that they are both flexible and diverse.

5 It is not inconceivable that we will live to a very old age and in some cases suffer a reduction in our mental ability to handle money matters. Before this may arise it is worth considering setting up an **enduring power of attorney**. This is a document providing for the management of a person's affairs in the event of their becoming mentally incapacitated. The appointed person (the 'attorney') may be allowed to take a wide range of actions on your behalf in relation to property, business and social affairs. He or she may make payments from the specified accounts, make appropriate provision for any specified person's needs and make appropriate gifts to the donor's relations or friends. You can appoint anyone you wish to be your attorney, including a spouse, family member, friend, colleague, etc.

6 **Know thyself!** There's no point in setting financial objectives that you're going to find impossible to attain. Your financial objectives may involve modest changes in your behaviour, but they shouldn't require a complete change in your personality!

TEN UNIVERSAL NEEDS

Ultimately, financial planning is about tailoring a solution to meet your precise requirements. Having said this, there are a number of 'universal' needs that most of us face. To my mind they are:

1 Having an emergency fund to cover unexpected expenses.
2 Paying off any expensive personal loans and credit card debt.
3 Short-term saving for cars, holidays, and so forth.
4 Income protection, in case you are unable to work for any reason.
5 Life assurance for you (and, if relevant, your partner).

6   Starting a pension plan (in my opinion it is never too early).
7   Buying a home with the help of a mortgage.
8   Saving for major purchases.
9   Planning for education fees (if you have children), whether for private school or university.
10 Building up your personal investments.

To this, I suppose I might add long-term care planning if you're worried that your pension and/or the state may not provide for you sufficiently in retirement.

SETTING REALISTIC AIMS

If you had unlimited funds, then you could achieve all your financial ambitions without difficulty and you wouldn't need a financial plan. As it is, for most of us life is more complicated. Since we can't have everything we want instantly, we need to set realistic targets and work towards them in easy stages. To make sure we have realistic targets we must test them. Let me give you an example:

> David is 40 and self-employed. His objective is to be financially independent by the age of 55. At that point he wants to be able to live comfortably without working. His current income is €40,000 a year and he feels that he'll be able to manage on much less, say €25,000 a year, once he retires. To achieve this, he'll need capital resources of between €500,000 and €600,000. At this point in time he has a pension fund worth €100,000 which, if it grows in real terms (i.e. after the effects of inflation) by 5% a year, will be worth some €208,000 in 15 years. He also has €25,000 of stocks and shares, which he expects to grow at a slightly faster rate, say 7% a year, which would mean an extra €74,000 in 15 years.

> In other words, David has a shortfall of between €212,000 and €312,000. To fill this shortfall, he would have to save at least €600 a month (assuming a growth rate of at least 7%) until he reaches 55. However, €600 a month, or more, is a lot of cash to find, so he may have to adjust his expectations. Perhaps he could live on less? Or postpone his retirement an extra five years? Or earn additional money?

> **Note: this example is just to give you a feel for what I'm talking about. Inflation would need to be taken into account when deciding what to do. I have ignored current pension returns and low growth rates. Everything is cyclical.**

Once you settle on your overall objectives, you'll have to decide which is the most important to you. For instance, would you rather pay off your mortgage ten years early, or take an annual holiday overseas? Is being able to retire early more important than putting your children through private school?

You must also weigh up other priorities. I always recommend that those with dependants take out income protection insurance before they take out life cover. Why? Anyone under retirement age is 20 times more likely to be unable to work for a prolonged period due to sickness than they are to die. Another recommendation I often make is that people with high personal debt pay it off or consolidate it before they start saving money. This is because it costs more to borrow than you can hope to earn from most forms of low-risk investment.

Anyway, the two key points I want to make are:

1 Keep your financial expectations realistic.
2 Test them to make sure.

HOW FAR HAVE YOU GOT?

If the first stage of a financial plan involves deciding what you want, then the second stage is all about working out where you've got to so far. You need to produce an honest and realistic assessment of:

- what resources you have
- what demands there are on your resources and
- what action you are already taking to meet your targets.

Once you have this information you'll know what surplus is available to you and whether you have a shortfall that needs to be made up.

If you visit my website – www.moneydoctor.ie – you'll find several aids to helping you make and reach your goals. Otherwise, you can use the questionnaire that follows.

YOUR MONTHLY INCOME AND OUTGOINGS

I usually suggest that people start with their income and – if relevant – their spouse/partner's income. The best way to calculate it is as follows:

Monthly income – gross	You €	Spouse/partner €
Salary or wages		
Profits from business		

	You	Spouse/partner
Investment income	_____	_____
State benefits	_____	_____
Pensions	_____	_____
Other earnings	_____	_____
Anything else	_____	_____
Subtotal A	€ _____	_____
Less tax (PRSI and income tax)	_____	_____
Subtotal B	€ _____	

The resulting figure (Subtotal B) is your disposable income. You now need to consider how you spend it.

Monthly outgoings	You €	Spouse/partner €
Rent/mortgage	_____	_____
Utilities (gas, electricity, telephone, etc.)	_____	_____
Food	_____	_____
Household items	_____	_____
Drink	_____	_____
Car(s)	_____	_____
Home insurance	_____	_____
Life insurance	_____	_____
Other insurance	_____	_____
Clothes	_____	_____
Child-related expenses	_____	_____
Credit cards	_____	_____
Other loan repayments	_____	_____
Spending money	_____	_____
Pension contribution	_____	_____
Regular saving plans	_____	_____
Anything else	_____	_____
Subtotal C	€ _____	

By subtracting your monthly outgoings (Subtotal C) from your disposable income (Subtotal B) you will arrive at your available surplus. Don't despair if this is a 'minus' figure. That's why you are reading this book – and, together, we are going to do something about it!

YOUR ASSETS

Working out what assets you have involves the same process as working out
what your surplus income is. You need to tot up the value of everything you
own and subtract any debts or other liabilities you may have.

Start with a list of the assets themselves:

Assets	You €	Spouse/partner €
Home		
Personal belongings		
Furniture and contents of home		
Car(s)		
Other property		
Other valuables		
Cash		
Savings		
Shares		
Other investments		
Subtotal D	€	

With regard to any investments you have – savings plans or a pension, for
instance – you may want to work out what they will be worth at whatever point
in the future you intend to cash them in. This can be a complex business. A
pension fund, for instance, may grow by more or less than the predicted
amount. Therefore, it could be well worth your while to get professional
assistance with your calculations.

YOUR LIABILITIES

Liabilities	You €	Spouse/partner €
Mortgage		
Credit card debts		
Personal loans		
Hire purchase		
Overdraft		
Other loans		
Tax		
Other liabilities		
Subtotal E	€	

By subtracting your total liabilities (Subtotal E) from the value of your assets (Subtotal D) you will arrive at what financial experts call your 'net worth'. While it not good if this is a 'minus' figure, once again you shouldn't despair. The whole purpose of a money plan is to strengthen your finances.

THE IMPORTANCE OF MAKING ASSUMPTIONS

All financial planning requires 'assumptions'. Some of these assumptions will be personal to you, such as how much income you expect to earn in the future or how many children you anticipate supporting. Other assumptions will be related to factors only partly within your control, such as the return you can expect to receive for a particular investment. You'll also need to allow for financial factors beyond your control, such as the state of the economy. When making assumptions, the longer the period you're planning for, the less accurate your assumptions will be. It's very hard to predict exactly what you'll be earning in, say, five or ten years, let alone what you'll be earning in twenty years.

In order to improve the quality of their assumptions, many people use historic figures for guidance. Below, I've detailed some statistics that you may find of help.

Inflation. There was a time when inflation had the single greatest influence on the economy and thus on financial planning. Although inflation has been quite low for the last few years, it still has a marked effect on the cost of borrowing and the value of your investments. Over the last ten years inflation has averaged 3.2% a year in Ireland. Over the last twenty years it has averaged 3.5% a year. At its peak, in the 1970s, inflation was running at 18% a year.

Interest rates. Interest rates vary enormously, especially when you are borrowing. For instance, in 2010, when a typical mortgage cost 2.6% per year, you could pay up to 18% on a typical store card. Over the last ten years the average mortgage rate has actually been c.6% a year, though in 1995 it did reach 12% a year. During the same period the average personal loan rate has been 12% a year, and the average rate for deposits in a bank or building society has been 3% a year.

Investments. Not only do the returns on different types of investment vary dramatically, so do the returns within each sort of investment vehicle. So, while investing in the stock market could bring a better average return than investing in property, an individual investor might do substantially better or worse in one or the other. In general, it is best to spread your money between different types of investment, and to assume an average return of between 4% and 7% a year in real terms. For instance, over the last ten years the average return from government bonds has been 4.7% a year, while the average return on the stock market has been 10.1% (not including the last three years).

MONEY DOCTOR WEALTH CHECK

How much capital will you need?

One of the hardest calculations anyone has to make is how much capital they need to provide a sufficient income for their needs. There are different factors affecting this: inflation, tax and investment performance.

On the whole, my advice is to assume a 2.5% return after inflation and tax. This means that for every €1,000 of annual income you require, you'll need €40,000 of capital. Put another way, if you want an annual income of €20,000 a year you'll need at least €800,000 worth of capital.

MONEY DOCTOR WEALTH WARNING

An important reminder

Do you have a will? If you do, when did you last update it? Are you taking *full* advantage of all the tax allowances and exemptions to make sure that your beneficiaries don't have to pay unnecessary inheritance tax?

If you are over 18 (or if you are younger, but married) you should draw up a will because if you don't, your money will be distributed in accordance with the Succession Act of 1965. This means that your estate could end up not going to your chosen beneficiary or beneficiaries and could even end up filling the government's coffers.

You'll find more information about using your will to save capital acquisition tax on the Money Doctor website (www.moneydoctor.ie). Don't forget, both you and your partner should draw up a will and you should also consider:

- giving a power of attorney to someone you trust should you become physically incapacitated – an enduring power of attorney
- a living will explaining anything you would like done should you become so unwell as to be unable to communicate.

WHERE DO YOU NEED TO TAKE ACTION?

Which areas of your personal finances should you be dealing with first? Answer the questions below with a 'yes', 'no', or 'maybe'. Every question you answer with a 'no' or 'maybe' suggests an area where you need to take action.

- Do you spend less than you earn each month?
- Are you satisfied with your standard of living?
- Do your pay your credit card and charge card bills in full, on time, every month?
- Have you taken out sufficient life cover to ensure that your family's lifestyle won't be adversely affected if you die?
- Are you happy with where you live? Is it costing more than you can afford?
- If you had to manage without an income, would you be able to support yourself for at least three months using money you have saved?
- Do you have a clear sense of financial goals? Have you spent any time thinking about how you're going to achieve them?
- Do you have a pension? Will it be sufficient to support you in reasonable comfort?
- Do you have a will?
- Do you have other investments designed to bring you long-term capital growth?

THE MONEY DOCTOR SAYS...

- If you are not sure where to begin – begin at the beginning. Work out what you want from your money – what your priorities are.
- Although everyone's circumstances are different, we all have the same basic needs – to secure our future regardless of what happens. This is done through a combination of saving, investment and insurance.
- Take a little time to work out where you are financially – it may be the most profitable half hour you ever spend.
- Don't be shy about asking for help. If you know you want to sort out your finances, but find it difficult, call in expert help.

3
MONEY IS A FAMILY AFFAIR

HOW FAMILIES CAN WORK TOGETHER TO ACHIEVE LONG-TERM FINANCIAL SECURITY

Anyone who has been in a settled relationship will know that money and love can be a potent combination – both good and bad. If you and your partner share the same attitude to money, then obviously you'll be able to build a secure future for yourselves faster, more efficiently and more enjoyably than if you are in conflict.

However, it would be ridiculous not to acknowledge that many relationships are blighted by arguments about money and that reaching a compromise isn't always easy. In this chapter we look at how couples – and families – can work together to reach their financial goals. And we also look at the importance of educating children about money.

PROBLEM? WHAT PROBLEM?

All relationship money problems tend to boil down to one or more of the following issues:

- how the money is earned and who is earning it
- how the money is spent and who is spending it
- how the money is being managed and who is managing it
- how the money is being saved (if it is being saved at all) and who is doing the saving
- how the money is being invested (if it is being invested at all) and who is handling the investment decisions
- what debts you have – both individually and jointly – and why they were incurred.

Of all the subjects which couples argue about – from the choice of holiday destination to who should do the washing-up – money arguments are the hardest to resolve. This is because our money beliefs tend to be (a) firmly held, (b) unconscious and (c) non-negotiable.

Couples who are serious about building a financially secure future for themselves need to keep an open mind regarding their partner's viewpoint. One of you may be a saver, the other a spender, but that doesn't mean a compromise isn't possible.

ARE YOU AND YOUR PARTNER FINANCIALLY COMPATIBLE?

When a couple disagree about money, it is almost always because they each hold different money beliefs. Which of the following categories best describes you and your partner?

Worry warts. People who worry so much that they never really enjoy money – even when they have plenty.

Big spenders. People who spend money whether or not they have it. They don't mind going into debt to fund their lifestyle.

Careful savers. People who are committed to saving. Sometimes they can be obsessive about it to the point of miserliness, however.

Optimistic dreamers. People who believe that through some miracle – perhaps an unexpected legacy or a lottery win – all their financial worries will be solved overnight.

Outright fools. People – sorry to be harsh – whose spending and borrowing is reckless.

Clever planners. People who plan for a secure financial future but still manage to enjoy a good lifestyle now.

Where a couple consists of two 'clever planners' you tend to get minimum friction. Otherwise, sooner or later, disagreements are bound to arise.

In an ideal world ...

In an ideal world, one would discuss money with a future partner before making any sort of commitment, as this would allow you to check that you are financially compatible. However, we don't live in an ideal world and so most couples will find themselves tackling financial issues after they have been together for some time. Looking on the bright side, maybe this is preferable. After all, you now know and understand each other better.

OPENING A DIALOGUE

The first and most important step for anyone in a relationship is to **open a dialogue** with their partner. If you don't communicate you won't know what they are thinking, and they won't know what you are thinking. My advice is to have a gentle discussion in which you discuss some or all of the following topics:

- Your individual values in relation to money. What do each of you think is important?
- Any assumptions either of you may have. One of you may assume that finances should always be joint, the other may have fixed ideas about keeping them separate.
- *Your* dreams and desires and *your partner's* dreams and desires. How do you both envisage the future?
- *Your* fears and *your partner's* fears. What are you both most worried about?

Both of you will have inherited traits and you need to recognise what they are before any sort of agreement can be reached between you.

ANYTHING TO DECLARE?

There are so many tricky areas when it comes to discussing personal finance with your partner that it is hard to decide which is potentially the most controversial. One subject which never fails to cause problems is that of 'secret debts' and 'secret savings'. By this I mean:

- One or both partners have borrowed money without telling the other one.
- One or both partners have tucked money away without telling the other one.

Other 'secrets' which couples keep from each other include:

- How much one or other really earns.
- Money that one or the other has given away or promised (this often arises where one or other has been married before).

If you are harbouring a money secret from your partner, my advice is come clean. The longer you leave it, the worse it will be if you are discovered. Also, it is much harder (and sometimes impossible) to tackle your joint financial position if one of you is holding out.

MONEY DOCTOR WEALTH CHECK

The gentle art of confession

You have a money secret that you need to tell your partner. How can you do it without risking a break-up? Here are some tips:

- The longer you leave it, the worse it will be and the more chance that it will cause a serious rift.

- Pick your moment. No one likes to receive bad news just when they have to go to work or do something else. Better to raise the topic when you are alone and there is a chance to talk about it.

- If appropriate, don't forget to say 'sorry'.

- A medical doctor once told me that he always prepares family members for news about the death of a loved one a day or two before it is likely to happen with the words 'I am afraid you should expect the worst' – this gives them time to get used to the idea. If you start by saying you have a confession to make and it may shock or anger them, the conversation is unlikely to be as acrimonious.

- Don't fool yourself that – say – borrowing or spending money without telling your partner won't upset them. But, equally, remember that it is only money. The important thing is that there should be honesty in your relationship.

BUILDING A JOINT APPROACH TO MONEY

Disagreements about personal finance can be very divisive – I have seen figures that suggest half of the couples who break up do so because of a disagreement about money. So when I say that you need to agree a joint financial strategy with your partner I don't say it lightly. One approach that I have found works well is to:

- **Look for common ground.** It is likely, for instance, that you both want the same thing – to be free of debt and have plenty of spare cash.
- **Communicate freely and honestly.** Assess where you are and how each of

you have contributed to the current state of affairs. Be honest. Discuss each of your strengths and weaknesses – the things you are doing right, and the things you are doing wrong.

- **Compromise.** Don't allow past behaviour and events to poison your chance of success. Put grievances behind you. Start afresh and in doing so accept that you will both have to agree to do things differently in the future.

SHARING OUT THE CHORES

There are certain basic money chores that have to be done and one of the most useful things any couple can do in relation to their personal finances is agree who is going to take on which responsibilities. My recommendation is that all major decisions are made jointly and that each partner should keep the other informed about what they are doing. The tasks that need to be divided up include:

- paying household bills
- filing and organising financial paperwork
- doing the household shopping
- checking the bank accounts and reconciling the balances
- looking after the spending money and accessing cash
- shopping for larger purchases
- saving money and arranging any loans
- investment decisions
- keeping an eye on investments
- dealing with financial institutions, banks, insurance companies and so forth.

In many relationships, one or other partner will take over management for the financial affairs. Even where this works without a hitch I feel it is not entirely a good idea. Supposing one of you should die unexpectedly – how would the other cope? Also, what happens if you go your separate ways at some point? I can't stress how important it is to share information and decisions.

MONEY DOCTOR WEALTH CHECK

How to make yourself financially compatible

Here are some valuable tips on handling joint finances – whether with your partner or with someone else, such as a flatmate or friend.

- Maintain your independence. A joint account is perfect for joint responsibilities but it is a good idea to keep an account for yourself so that you have money available to spend as you want. Decide which areas are joint expenditure and which you are each going to handle alone.

- If one half of a partnership takes over all the money management it can lead to big trouble. The person 'in charge' may end up resenting the fact that he or she is doing all the work and he or she may also become controlling. The person not involved is leaving himself or herself vulnerable and is adopting an essentially childlike position. Both of you should take decisions together – even if one of you does the day-to-day accounting.

- Be honest about how you each feel. If one of you wants to save and the other wants to spend, admit it and work out a strategy that allows each of you to do as you please. Compromise!

- Plan for a future that isn't completely dependent on staying together. I realise that this may seem pessimistic but I frequently find myself counselling people who unexpectedly find themselves having to deal with money for the first time.

THE IMPORTANCE OF INVOLVING AND EDUCATING YOUR CHILDREN

How did your parents' approach to money influence you? Now consider how your attitude will influence your own children. Regardless of your level of wealth, everything you say or do in relation to money will have an effect:

- If you don't discuss money in front of them they won't learn anything about it.
- Whatever emotions you display – such as fear, worry or indifference – will colour their own relationship with money.

- If you are mean with money or overly generous, if you never waste a penny, or if you spend like there's no tomorrow, your children will be watching and learning.

Given that they are unlikely to learn much about money from any other quarter – and given the way debt is spreading through society like some super virus – it is obviously important that you educate your children about personal finance. You need to teach them the key principles, including how to:

- save for a specific purpose
- stick to a budget
- choose competitive products
- shop around
- spend money wisely.

THE MONEY DOCTOR SAYS...

My upbringing was fairly typical for Ireland in the 1960s. There were six of us squeezed into a three-bedroom house. My father was a manager and although we never went without, money was always tight. I am reminded of the comedian Les Dawson's self-deprecating quip, 'We were so poor, the first time I saw a butcher's shop, I thought there'd been an accident!' Of course, we didn't have the luxuries that today's generation are now so used to and have come to expect. In Ireland today, our children really do not appreciate some of the hardship their parents went through and, in some respects, this is a pity, because parents' values are so much different to their children's.

Clearly, what you *don't* want to do is worry your children about money. Still, I believe there is a lot to be said for showing them where your income comes from, and what you then do with it.

When your children realise how well you manage money they can't fail to be proud of you. Naturally, they will grow up not just wanting to be debt free and rich enough to retire when young – but actually understanding how this can be achieved. What better legacy could you leave?

THE MONEY DOCTOR SAYS...

- If you are in a relationship, it is vital that you discuss your financial objectives together, sort out your differences and formulate a joint plan.
- Honesty is vital! You have to work together, not against each other.
- Remember, two heads are better than one. If you are working together you'll reach your objectives sooner – and it will be more fun, too.
- Don't forget, it is important to educate your children about finance. Don't let them leave home without good money habits and a genuine understanding of how money works.

4
GETTING HELP

Should you adopt a DIY approach to your financial planning or should you get professional help? And, if you seek help, who can you trust to give you the best advice?

Are you the sort of person who relishes the challenge of managing their own financial welfare? Or are you the sort of person who would feel happier passing the whole task to someone else?

HOW FAR SHOULD YOU GO?

You want to make the most of your money. In practical terms this means:

- keeping the cost of your borrowing (including your mortgage) to a bare minimum and making sure that you have the most suitable mortgage for your needs
- earning the highest possible return from your savings and investments without taking undue risk or paying unnecessary fees or commission
- obtaining the best possible pension plan
- taking out only the most appropriate insurance at the lowest possible price
- not paying a penny more tax than you have to
- not paying a penny more for any other financial services or products than you have to
- not being caught by any unscrupulous operators.

With the help of this book (and by visiting my website www.moneydoctor.ie) you will certainly be able to achieve all of the above by yourself. However, does the DIY approach make sense for you? The following questions may help you to decide:

Have you got the right temperament? Financial planning can be stressful and time-consuming. If you hate figure work, don't like making decisions and worry about taking risks then maybe you would be better off seeking professional assistance.

Do you have the time? Are you willing to give up a few hours a month to make sure you are optimising your finances? Do you see this as being quite good fun? If not, then maybe the DIY approach isn't best for you.

Can you access the information you need? Financial planning requires access to information. If you can't gain access to the web, and if you aren't near a good library, then it is possible you should let someone else do the legwork for you.

GETTING HELP

How to get help from someone you can trust

Whenever I do a radio phone-in as the Money Doctor I find that the question I get asked most is: 'Who can I turn to for help with my money problems?'

Consumers, understandably, want independent and expert advice. The trouble is that most people offering advice actually work for financial institutions and have products to promote. Bluntly, if you talk to a life assurance salesperson about your retirement planning you know she or he isn't going to recommend anything except one of the products her or his own company sells.

The only solution is to get your advice from someone who isn't under any pressure to *sell* anything, but is in a position to do what is best for you.

For insurance and investments, about 400 such professionals exist in Ireland. They are called **Authorised Advisors** and they are legally obliged to do the best for you by giving 'best advice'.

This book is designed to give you all the information you need to organise your finances, save you tax and find the most appropriate products for your needs. (If you have any questions, remember you can also take advantage of my web-based service at www.moneydoctor.ie)

However, if you want to discuss your situation through with someone – face to face – make sure you talk to a professional who is experienced in all financial areas. In other words, contact an Authorised Advisor or for credit issues (mortgages, loans), an adviser who deals with and has access to all the lenders.

What can you expect from your independent professional Authorised Advisor or mortgage intermediary?

One of the key advantages to appointing an Authorised Advisor (someone who is independent, professional, qualified and stringently regulated) for insurances and investments is that they owe their allegiance to you and not to any particular financial institution or investment house. *Your needs* will be paramount. As a result, you can expect them to provide you with the following services:

Strategic planning. They will look at your complete financial position, agree your financial objectives with you, and advise you on how to reach your money targets. When doing this he or she should also assess your existing position and review any financial products you have in place to make sure they meet your requirements.

Competitive analysis. Having decided what products you need, your adviser should search the market for the best product offering the best value for money.

Negotiation services. When an insurance company quotes a rate, it isn't necessarily fixed in stone. In fact, it is possible to negotiate discounts on a huge range of financial products. Your adviser will know what else is available in the market and should negotiate to get you the best possible deal.

Background information. Your adviser should provide you with background information on any products or companies they recommend.

Administration. Your adviser should deal with all the paperwork on your behalf and will assist with the filling-out of any forms.

Regular reviews. Your adviser should monitor your needs without being asked. They should constantly be thinking about your situation and making sure that whatever they have recommended is performing in the desired manner.

Your adviser should also be able to look after all your financial and money needs, including:

- mortgages
- re-finance
- commercial loans
- personal loans
- asset finance and leasing
- life cover
- income protection and other insurance
- health cover

- all savings and investments
- pensions
- property and other general insurance.

Where even more specialised advice is needed (say in the selection of shares to build a portfolio, or specific tax planning), then your adviser should be able to recommend other professional experts.

Saving tax

A first-class financial adviser will be able to advise you on tax-saving products. Keep in mind though that for specialist tax advice you should always go to an accountant or qualified tax consultant. If the size of your tax bill doesn't warrant appointing an accountant, then your financial adviser should still be able to assist you. Tax is a big part of financial planning. After all, what's the point of making a better return on your investments only to lose it through poor tax advice? *Always* check that your adviser is taking your tax position into account and is properly qualified to assist you.

A very short history lesson

Prior to November 2001 there were over 9,000 'insurance brokers' offering financial advice. After that, the Central Bank took over regulation and forced them to register.

- Six thousand dropped out immediately, mainly because the scale of their operations meant they did not have the time or resources to provide the level of product research required.

- Of the two authorisations available, there are currently around 400 Authorised Advisors, who must give 'best advice' irrespective of agencies held.

- The balance of about 2,500 are called multi-agency intermediaries (originally called RAIPIs, then 'restricted intermediaries') and they can only give advice on the insurance and investment appointments held.

Then, in 2003, in order to make sure that consumers receive reliable and independent advice the government set up the Irish Financial Services Regulatory Authority (IFSRA, now called the 'Financial Regulator'), an independent agency set up to take over the regulatory role previously filled by the Central Bank.

One of the first things to do when considering any professional adviser is to check:

- that they are regulated by the Financial Regulator, now retitled the Central Bank of Ireland

- what services they are authorised to provide and at what cost.

Financial advisers must give you a **Terms of Business** booklet, which outlines their terms of business, appointments with product providers, Central Bank of Ireland authorisation and notification of the Investors' Compensation Act.

MONEY DOCTOR WEALTH WARNING

Some things are best not delegated

There is an enormous amount to be said for getting a really good professional adviser to sort out everything for you. You'll save money. You'll save time. And you will end up with the best possible products for your needs. But no matter how good your adviser, you should always take time to:

- understand what he or she is proposing, and why
- learn about the products you are committing to
- check up on the financial institutions that will be supplying those products.

THE MONEY DOCTOR SAYS...

It is possible to handle all your financial decisions without reference to anyone else. However, it requires time and commitment.

If you do decide to use a professional adviser, make sure that they are fully authorised and don't be shy about asking them questions.

Remember, it is important to have clear financial objectives.

PART 2

YOUR FINANCIAL RIGHTS

Are you entitled to claim any government benefits? How does the law protect you as an employee? What do you do if you buy something and are unhappy with the way you have been treated?

This section of the book will answer all your questions with regard to your financial rights. In Chapter 5 you'll discover how the Social Welfare system works and be able to assess what you may be entitled to. In Chapter 6 you'll learn about your rights as an employee. And in Chapter 7 you'll find out what your consumer rights are. I've also included useful sources of additional information and important contact information.

5
YOUR RIGHT TO SOCIAL WELFARE

HOW THE SYSTEM WORKS AND HOW TO MAKE SURE YOU RECEIVE YOUR ENTITLEMENTS

The Irish state provides its citizens with one of the most advanced, generous and comprehensive social welfare systems in the world. It isn't, however, what you would call a simple system, being made up of a bewildering array of:

- assistance payments
- benefits
- supplements
- allowances
- grants and
- pensions.

Many of the financial benefits available are 'contributory', meaning that you are only entitled to them if you have made **PRSI** (pay related social insurance) contributions in the past. Others are available to everyone, including people who have moved here from abroad.

As one would expect, the state only provides social welfare when certain conditions are met. Sometimes these conditions are very straightforward. For instance, with very few exceptions, a special grant of €4,000 is paid to widows or widowers with dependent children following the death of their spouse. In other instances you have to meet stringent requirements, often related to the size and number of your PRSI contributions. A good example of this is the invalidity pension, which is payable if you have been 'incapable of work for at least twelve months and are likely to be incapable of work for a further twelve months, or you are permanently incapable, or you are over age 60 and suffering from a serious illness or incapacity'. Furthermore, to claim this pension you must have paid PRSI at Class A, E or H for at least 260 weeks, and you must have had at least 48 weeks PRSI paid or credited in the last tax year before you apply!

I am afraid the system is made even more confusing by the fact that the government frequently changes the nature, value, names and conditions attached to the various benefits available.

So, how can you discover exactly what you are entitled to?

In this chapter I outline, in broad terms, all the various forms of social welfare that are available, along with the more important conditions which must be fulfilled in order to claim them. Using this, you should be able to ascertain benefits to which you might be entitled.

Your next step should be to contact your local Social Welfare Office or Citizens Information Centre for further assistance. You'll find both listed in your local phone book.

Another approach is to write directly to:

> The Information Service, Department of Social & Family Affairs
> Áras Mhic Dhiarmada, Store Street, Dublin 1
> Tel. (01) 704 3000.
> or
> Retirement/Old Age Contributory & Non-Contributory Pensions
> College Road, Sligo
> Co. Sligo
> Tel. (071) 915 7100/LoCall: 1890 50 00 00.

Or, if you have access to the internet, you can go to www.welfare.ie.

THE DIFFERENCE BETWEEN CONTRIBUTORY AND NON-CONTRIBUTORY PAYMENTS

The terms 'contributory' and 'non-contributory' are bandied about a good deal in relation to social welfare benefits. The terms are slightly misleading because they imply that you have to have contributed personally to be eligible for certain payments. The contribution being referred to is generally assumed to be PRSI payments, the health levy, and the employment and training levies. However, a completely different system operated prior to 1974, a third system was in place until 1953, and both may entitle you to contributory benefits.

The word 'contributory' is confusing in another respect, too. You may well be eligible to receive a contributory benefit if you are married to someone who has made contributions, or if you are the child or dependant of someone who has made contributions.

Another point to bear in mind is that you may have been in regular employment but earning so little that you were not liable to make any PRSI payments. If you are a public servant your entitlements will be linked to when you joined, and if you're self-employed a completely different set of regulations applies.

My advice, therefore, is never to assume that you won't be entitled to a particular form of social welfare until you have fully investigated each and every one of the conditions attached to it. Don't ever assume that because something is 'contributory' or 'non-contributory' it won't apply to you.

THE DIFFERENT TYPES OF SOCIAL WELFARE

I've already listed off all the different names used to describe the variety of social welfare payments. What do these various terms mean?

On the whole, social welfare **benefits** tend to be available only to those who have made PRSI contributions. Furthermore, though there are a few exceptions, social welfare benefits are not affected by your level of wealth.

Social welfare **assistance**, on the other hand, is given only to those who satisfy what's called a 'means test'.

A good example of the difference is Jobseeker's Benefit, which has PRSI conditions attached to it but for which there is no means test, and the non-contributory old age pension, which is classified as social assistance and is subject to means testing.

SO, WHAT IS MEANS TESTING?

In order that financial assistance only goes to those who are most needy, the government checks each claimant's financial circumstances first. This check is called a 'means test'.

Your means are considered to be:

- any cash income you have
- the value of your assets (your home will be excluded, but if you own a farm that would be included)
- your savings and investments.

In some cases your residential situation will be relevant. For instance, if you are unemployed but live at home with your parents and you are under the age of 24, this could reduce your entitlement.

When you apply for a means-tested form of social assistance, a 'means test officer' will consider your case. The criteria he or she uses in order to assess your entitlement will vary – of course – according to the form of social assistance you are applying to receive. You should expect, however, to be asked about your entire financial situation. This could include:

- your income
- your spouse's income
- your partner's income (if co-habiting)
- your farm income (if relevant)
- any savings, investments or other assets you may own, such as property
- your general circumstances, such as where you live, whom you live with, who is dependent on you, and so forth
- any debts you may have
- your weekly outgoings, including rent
- any other benefits you may be receiving.

Naturally, any information you provide will be treated in the strictest confidence.

There will, of course, be other conditions as well. For instance, you have to be genuinely unemployed to claim Jobseeker's Allowance. But it is your means that will be the deciding point. Note that even if you're not eligible for the maximum amount of assistance, you could still be entitled to a reduced amount.

WHAT ARE YOU ENTITLED TO? SOCIAL WELFARE PAYMENTS IN DETAIL

Below is a summary of all the main social welfare payments. You'll also find an explanation of what they could be worth to you, together with some of the more notable conditions.

Remember, the Department of Social & Family Affairs is there to help you. You shouldn't hesitate to ask their advice about what you are entitled to.

Social welfare pensions

The state makes available two different types of social welfare pension:

Contributory pension. So-called because your entitlement is linked to the amount and class of PRSI you have paid during your working life.

Non-contributory pension. Means-tested and available to those who haven't made any contributions during their working lives.

Contributory pensions in turn also fall into two categories: state pension (transition) (paid if you're aged 65 and over and have actually stopped working) and state pension (contributory) (paid from the age of 66 with no requirement that you should have stopped working).

The maximum standard amount for a contributory pension is €230.30 per week, but the actual sum you receive will be determined by the number and value of contributions you made during your working life – and your age. Additional sums are payable if you have dependent children and live alone.

The maximum standard amount payable as an old age non-contributory pension is currently €219 per week or €229 per week for those aged over 80. Again, you may be able to claim more if you have dependent children or live alone.

Regardless of whether you have made contributions or not, additional amounts may also be available if you're blind, or if you live on certain offshore islands.

Pensions for widows and widowers

If you are – or become – a widow or widower then you will also have pension entitlements. These are:

The contributory widow(er)'s pension. This – as its name implies – is available to widows or widowers where sufficient PRSI contributions have been made and is worth up to €230.30 per week for those aged 66 to 80, increasing to €240.30 for those aged over 80.

The non-contributory widow(er)'s pension. This is means-tested and could be worth as much as €196 a week.

In both instances if you have a dependent child, live alone and/or are resident on certain offshore islands you may be entitled to receive an additional sum.

Other age-related benefits

If you are aged 66 or over and you qualify for a contributory or non-contributory pension – or you satisfy a means test – you may be entitled to a number of other household benefits, including:

- free travel
- free electricity
- a natural gas allowance
- a free television licence
- a telephone line-rental allowance.

These benefits are referred to as the **Household Benefits Package Scheme**.

MONEY DOCTOR WEALTH CHECK

You don't have to be retired to claim free electricity and other benefits

The Household Benefits Package Scheme is also available to those entitled to other payments such as an invalidity pension or a carer's allowance (see below). Under these circumstances your age will not be relevant to your eligibility.

Supplementary welfare allowance

Supplementary welfare allowance provides a basic weekly allowance as a right to eligible people who have little or no income. If you have a low income, you may also qualify for a weekly supplement under the scheme to meet certain special needs. In addition, payments can be made in respect of urgent or exceptional needs.

There are four types of payments – **basic** payments, **supplements**, **exceptional needs** payments and **urgent needs** payments. To find out more about the scheme, contact the:

Supplementary Welfare Allowance Section
Department of Social & Family Affairs
Áras Mhic Dhiarmada
Store Street, Dublin 1
Tel. (01) 704 3000.

One-parent family payment

If you are bringing up a child (or children) without the support of a partner, you may be eligible to apply for the **one-parent family payment**, which is available to both men and women. You may earn up to €146.50 per week and still qualify for the full payment, while a reduced payment will be made to you if you earn between €146.50 per week and €425 per week. If your weekly income exceeds €425 a week, a half-rate payment will be made to you for six months from date of application.

Deserted wife's benefit

Deserted wife's benefit is a payment made to a woman deserted by her husband. Entitlement to payment is based on PRSI contributions paid by the wife or her husband. The deserted wife's benefit scheme was closed off to new applications with effect from 2 January 1997, when the one-parent family payment was introduced.

Guardian's payment (contributory)

This allowance is payable where both parents have died, or one parent has died and the other has abandoned the child. Being a contributory allowance, one or other of the parents must have made sufficient PRSI contributions. The payment is made up to the age of 18, or 22 if the child is in full-time education. It can be as much as €169 a week.

Guardian's payment (non-contributory)

If a child does not qualify for the contributory guardian's allowance, he or she may instead be eligible for the **non-contributory guardian's payment**. This pension is means-tested. It can be as much as €169 a week.

Invalidity pension

This is a contributory pension, so it is only available to those who meet the PRSI payment qualifications. It is payable instead of a disability benefit if you've been incapable of work for at least 12 months and are likely to be incapable of work for a further 12 months, or if you're permanently incapable of work, or if you're over the age of 60 and suffering from a serious illness or incapacity.

As with many other pensions, the amount you receive will increase if you have dependent children, live alone, or live on certain offshore islands. If you are eligible for an invalidity pension you may also be able to claim an additional sum if you support someone else. It can be as much as €230.30 a week at age 65.

Medical cards

Medical cards entitle you to a range of free medical care. Eligibility is normally means-tested, although there are a number of exceptions including exceptions for those aged 70 or over, and anyone drawing a state pension from other EU countries. Different income limits exist for those aged under 66 and those aged between 66 and 69 and vary depending on the number of children or dependants and whether they are aged over 16 and in full-time education.

Although your circumstances may not entitle you to a medical card, you could still be eligible for a **doctor visit card**, which would allow you to receive free care from your GP. If this section is relevant to you, you should seek assistance from the Department of Social & Family Affairs – see contact details on p. 35.

Treatment benefits

The state provides a range of contributory **treatment benefits** covering dental care, eye testing, glasses, contact lenses, and hearing aids. In some instances, the benefits are entirely free and in others you must pay a part of the cost. There may also be upper limits on the amounts which can be claimed.

Maternity benefit

A contributory **maternity benefit** is payable to women in current employment or self-employment who have been paying PRSI. It is only payable where the mother has been making contributions – the father's contributions have no bearing on eligibility. It can be as much as €270 a week for 26 weeks.

Adoptive benefit

If you adopt a child you may still be eligible for a payment equivalent in value to the maternity benefit. This is a contributory benefit. It can be as much as €270 a week for a continuous period of 24 weeks from the date of placement of your child.

Asylum seekers

If you are applying for refugee status, you can obtain rent-free accommodation at a regional centre. Each adult is entitled to a personal allowance of €19.10 per week and €9.60 for each child. Child benefit may also be applicable. More information can be obtained from:

> Reception and Integration Agency
> PO Box 11487
> Dublin 2
> Tel. (01) 418 3200, LoCall: 1890 777 727.

MONEY DOCTOR WEALTH WARNING

A tightening-up of the rules: Habitual Resident's Test

Since 2004 the government has introduced a new Habitual Resident's Test, which means that in order to receive a whole range of payments you must be able to prove that you are 'habitually resident in Ireland'. However, the rules do allow you to be resident in the UK, Channel Islands, and Isle of Man, too. Payments affected by this include unemployment assistance, old age contributory pension, one-parent family payment, and supplementary welfare allowance.

Child benefit

Child benefit is not means-tested, nor do you have to make any contribution in order to receive it. It is paid each month, and the amount you receive will depend on the number of qualifying children living with you and their ages. In some instances the payment may be made until the children reach the age of 18. For the first and second child it can be as much as €150 each per month and €187 for the third and subsequent children (2010 rate). It also pays to have multiple births – 1½ times the child benefit rate for twins (each) and double for triplets or greater (each) PLUS three one-off payments: at birth, aged four and aged 12, or €635 for each child.

Early childhood care & education scheme (ECCE)

This scheme provides a free year of early childhood care and education for children of pre-school age. Children are eligible for the scheme if they are aged between 3 years and 2 months and 4 years and 7 months on 1 September of the year they will be starting. The state pays a capitation fee to participating playschools and daycare centres.

Jobseeker's benefit

Jobseeker's benefit is only paid to those who satisfy the PRSI conditions. The amount you receive will be linked to your age and the amount of PRSI paid. It can be as much as €196 a week.

From January 2009 changes to income limits and the number of PRSI contributions required were introduced.

Jobseeker's allowance

This was previously known as Unemployment Assistance and is a means-tested payment available to those who are unemployed and have not made sufficient PRSI contributions or have used up their entitlement to Jobseeker's Benefit.

It can be as much as €196 per week for those aged over 25, with proportionate increases for qualified adult or child dependents.

If you want to find out why you have been turned down for a benefit, or considered ineligible, contact the:

Social Welfare Appeals Office
D'Olier House
D'Olier Street, Dublin 2
Tel. (01) 673 2800.

Back-to-work allowance and back-to-work enterprise allowance

Two different schemes exist for those who have been unemployed for a period of time and then return to work: the back-to-work allowance and the back-to-work enterprise allowance. The first is available if you move into paid employment after being unemployed; the second is given if you become self-employed. Back-to-work allowance was closed to new applicants from 1 May 2009. Note that other support is also available to those who start their own businesses, including training grants, loans, and assistance towards the cost of public liability insurance. Apply to:

Employment Support Services
Department of Social & Family Affairs
PO Box 3840
Dublin 2
Tel. (01) 704 3867.

Carer's benefit

If you leave work in order to look after someone in need of full-time care and attention, then you may well be eligible for the contributory carer's benefit. Additionally, you may be entitled to an annual respite care grant, which would be paid to you in June each year. This grant is, in fact, available to all carers providing full-time care, subject to certain conditions. The respite care grant is currently worth €1,700 per person cared for. The carer's benefit can be as much as €319.50 a week if you are caring for more than one person.

Disability and injury benefits

A range of disability and injury benefits – all contributory – is available to those unable to work due to a disability, injury or some form of disablement. If you are disabled, suffer an injury or have some form of disability you may also be eligible, without means testing, for a range of other benefits including medical care, and a constant attendant's allowance. If you are a public servant and have to give up work due to ill health, you will be eligible for an early retirement pension. These benefits can be worth anything up to €204.30 a week.

Bereavement grant

A bereavement grant of €850 is available subject to certain conditions based on PRSI contributions.

Widowed parent's grant

In addition to the bereavement grant mentioned above, a special grant of €6,000 is available to widows or widowers with dependent children following the death of their spouse. This is not means-tested and only minimal conditions are attached to it.

Family income supplement

The purpose of this scheme is to help families on low incomes. However, to be eligible it is necessary for one member of the family to be working at least part-time, and for the family income to be below a certain level. Although the family income supplement is based on the family's weekly income, once it has been set it doesn't normally fluctuate. However, if your circumstances change (for instance, if you have another child) you can apply to have it increased. The supplement is based on 60% of the difference between your net family income and the income limit that applies to your family circumstances (see Department of Social & Family Affairs leaflet SW19).

Drugs payments scheme

Even though you may not be eligible for a medical card, you could well be eligible to receive support under the drugs payment scheme. Once you are registered, no individual or family is expected to pay more than €120 a month for prescription drugs included on the list of 'essential medicines'. In order to register you should contact your GP, local pharmacy or health board.

The nursing homes support scheme

Someone aged 65 or over needing nursing home care may be eligible to have some or all of it paid for by the local health board. Financial support is only forthcoming if:

- the claimant clearly needs to be in a nursing home.
- he or she is unable to pay for it himself or herself.

In other words, it is linked to need and is means-tested.

With regards to the means-testing, if the claimant has recently (within the past five years) sold or given away assets then he or she may cease to be eligible. This is because many elderly people were voluntarily changing their financial circumstances in order to avoid paying nursing home fees.

A family home, if occupied by a dependent spouse, child or other close relative will not count as an asset for means-testing.

Disabled persons

A host of grants and allowances exist for disabled and incapacitated persons. These include the blind welfare allowance, blind person's pension, carer's allowance, disability allowance, motorised transport grant, domiciliary care allowance and many more. Various tax credits and allowances are also available to disabled people.

Free travel

Free travel on public transport is available to almost everyone aged 66 or over. It is also available to anyone receiving an invalidity pension, a disability allowance, a blind person's pension or a carer's allowance. Note that if you are entitled to free travel, and you're married or co-habiting with someone, they may travel with you free of charge at the same time.

MONEY DOCTOR WEALTH CHECK

What you're entitled to elsewhere in the EU

As Ireland is part of the European Union, you are entitled to a wide range of benefits in other EU member states. However, since EU member states each have their own social welfare system, claiming entitlements in other countries can be fraught with problems. Keep in mind too that contributions made in one member state do not necessarily qualify you for benefits in another. For instance, if you have been working overseas and return home to Ireland, you will not automatically be eligible for unemployment benefit. However, if you have been registered as unemployed for four weeks in Ireland you are then entitled to move to another EU country to look for work and still receive the benefit for up to three months.

If you are thinking of living or working in another EU member state, then you should ask at your local Social Welfare office for a special leaflet describing the benefits which will be available to you.

Incidentally, not only are you legally entitled to look for work in any EU member state without a work permit, but you can also take advantage of each member state's national placement service. To do this, contact your local FÁS Employment Services office. Details of your application will be sent overseas through the SEDOC system free of charge.

MONEY DOCTOR WEALTH WARNING

Social welfare benefits are not necessarily tax-free

Social welfare benefits are not automatically tax-free. Whether they are taxable will largely depend on the income level of the recipient. Although tax will not be deducted by the Department of Social & Family Affairs on any payments made to you, the Revenue Commissioners will often take the tax directly from some other source of income which may be payable to the recipient. However, on the plus side, four of the 'taxable benefits' you may be entitled to will also qualify you for the PAYE tax credit. These are:

- state pension (contributory)
- state pension (transition)
- contributory survivor's pension
- guardian's payment.

A number of other benefits may also be liable to income tax. These are:

- invalidity pension
- one-parent family payment
- carer's allowance
- Jobseeker's Allowance
- blind person's pension
- non-contributory widow(er)'s pension
- non-contributory guardian's pension
- social assistance allowance for deserted or prisoners' wives.

The Revenue Commissioners do, however, make a number of useful concessions:

- If you are receiving a disability benefit the first six days will not be subject to tax.
- If you are receiving social welfare payments, child-dependent additions are not taxed (except for invalidity pensions).
- If you are a 'short-term worker' (that it is to say, you work in a trade where short-term employment is the norm) then any Jobseeker's Allowance you receive will not be taxed.
- The first €12.70 a week is not liable to tax.

MONEY DOCTOR WEALTH CHECK

Don't forget to apply for a European Health Insurance Card

If you're travelling or staying temporarily in another EU member state (excluding the UK), then you should apply for a European Health Insurance Card. This will ensure that you are eligible for free health care if you become ill or have an accident when overseas. You can do this through your local health board.

THE MONEY DOCTOR SAYS ...

- You may be entitled to all sorts of social welfare payments that you weren't aware of.

- Check through all the allowances, benefits and grants summarised in this chapter to see which might apply to you.

- Contact your local Department of Social & Family Affairs to find out more and to make a claim. Remember, they are there to help you.

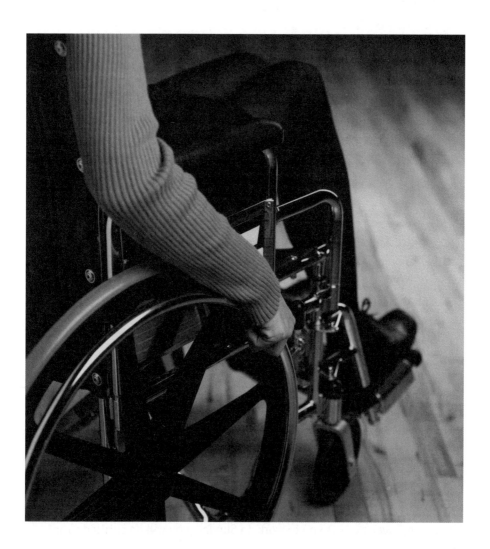

6
YOUR EMPLOYMENT RIGHTS

When most people think of 'employee rights' they think of legal rights relating to things like discrimination and redundancy. But if you are an employee you have financial rights, too. For instance, you have the right to be paid a minimum wage and the right to holiday pay. This chapter explains these rights in plain English.

You may be more protected than you imagine.

In the last few years the Irish government has enacted a considerable amount of new legislation to protect employees. One reason for this was that many employers were seeking to get around the existing employment legislation by putting their workers on 'contract'. Seasonal and part-time workers were also at a disadvantage. Since 2003, however, workers on fixed-term contracts must be treated just as well as full-time employees. Furthermore, an employee cannot be expected to work on a fixed-term contract for more than four years.

MINIMUM WAGE

Since 1 April 2000 all but a tiny minority of workers over the age of 18 are entitled to be paid a minimum amount of money per hour, known as the national minimum wage. From 1 July 2007 the national minimum wage has been set at €8.65 per hour. However, you should note that:

- If you're in a new job you are only entitled to 80% of the minimum wage for your first year, and 90% in your second year.
- If you're under 18 you also have reduced entitlements (70% until your 18th birthday, 80% between your 18th and 19th birthdays, and 90% for the following year).
- If you are still in training or attending an educational course your employer is also entitled to reduce your wage.

A SUNDAY BONUS

If your employer expects you to work on Sunday, you will be entitled to an increased hourly rate. If you are not automatically receiving this then you should contact the Department of Enterprise, Trade and Employment at the address given on p. 52.

ANNUAL LEAVE ENTITLEMENT

You are entitled to a minimum of four weeks annual leave plus public holidays, of which there are nine per year.

HOLIDAY PAY

If you are in paid employment, then you are legally entitled to paid holidays. The holiday year usually runs from 1 April–31 March. However, your employer is entitled to use an alternative twelve-month period. Broadly speaking, if you're working full time, you should be entitled to a minimum of four working weeks over the year. Of course, if you switch jobs this may have the effect of reducing your entitlement.

YOUR WORKING WEEK

Under something called the 'Organisation of Working Time Act', employees cannot be expected to work more than 48 hours a week. However, there are innumerable exceptions to this. For instance, the Act does not apply to junior hospital doctors, transport employees, fishermen, and family members working on a farm or in a private house, or to the Gardaí.

There are also rules regarding rest periods. You're legally entitled to an 11-hour rest period every 24 hours; one period of 24 hours rest per week preceded by a daily rest period – in other words a total of 35 hours in a single block; and rest breaks of 15 minutes where up to four and a half hours have been worked, or 30 minutes where up to six hours have been worked. Slightly different arrangements apply to night workers.

ON-CALL WORKERS

If you are expected to be on call for work, then you should be paid for it. The rule is that you are entitled to receive pay for at least a quarter of your on-call hours even if you don't end up working. The maximum amount your employer has to pay you is for 15 hours a week.

DISMISSAL RIGHTS

Your employer can only dismiss you if he or she can prove that you aren't capable, competent or qualified to do the work you were employed to do. Alternatively, your employer must show that your conduct was in some way unacceptable; or that by continuing to employ you he or she would contravene another statutory requirement. The only other reason an employer may dismiss you is if he or she is making you redundant (see over, p. 52). This said, unfair dismissal normally only applies to those who have been employed for at least a year's continuous service with the same employer. Furthermore, there are many exclusions, including those who are aged 65 and over.

If you feel that you've been unfairly dismissed then you must make your complaint within six months.

Note that once you've completed at least 13 weeks with the same employer you are entitled to pre-set periods of notice. This ranges from one week's notice if you've been working for 13 weeks to two years, to eight weeks' notice if you've been working for over 15 years.

TIME OFF WORK

There are various other reasons why you can legitimately claim time off work. For instance, you can take:

- **Emergency time** off in order to deal with family emergencies resulting from an accident or illness. You are entitled to up to five days over a period of 36 months, and such leave is paid.

- Up to 26 weeks **maternity leave** if you become pregnant, during which time you can claim maternity benefit. Your employer is not obliged to give you any additional income over and above this maternity benefit. When the maternity benefit period ends, you're entitled to take up to a further 16 weeks of unpaid leave.

- Up to 14 weeks parental leave if you are a **new father**, but this is unpaid and without any social welfare entitlement.

- Time off if you are an **expectant mother**, **parent** or **carer** with a special need. For instance, expectant mothers can take time off without loss of pay to go to medical examinations.

WHAT TO DO IF YOU ARE UNHAPPY WITH YOUR EMPLOYER ...

If you feel that your employment rights are being abused, you can obtain further information from:

The Department of Enterprise, Trade and Employment
Employment Rights Section
Davitt House, 65A Adelaide Road, Dublin 2
Tel. (01) 531 3131/LoCall: 1890 201 615.

The Labour Relations Commission will also assist you. Their address details
are:

Rights Commissioner Service
Labour Relations Commission
Tom Johnson House, Haddington Road, Dublin 4
Tel. (01) 660 9662.

REDUNDANCY

If you have worked for the same employer for at least two years – even if it is
part-time – and you are made redundant, then you may well be eligible for a
redundancy payment. Various conditions apply. For instance, you must be
aged between 16 and 66, and you must have normally worked at least eight
hours a week. Also, 'redundancy' only covers the situation where you've been
dismissed because – essentially – your employer no longer needs your
services. This could be for a variety of reasons, including a change in location,
or a decision by the employer to carry on the business with fewer employees.
The amount you receive will be based on the number of years you've worked.
You should receive two weeks' pay for every year of service to a maximum of
€600 a week, topped up with one additional week's pay. If you receive a large
lump-sum redundancy payment then you may be liable to pay tax on it. For
further information about this, turn to Chapter 33.

THE MONEY DOCTOR SAYS...

- Know your financial rights as an employee and don't let your
  employer bully or cajole you into accepting anything less.
- Remember, there are lots of circumstances where your employer
  must pay you. And lots of circumstances where your employer must
  let you have time off.

7
YOUR RIGHTS AS A 'FINANCIAL' CONSUMER

Do you suspect your bank of over-charging you? Have you felt that an insurance salesperson has sold you a product you don't need? Are you worried about personal financial information being used for marketing purposes?

If you have any concerns about the way you've been treated by a financial institution, then this chapter is for you. In it you'll learn how the law protects you and what you can do if there's something you are unhappy about.

Your basic rights

As the customer of a financial institution you have a wide range of rights. You don't need to suffer poor service, over-charging, mis-selling or fraud. If you're unhappy, there are dedicated, independent organisations which will assist you. Furthermore, if you have lost money you may also be entitled to compensation.

HOW TO COMPLAIN

If you are unhappy and wish to complain, then, in the first instance, you should write to the financial institution concerned and offer them an opportunity to redress the situation. If you are not satisfied with the response you receive, follow the appropriate course of action outlined in the relevant section below.

If you're unhappy with your bank, building society, credit union or insurance company

If you're unhappy with your bank, building society or credit union, you can appeal to the Financial Services Ombudsman. This body also covers insurance complaints and is authorised to make awards of up to a limit of €250,000.

All the banks in Ireland now offer a wide range of financial services including insurance and pensions, so this body will cover all that area should you have a complaint to make.

Insurance companies and banks are bound by the Ombudsman's decision but the complainants are not (e.g. a policyholder who does not agree with the Ombudsman's decision).

The details are:

Financial Services Ombudsman's Bureau
Third Floor
Lincoln House
Lincoln Place
Dublin 2
Lo-Call: 1890 88 20 90
Tel. (01) 662 0899
Fax (01) 662 0890
Email: enquiries@financialombudsman.ie

If you're unhappy with your financial advisers

In order to make sure that consumers receive reliable and independent advice, the government set up the **Financial Regulator**, now operating within the Central Bank of Ireland. Before you even consider dealing with any professional adviser, you should check that they are regulated by the Central Bank of Ireland and what services they are authorised to provide. They must give you a **Terms of Business** letter, which outlines their terms of business, appointments with product providers, Central Bank of Ireland authorisation, and notification of the Investors' Compensation Act. You'll find more information about choosing a professional adviser in Chapter 4.

There are, in fact, four different bodies to which your adviser may belong:

1   The Independent Mortgage Advisers Federation (IMAF).
2   The Irish Brokers Association (IBA).
3   Professional Insurance Brokers Association (PIBA).
4   Life Insurance Association (LIA).

If you're unhappy with your pension company

If you feel that you have been given poor pension advice, then you should contact the Financial Services Ombudsman's Bureau and you should also get in touch with the Ombudsman in charge of pensions. The latter can be contacted at:

The Office of the Pensions Ombudsman
PO Box 9324
36 Upper Mount Street, Dublin 2
Tel. (01) 847 1650.

HAVE YOU BEEN TURNED DOWN FOR A LOAN OR CREDIT CARD FOR NO APPARENT REASON?

If you have been turned down for a loan or credit card, it is probably because of your **credit rating**. Almost all the lenders in Ireland rely on credit bureaux to provide them with information about their potential customers. If the information that any particular credit bureau holds is incorrect, it can result in you being turned down for credit. The two bureaux which operate in Ireland are legally obliged to advise you of the information they hold about you. Their details are:

The Irish Credit Bureau (ICB)
Newstead House
Newstead, Clonskeagh, Dublin 14.
www.icb.ie

and

Experian Ireland
Newenham House, Northern Cross,
Malahide Road, Dublin 17.

You will pay a small charge for this service. For instance, ICB will charge €6. Do note that they respond only to written or on-line requests and the service usually takes no more than three days. You should get in touch with the Ombudsman for Credit Institutions and the Ombudsman for the Financial Services if you're not satisfied with the response you get.

If you're worried about Big Brother

Many of us, with a certain amount of justification, worry that large organisations – such as banks and insurance companies – hold incorrect and unnecessary information about us on their files. Under the Data Protection Act you have the right of access to any personal file relating to yourself held by either a company or other type of organisation. To discover what data a company or organisation holds about you, you simply have to write to them saying that you're making your request under the Data Protection Act. If you encounter any resistance, then you should contact the Data Protection Commissioner at:

The Data Protection Commissioner
Canal House
Station Road
Portarlington, Co. Laois
Tel. (01) 674 8544.

If you discover that an organisation has incorrect information about you, you are entitled to have it corrected.

MONEY DOCTOR WEALTH CHECK

The Deposit Protection scheme

With the level of uncertainty about the future of some of our financial institutions it should be reassuring to know the details of this scheme. This has been in place since 1995 and guarantees individual deposits of up to €100,000 held in any bank, building society or credit union regulated by the Central Bank of Ireland. This consists of 14 Irish and non-Irish deposit-taking institutions operating in the Irish market.

Other institutions such as Rabobank and Investec are covered by similar guarantees, the former from Dutch bank Rabo Group, the only AAA-rated bank in Ireland, and the latter through the UK Financial Regulatory Authority (from January 2011 and covers up to €100,000 per person).

IF YOU'RE STILL UNHAPPY AND WANT TO TAKE IT FURTHER

What do you do if you've made a complaint to a financial institution and the relevant Ombudsman and you're still not happy with the result? You have two basic choices:

1 You could institute legal proceedings.
2 You could contact the European Ombudsman.

The European Ombudsman investigates complaints about poor administration by financial institutions and other bodies throughout the EU. You can write to the Ombudsman at:

The European Ombudsman
1 avenue du President Robert Schuman
CS 30403, F-67001
Strasbourg, Cedex
France.

THE MONEY DOCTOR SAYS...

- If you are unhappy with the service you have received from a financial institution you should, in the first instance, offer them the opportunity to put things right. The best way to do this is to put your complaint in writing.

- If you aren't satisfied with the response you receive – take it further. Complain to the relevant Ombudsman.

- Legal action is always an option – but remember, it will cost you money, whereas there is no charge involved in asking an Ombudsman.

PART 3

BANKING, BORROWING AND GETTING
OUT OF DEBT

This section deals with three extremely important topics. Firstly, it offers a comprehensive guide to modern banking services in Ireland, together with tips on getting the most from your bank at the lowest possible cost. Secondly, it explains how you can pay off all your debts – including your credit cards, loans, overdrafts and even your mortgage – quickly and easily. Thirdly, it looks at the different ways in which you can borrow money and suggests the most inexpensive ways to do so.

8
BANKING

HOW TO ENJOY THE BEST BANKING IN IRELAND

What do you demand from your bank? A first-class service? Free banking? Total security? A range of competitively priced financial products? With a little careful planning, as I will explain in this chapter, you can enjoy the best banking in Ireland.

UNDERSTANDING THE BANKING SYSTEM

The first step to enjoying better banking is to understand how the banks themselves operate.

To begin with, despite the charges they make, banks don't make their profits from providing day-to-day banking services. This is because it is incredibly expensive running a branch network, handling millions of transactions, dealing with vast quantities of cash and providing customers with all the other services we (rightly) demand.

So, how *do* banks make their profits? The answer is by selling their customers a wide range of other financial services – everything from mortgages to credit cards, and from insurance to stockbroking.

Every time you use your bank, whether you are withdrawing cash from a machine, paying a bill, or ordering a statement, you present your bank with another opportunity to sell you something. Much in the same way as supermarkets use 'loss leaders' (popular products sold at below-cost price in order to attract customers), banks offer banking services – especially current accounts – as a way of attracting and keeping customers.

In fact, *operated properly* a current account is one of the greatest financial bargains of all time.

Why have I put the words 'operated properly' in italics? Because in order to recoup some of their expenses, banks stipulate that you must follow the terms and conditions relating to your account. If you don't, they hit you with all sorts of extra charges.

MONEY DOCTOR WEALTH CHECK

Loyalty doesn't pay

Don't imagine for a moment that by being loyal to a bank you'll get a better service. The era of 'relationship banking' is long gone. For instance, the decision over whether to lend you money is no longer made at branch level but by a centralised team. Of course, no bank wants to lose its customers, but the threat to take your business elsewhere is no longer as powerful as it once was.

Making the banking system work for you

How, then, can you get the most from your bank? I would offer you four straightforward and easy-to-follow rules:

1 Only buy the services and products you need from your bank. Don't allow them to persuade you into buying something you don't really require.

2 Make sure the services and products you buy are competitively priced. Buying a financial product from your bank may be more convenient – but it could cost you a lot of money.

3 Don't hesitate to shop around or move your business. Banks rely on customer inertia. In other words, they know that many people can't be bothered to ring around for a better price, let alone move their account elsewhere for a better deal.

4 Avoid breaking the terms and conditions attached to any product you purchase from your bank, as the consequences will undoubtedly be expensive.

You may imagine from what I am saying that I am 'anti-bank'. Far from it. Today's modern banks offer customers a fantastic choice and – if you buy wisely – a chance to pay little or nothing for your day-to-day banking.

WHAT BANKS DO BEST

At the heart of all banking lies the current account. This basic bank account should provide you with the following facilities:

- a safe and secure place to deposit cheques or cash
- somewhere convenient to keep your money in the short to medium term, until you need to spend it
- access to your cash via branches and cash machines
- a simple and easy way to pay your bills
- a comprehensive record of all your day-to-day financial transactions.

In order to provide all this, the typical current account will offer you some or all of the following services:

- a **cheque book**
- an **ATM** (this stands for automated teller machine) **card** allowing you to get cash 24 hours a day
- a **direct debit facility** so that you can pay your bills automatically
- a **standing order facility** allowing you to make regular payments
- a **cheque guarantee card**, making your cheques (up to a certain value) as good as cash in the hands of the recipient
- a **debit** (Laser) **card** so that you can arrange direct payments without having to write a cheque in-branch, buying in shops, on-line and even overseas
- **regular statements**
- **overdraft facilities.**

Your current account should also give you access to a telephone banking facility and – if you use the internet – on-line banking. Both should allow you to access your account – and arrange for other transactions – without having to go into a branch.

Although you can obtain some of the services listed above from building societies and credit unions, only five banks in Ireland offer you full current account banking facilities. These are:

 Bank of Ireland

BASIC BANKING SERVICES EXPLAINED

There are various banking terms that regularly cause customer confusion. I know, because I used to be a banker. Below, I explain them in plain English.

Standing orders

A standing order is exactly that – a regular ('standing') instruction ('order') to your bank to make the same payment to the same person or organisation on an agreed date. For instance, you might order your bank to pay €200 a month to me because you appreciate this book so much. Or, for that matter, you might instruct them to pay me a much larger amount every other month or every quarter, six months or year. You can instruct them to do this until further notice or until a date you specify.

Direct debits

A direct debit is basically an authorisation to your bank to pay a regular bill on your behalf. For instance, you might sign a direct debit instructing them to pay your ESB bill when it's presented. With a direct debit you don't specify the amount that is going to be paid and because of this there are some very strict safeguards in place to protect you. One of these is that only reputable organisations are allowed to use the direct debit system.

Laser cards (debit cards)

A Laser card works exactly like a cheque book – but using plastic instead of paper. When you pay someone with a Laser card they apply to your bank for the money, which is then transferred to their account. The upper limit for a single payment is €1,500. With cheques, of course, the bank only guarantees payment up to the maximum amount on your cheque guarantee card.

You should only make a payment by Laser card if you have sufficient funds in your account or if your overdraft credit is large enough to meet the payment. There is an annual €5 stamp duty charge on Laser cards. All Laser cards also double as ATM cards. Thanks to Laser cards you no longer need to take cash when shopping or wait for a cheque to clear before collecting goods.

Overdrafts

An **overdraft** is a short-term loan offered by your bank as part of your current account facility. There are two types:

> An **authorised overdraft** is one that has been arranged in advance – though you don't, necessarily, have to use it. The bank normally charges for agreeing this facility, usually €25.

> An **unauthorised overdraft** is where the bank decides that despite the fact that you have no agreement to borrow from them, they will still make some payment on your behalf. Unauthorised overdrafts attract penalties and high rates of interest called surcharges. With one bank, it can amount to over double the normal overdraft rate!

What many bank customers do not realise is that banks expect your current account to be in credit for 30 days a year and will charge you extra if it isn't.

WHAT PRICE BANKING?

So, what can you expect to **pay** for your current account banking? There isn't an easy answer. All banks have different pricing structures so that what one bank offers for free, another will charge for.

In 2004 the Irish Financial Services Regulatory Authority (now known as the Central Bank of Ireland) surveyed bank customers and found that on average they were being charged between €50 and €137 for current account transactions. The level of charges was linked to the customer's choice of bank and level of usage. Today these charges are greater.

A direct comparison of current account charges isn't possible because all five banks offer different products and make different charges. If you want to save money on your own current account fees, the best way is to follow the money-saving tips detailed below.

CUTTING THE COST OF YOUR CURRENT ACCOUNT

There are a number of ways in which you can dramatically reduce the cost of your current account banking. These include:

1 With competition hotting up, all the banks now offer free banking, subject to various conditions. Shop around for the best package to suit your individual circumstances.

2 Don't use a bank overdraft facility. Banks will charge you for setting it up. They'll charge you interest on it and if you exceed the overdraft, a surcharge and an additional cost on top of this interest! Also, they'll use it as an excuse to charge you for other facilities.

3 Don't, whatever you do, go overdrawn without formal agreement. An unauthorised overdraft will result in you being charged an extremely high rate of interest plus huge additional fees. Even going overdrawn for a couple of days could result in you paying anything from €20 upwards for the privilege.

4 Don't allow your cheques to 'bounce', referred to as being 'Returned Unpaid'. All five banks make heavy charges if your cheque or direct debit has to be returned unpaid. This happens, of course, if you haven't sufficient money in your account or you don't have a large enough overdraft limit. '**Refer to Drawer**' or '**Payment Stopped**' are stamped on the cheque. With the former, your credibility is shot, and there is a question mark on your ability to honour a debt. With the latter, you might wish to stop payments to a supplier of faulty goods if it is outside the cheque card guarantee (capped at €130).

5 Don't bank a cheque that might not clear. A cheque which is lodged to your account, but not honoured, could cost you as much as €17.14 including unpaid charges and referral fees per transaction.

6 Consider using a building society, An Post (their BillPay service is excellent, with over 120 bills payable through any of the 1250 post offices throughout Ireland, six days a week and completely free of charge) or credit union account for limited banking facilities – a far more economical way to do one's banking, see pp 67–8.

7 Consider using a credit card to pay all your bills. If you settle your credit card statement in full every month, this won't cost you anything. See the section on credit cards below for more information about this.

8   Internet and telephone banking eliminate cheque costs and other bank charges by enabling you to make payments and transfers between accounts on-line or over the telephone with a secure password.

MONEY DOCTOR WEALTH CHECK

The advantage of a joint account

If I am advising someone who is married, co-habiting or has other dependants I often recommend that they open a joint account and keep a bit of emergency cash in it. Why? When someone dies, it often takes months before his or her affairs can be wound up. During this time all bank accounts and other assets will be frozen. This frequently leaves the bereaved worrying about money. If you have a joint account, however, no such problem arises. Joint accounts are useful in other circumstances too, as everyone named on the account has the right to operate it, subject to the signing authority given.

Note: Joint accounts do not automatically escape inheritance tax.

OTHER TYPES OF BANK ACCOUNT

In addition to offering current accounts, all five banks offer a range of **deposit** and **saving accounts**. The usual rule with these is that the longer you leave your money, and the more money you deposit, the better the rate of interest you will receive.

In the current climate of low interest rates, many bank deposit accounts offer an extremely poor return.

To put this in perspective, if you deposited €1,000 with your average high street bank for one year you would earn €10 before tax. Unless you are not liable to income tax, you would have to pay Deposit Interest Retention Tax (DIRT tax) on this at 25%, meaning you would be left with a rather modest €7.50 for your trouble.

I examine the whole question of what to do with your savings in Part 6. In the meantime, my only comment would be that you should not leave your short-term savings in a current account, where it's unlikely to be earning any interest at all, but instead you should shop around and put any spare money where it gets the best rate.

Other bank services to consider

As already mentioned, all five banks offer a wide range of other services, from credit cards to personal loans, and from pensions to mortgages. There is a great temptation if you have your current account with a particular bank to use them for one or more of these other services. I would advise you to resist this temptation. Let me give you two examples of why it's such a bad idea.

At the time of writing I checked the market for the best and worst mortgage rates.

- The best 92% mortgage for a first time buyer is at 3.00% (standard variable rate).
- The worst 92% mortgage for a first time buyer on a standard variable rate (no interest-only facility) is at 3.65%. Some existing borrowers can pay up to 5.9%.

At the same time I also checked credit card interest rates:

- Best credit card interest (after the 'loss leader' rates) is 9.5%.
- Worst credit card is a store card in the range of 17.9–24%.

As you can see, it definitely pays to shop around.

MONEY DOCTOR WEALTH CHECK

Switching is easy!

All five banks have adopted a code of practice to make it easier to move from one bank to another. Under this code, it should take you less than ten days to get a new account up and running, and all your standing orders and direct debits should be transferred from your old account within one week after that. If you have any trouble changing your bank you should contact the Financial Services Ombudsman's Bureau. You'll find their address on p. 54.

THE BUILDING SOCIETY OPTION

Building societies are owned by their members or – in plain English – their customers. Over the last decade all but two of Ireland's building societies have been sold to other financial institutions or have gone public. The remaining two, however, the EBS and Irish Nationwide, do offer an alternative to the traditional banks. Because of their slightly unusual status in the Irish financial services market place, they no longer offer current accounts to new customers. Nevertheless, thanks to their ATM network, competitive interest rates and other services, using them for your day-to-day banking can be feasible and may save you quite a bit of money.

THE AN POST OPTION

An Post is another option if you would rather not deal with one of the five major banks. Although they don't have any ATM cash machines, there are 1,250 branches of An Post and, of course, they're open six days a week. An account with An Post pays a higher level of interest than the equivalent bank account, and you can pay (without cost) a range of household bills (up to 120 bills) and buy money drafts at minimal cost.

THE CREDIT UNION OPTION

Credit unions, like building societies, are owned by their members. There are 430 credit unions in Ireland – each one serving a local community. Their original role was to help people to save and also to provide inexpensive loans. In the last few years,

though, many have expanded the range of financial services they offer dramatically. For instance, many credit unions now offer budget accounts, which are perfectly suitable for paying regular bills. The main drawback to using a credit union for your day-to-day banking is that you can't take advantage of a national branch network or ATM machines. However, for some people they do offer an acceptable option.

BANKING ON HOLIDAY

You're going abroad, what should you do about money? Here are a few useful tips:

1   Since Ireland is one of the 16 countries that comprise the eurozone, you can pay with **euro** when visiting Austria, Belgium, Cyprus, Finland, France, Germany, Greece, Italy, Luxembourg, Malta, The Netherlands, Portugal, Slovakia, Slovenia and Spain. Like the American dollar, the euro is widely accepted in many other countries, while not legal tender. Unfortunately, euro cheques from Ireland cannot, yet, be used for

payments when visiting another eurozone country.

2 Wherever you're travelling in the world – whether it's in the eurozone or not – a **credit card** is probably the least expensive, most secure and most convenient way of paying. Visa and MasterCard are the most widely accepted credit cards overseas. The exchange rate you receive will, broadly speaking, be competitive. However, I would not recommend credit cards as a means of obtaining cash when overseas as all the credit card companies charge a fee for cash advances plus a high rate of interest from the day of withdrawal.

3 If you have an **ATM card** from one of the five Irish banks you'll find that you can use it extensively all over the world. The advantage of this is that you need not carry a great deal of cash with you, providing you have sufficient funds in your current account. Note, however, that you may not get the best rate of exchange and there could be special charges. Check with your bank before you head off.

4 **Traveller's cheques** are, in fact, quite expensive. Although they are obviously much more secure than cash, between the commission and exchange charges you could lose as much as 6% of your money – which is a high price to pay in my opinion. In fact, the demand for traveller's cheques has fallen so much that Ireland's biggest bank no longer stocks them.

5 The practical option is to ask for the minimum credit limit on your current credit card and pre-lodge all the funds you expect to spend on your holiday. Simple, but sensible.

THE MONEY DOCTOR SAYS...

- It is possible to enjoy free or very low-cost banking if you take advantage of the system.
- Unauthorised overdrafts are very expensive and should be avoided if at all possible.
- Bank loyalty doesn't pay. Always shop around for the best deal.
- If you settle up each month in full, a credit card can be a very inexpensive way to manage much of your banking.
- There are alternatives to the banks – building societies, An Post and credit unions.

9
GETTING OUT OF DEBT

HOW TO PAY OFF ALL YOUR LOANS – INCLUDING YOUR MORTGAGE – QUICKLY AND EASILY

The greatest threat to your financial well-being is borrowing. I am not talking about reckless borrowing, either, but ordinary borrowing in the form of personal loans, overdrafts and credit cards. This is because the cost of borrowing money is a huge drain on your most valuable asset – your income.

What's more, the cost of borrowing can't just be measured in terms of the interest you are paying. You must also factor in the opportunity cost – the money you would otherwise be making if you were investing your income instead of spending it on servicing your debts. Let me give you one simple example:

> €10,000 repaid over seven years at an interest rate of 10% will require monthly repayments of €166. Total interest cost €3,945.

> Invest €166 a month into – say – the stock market for the same period and assuming the same sort of growth as we have seen over the last ten years bar the last two – you'll have a lump sum of almost €20,000 in seven years.

Which is why, in this chapter, I explain the benefits of being debt-free, together with two proven methods to make paying off all your loans fast and painless.

YOU MAY NOT EVEN REALISE YOU HAVE A PROBLEM

Most people borrow money but fail to think of themselves as being in debt. The fact is:

- You don't have to be in any sort of financial difficulty to be in debt.
- When you add up the cost of servicing your debt – including your mortgage – it may come to more than you imagine.

- Debt is the single greatest threat to your financial freedom and security. It is sucking away your most valuable asset: your income.

- The first benefit of being debt-free is that your money becomes your own to spend or invest as you prefer.

- Not having any debt will make you less vulnerable. You won't need so much insurance, for instance.

SIZING UP THE PROBLEM

Over the last twenty to thirty years consumer debt has increased at a frightening pace. Why should this be? Some borrowing is unavoidable – for instance, loans taken out when ill or unemployed. Some can be attributed to other factors such as changing social values, lack of education at school, our consumer society and 'impulse' spending. However, I believe the main reason for the borrowing boom is that debt has become a hugely profitable business. Bluntly, lenders use clever marketing tricks to 'push' debt onto innocent consumers. They are doing this because the returns are irresistible. Look at how much money they can make:

- If you leave money on deposit at a bank you'll typically earn less than 1% (€1 for every €100) a year by way of interest.

- That bank, however, can lend your money to someone else at anything up to 24% (€24 for every €100) a year.

Under the circumstances, is it any wonder that financial institutions are falling over themselves to lend money? Or that they devote themselves to coming up with new ways to sell loans to their customers?

DEBT COMES IN MANY DISGUISES

The trouble with the word 'debt' is that it has all sorts of negative connotations. Many people believe that providing they are never behind on their repayments they are not in debt. This isn't true. A debt is when you owe someone money. It could be:

- an unpaid balance on a credit card

- an overdraft

- a personal loan

- a car loan or loan for some other specific purchase

- a mortgage on your home

- a secured loan

- a hire-purchase agreement

- an unpaid balance on a store charge card

- a business loan

- a loan made by a friend or family member.

It is important to remember that just because you are never in arrears and have an excellent credit rating, it doesn't mean you are debt-free.

MONEY DOCTOR WEALTH WARNING

It is compound interest that makes debt so expensive

When you are earning it, it has the power to make you very rich. When you are paying it, it has the power to make you very poor. Albert Einstein described it as 'the greatest mathematical discovery of all time'. It is the reason why banks, building societies, credit card companies and other financial institutions make so much profit from lending money. And it is the reason why ordinary investors can make themselves rich simply by doing nothing. It is a fiendishly simple concept called **compound interest.**

Perhaps the easiest way to understand compound interest is to look at two hypothetical examples:

Imagine that you borrow €1,000 at a rate of 10% a year. At the end of one year – assuming you have made no repayments – you will owe €100 in interest (10% of €1,000) or a total of €1,100. If you wait another year then you will owe an additional €110 in interest (10% of €1,100) or a total of €1,210. In other words you are paying interest on the interest.

Now imagine that you have €1,000 to invest and you deposit it in a savings account, which pays interest at a rate of 10% per year. At the end of one year you will be entitled to €100 interest. If you withdraw this interest but leave your capital, at the end of the second year you will be entitled to another €100 interest.

Supposing, however, that you don't withdraw the interest but leave it to 'compound'. At the end of your first year your €1,000 is worth €1,100. At the end of your second year you will have earned €110 interest, meaning that your original €1,000 is worth €1,210. Put another way, your interest is earning you more interest.

When you borrow money, compound interest is working against you. Supposing, for instance, you borrow €5,000 on a credit card at an interest rate of 15% – which isn't high by today's standards. The credit card company allows you to make a minimum payment of 1.5% each month. After two years you will still owe approximately €4,700, having made repayments of €1,750, of which €1,450 has been swallowed up in interest.

Compound interest is your greatest enemy and your greatest ally. When you are in debt, it works against you. But when you have money to invest you can make compound interest really work for you.

'Compounding is man's greatest invention as it allows the reliable systematic accumulation of wealth.' – Albert Einstein

BEWARE THE MINIMUM PAYMENT TRAP

You make your lender happy when you:

- borrow as much as possible

- pay it back over as long a period as possible

- borrow at the highest possible interest rate

- make the minimum monthly payment.

You should be particularly wary of the **minimum payment trap** – where the lender allows you to pay back very little of the debt each month. This is particularly prevalent in the credit card and store card sector. When you opt for the minimum monthly repayment your repayment will be made up almost completely of interest so that the debt itself hardly ever gets reduced. Another thing to watch for is 'revolving credit' – where the lender keeps upping your credit limit or offering you new loans. It can take up to 11 years to repay some credit card debt if you only make the minimum payment each month!

DEBT THREATENS YOUR FUTURE FREEDOM

I certainly wouldn't go so far as to say all debt is bad. There are plenty of instances where borrowing money makes financial sense – in order to buy your own home, for example, or to pay for education. *It is when you are borrowing money to finance your lifestyle that you are getting into dangerous territory.* Living beyond your means threatens your future financial freedom. Let me give you an example:

> Cathal is the manager of a supermarket and earns a good income. However, it isn't enough to cover all the things he and his family like to enjoy, so he borrows frequently. In a typical year he might borrow to pay for Christmas presents, a holiday or just to cover other shortfalls in his monthly expenditure such as clothes or eating out. He views this as 'short-term' debt but the reality is that every year between the ages of 35 and 55 he borrows an average of €4,000 more than he earns. Because this is short-term, unsecured debt he pays an average of 12% a year in interest. His monthly debt repayments (excluding his mortgage) are €360.
>
> Cathal's twin brother, Ray, is also a supermarket manager and earns exactly the same income. However, he lives within his means. He doesn't eat out as often, go on holiday as frequently or drive such a nice car. He saves the €360 his brother spends each month on servicing his debts and instead he invests the money. He manages a return of 6% a year on average between the ages of 35 and 55 and so he builds up a tax-free lump sum of €160,000.

The fact is, your most valuable asset is your income and there is only so much that each of us will ever earn during our lifetimes. By spending a large portion of it on servicing debt you are – basically – giving it away to your lenders. Surely your need is greater than theirs?

SEVEN EXCELLENT REASONS TO BECOME DEBT-FREE

Here are seven reasons why you should pay off all your debts – including, perhaps, your mortgage.

1 It will make you less vulnerable. If you are in debt and for some reason your income is reduced or stops altogether (suppose, for instance, you fall seriously ill and don't have permanent health insurance), then not being able to repay your loans could have serious consequences.

2   It will make your family less vulnerable. I don't want to depress you but when you die your debts won't die with you – your estate will have to pay them all.

3   You won't have to worry about inflation. If you owe money and interest rates rise (as recently as 1981 interest rates were as high as 20%) then you could easily find yourself struggling to make your monthly payments.

4   You won't have the stress which comes with debt. The fact is that owing money is stressful.

5   You'll enjoy a genuine sense of satisfaction. There is a real peace of mind which comes with not owing money and with owning your home outright.

6   It will open up new choices. Suddenly all the money you are spending on servicing your debts will be available for you to spend or save as you prefer.

7   It will ensure you have a comfortable retirement. Furthermore, it may allow you to retire early. Why should you have to wait until you are 60 or 65 to give up work?

MONEY DOCTOR WEALTH WARNING

How lenders will try to trick you

With so much profit at stake lenders put a lot of effort into persuading consumers to borrow. There is a catch to every offer! Let me give you just one example:

Josephine goes to buy a new bed in the local store sale. It is marked down from €1,300 to €1,100 and as she goes to pay the shop assistant persuades her to take out a store card as it will give her an extra 10% saving. So instead of €1,100 she pays just €990. However, Josephine doesn't pay off her store card at the end of the month but instead takes 36 months to do so. The result? Because she is being charged 15% interest, the bed ends up costing her €1,548. Not so much of a saving, after all!

A couple of other things to watch out for. Firstly, **loan consolidation**. When used properly – as I will explain in a moment – loan consolidation is an excellent way to speed yourself out of debt. However, unscrupulous lenders often lure borrowers into taking out expensive consolidation loans – even encouraging them to borrow extra for a holiday or other luxury item. Secondly, if **transferring credit card debt** to save money, only too often a low interest or zero interest period is followed by a much higher rate. Check the conditions carefully and don't be taken in by lenders.

THE FIRST STEP TO GETTING OUT OF DEBT

There is one thing you must do before you set out to eradicate all your debt: stop borrowing. After all, you can't get yourself out of a hole if you keep digging. Take a once-and-for-all decision to:

- not just to pay off your debts, but to stay out of debt
- not to borrow any more money unless it is absolutely unavoidable (or there is a very reasonable chance that you can invest the money you borrow to make more than the loan is going to cost you to repay)
- not to live beyond your means
- avoid 'bargains'. In my book a genuine bargain is something you need to buy but which you manage to get at a lower price than you expected to pay for it. Something that you don't need but you buy because it seems to be cheap is definitely not a bargain.

There are various actions you can take to make this easier on yourself. You can:

- Cut up all your credit cards and store cards.
- Cancel your overdraft limit. But remember, most banks will allow a 'shadow' overdraft on your account. This means that informally they may allow your account to overdraw by say €500 before you are contacted. This is costly and may eventually have to be formalised, so you are back in the overdraft trap again. Keep track of all transactions on your account.
- Use a charge card where the balance has to be paid in full at the end of each month.

- Avoid buying any unnecessary items.

- Do not take out any new loans, including hire-purchase agreements and overdrafts.

- Do not increase the size of any existing loans.

- Pay with cash whenever possible (nothing reduces one's tendency to spend money as paying with cash).

American money expert Alvin Hall (you may have seen him on television) suggests that anyone with trouble curbing his or her expenditure should keep what he calls a **money diary**. The basic idea is that you carry a small notebook with you wherever you go and write down details of every single penny you spend. You should include everything – from your daily newspaper to your mortgage repayments. After a couple of weeks you'll have a precise picture of where your money is going and this, in turn, will help you avoid spending money on things you don't really want or need. If you are prone to impulse spending or if you always spend more than your income I can see the good sense in this approach.

TAKING STOCK OF YOUR SITUATION

Once you have stopped making the situation any worse you need to take stock of your situation. In particular, you want to gather together full details of your debts. The information you require about each of your debts is:

- to whom you owe the money

- how big the debt is

- how long you have to pay it back (the term), if relevant

- what the rate of interest is and whether it is fixed or variable

- whether you will be penalised for paying back the debt early (and if so what the penalties are)

- what the minimum monthly payment is (if this is relevant)

- whether the interest is calculated daily, monthly or annually.

Obviously, it is important not to overlook any possible debts, so here is a quick checklist to remind you. Don't forget to include any money that your spouse or partner may owe, too!

- mortgages

- secured loans
- credit cards
- store cards
- overdrafts
- personal loans
- car loans
- hire- or lease-purchase
- catalogue company loans
- family or friends who may have lent you money
- student loans.

Most of the information you need should be supplied to you each month by your lenders. However, if it isn't, then you should telephone or write to them asking for full details.

MONEY DOCTOR WEALTH CHECK

The 'savings' conundrum

The Money Doctor often encounters 'patients' who have debts but who are saving money at the same time. If you cannot make a greater return on your capital than the deposit interest rate on your savings, it may well be to your advantage to reduce debt where the interest rate chargeable is far higher than that of the deposit interest rate.

In most cases, it makes sense to stop saving money and to use any existing savings to pay off some or all of your debts. Why? Because usually what you are earning from your savings will be substantially less than what you are paying out to borrow.

€100 in a savings account may be earning you as little as €1 after tax.

€100 owed on – say – a credit card may be costing you as much as €24 or even more a year.

So if you had savings of €1,000 and used it to pay off €1,000 of credit card debt you could be saving yourself as much as €240 a year. More if you have borrowed on a store card.

Note, however, it does not make sense to cash in your savings if, for example, you have an endowment policy where you may need to leave it mature. You would be well advised to take professional advice since some are worth more than others.

Overall, however, it does not make financial sense to be investing a small amount of money each month if – at the same time – you are spending a small fortune on servicing a debt.

THE ART OF DEBT ELIMINATION

You've taken the decision not to incur any extra debt. You've got a real grip on the size and nature of your problem. What next? You have two options:

- the consolidation approach
- the sniper approach.

Option 1: The consolidation approach

The idea behind 'consolidation' is to reduce the cost of your debt dramatically. Instead of having lots of different loans – all at different rates – you have a single loan at one, much lower rate. It works particularly well if you own your own home. What you do is:

- Add up all the money you currently spend making your debt repayments.
- Consolidate all your debts into a single, much cheaper loan.
- Keep on making the same monthly payments.

This is best explained with an example. Below I have listed off all the debts that Brian and Sheila have along with the interest rate they are paying on each one:

Type of debt	Monthly cost	Interest rate (%)
Mortgage	€900	5.5
Home improvement loan	€16	10
Credit card 1	€45	16
Credit card 2	€30	16
Store card	€71	17
Car loan	€225	10

The total amount Brian and Sheila are spending on their debts is €1,287 a month. Since they own their own home they can consolidate all their debts in with their mortgage. At the moment their mortgage is for €128,000 and has 19 years to run. Although consolidating their loans increases their mortgage to €152,000, by continuing to pay €1,300 a month they can shorten the length of their mortgage to just 14 years. At the same time they will save themselves €27,000 in interest! Incidentally, to optimise the benefit of consolidation it may be preferable to take out something called a **current account mortgage**. The full benefits of these mortgages are explained on p. 117.

Please remember, debt consolidation is a once-in-a-lifetime course of action. It only works to your advantage if you carry on making the same monthly payments, otherwise all you are doing is spreading the cost of your short-term debt over the longer term. I believe one should never borrow money for a longer period than the life of the asset you are buying.

Currently it is extremely difficult to obtain such a consolidation loan with any of the lenders in Ireland. I would strongly advise using professional help.

Option 2: The sniper approach

If you don't own your own home – or if you don't have sufficient capital tied up in your property to consolidate your debts in with your mortgage – you'll need to take what I call the 'sniper' approach. This involves 'picking off' your debts one at a time starting with the most expensive. What you do is:

- Find some extra money. Just because you don't have a mortgage doesn't mean that you can't consolidate your debt. Move your borrowing to where it is costing you the least.
- Use the money you are saving each month to pay off your most expensive debt – in other words, the one with the highest rate of interest.

Do you sometimes pay more than the minimum amount required each month? If you do then make sure you pay it to whichever of your debts is costing you the most. Incidentally, you may find that one or more of your existing lenders will be open to negotiation.

To use a typical example, imagine that Neil has the following debts:

Type of debt	Monthly/minimum cost	Interest rate (%)
Credit card €4,000	€60	16
Store card €5,000	€75	17
Car loan €8,000	€258	10

Every month he usually pays about €100 more off one or other of the debts – on a purely random basis. Also, he is able to find €100 from other sources (see below) to help speed himself out of debt. In other words, Neil has €200 extra to apply to getting himself out of debt. Therefore, what he needs to do is pay off his most expensive debt first – his store card. By paying an extra €200 a month he can do this within 20 months. This frees up the store card minimum payment of €75 to help pay of his next most expensive debt – which is his credit card.

MONEY DOCTOR WEALTH CHECK

Put your money to the best possible use...

The secret to getting rid of your debts is in putting your money to the best possible use. Your objective is to get your loans onto the lowest possible rate of interest and then to use the saving to speed up the process of paying off your debt.

Of course, if you could find some extra money each month, then you could get out of debt even faster. One way to find extra money is to look at the way you spend your income and see if you couldn't make some basic savings without necessarily cutting back. For example:

- Many people pay more than they have to for their banking. Review your arrangements. Could you be earning extra interest? Saving interest? Avoiding unnecessary costs?

- Don't pay for anything you neither need nor use. For instance, membership fees, internet charges and magazines.

- Double check you aren't overpaying your tax. Are your tax credits correct?

- Review all your insurance costs. This is a fiercely competitive market and you may be able to save a substantial amount.

In general, it isn't what you earn but how you spend it that will make the difference to your finances. You could be on an enormous salary but if you are up to your neck in debt (as many high-income earners are) it is useless to you.

THE MONEY DOCTOR SAYS...

- If you only take action on one aspect of your finances make it your priority to get yourself out of debt.
- The first step is to stop borrowing and to get a realistic position of what you owe and how much it is costing you.
- Consider consolidating your debt in with your mortgage, if you can.
- Remember, if you save money or have any spare cash you should put it towards paying off your debts, providing you still maintain a Rainy Day Fund or Emergency Fund.
- Pay your most expensive debts off first.

10
BORROWING

IF YOU DO HAVE TO BORROW I WILL SHOW YOU HOW TO BORROW SENSIBLY

HOW TO BORROW SENSIBLY AND INEXPENSIVELY

There are times when it makes sense to borrow. And times when borrowing is unavoidable. Either way, you want to make sure that you don't pay a cent more than you have to. If there is one area of personal finance where consumers get 'ripped off' regularly, then it is when they borrow.

Look at the difference!

Nothing better illustrates the way in which consumers can overpay for a loan than a quick comparison of rates:

Secured loan from one of the specialist lenders	6%
Personal loan (unsecured) from any high street bank	10%
Credit card from any of the main providers	17%
Store card from any of the major retail outlets	19%

As a consumer it is not impossible that you might simultaneously be paying anything from 6% to 20% to borrow money – which is ridiculous.

MONEY DOCTOR WEALTH CHECK

How to compare loan rates

In order that consumers can compare interest rates, the government insists that the cost of loans is expressed in terms of an **annual percentage rate** (APR).

Confusingly, there is more than one way to calculate the APR – but broadly speaking it is an accurate way of assessing how much a loan is going to cost you including all the hidden costs such as up-front fees.

> Clearly, the lower the APR, the cheaper the loan, the better it is for you.
>
> Remember, financial institutions make enormous profits from lending money. You should never, ever be shy about shopping around or asking for a lower rate.

SO, WHAT IS 'SENSIBLE BORROWING'?

There are times when it makes excellent sense to borrow. For instance, if you want to:

- buy, build or improve your home
- finance a property investment
- pay for education
- pay for a car or other necessary item
- start a business.

There are also times when it is impossible not to borrow money – if you are temporarily unable to earn an income, for instance, for some reason beyond your control.

There is no intrinsic harm, either, in genuine short-term borrowing for some luxury item. What is really dangerous, however, is short-term borrowing that becomes long-term borrowing without you meaning it to do so. This is not only extremely expensive but makes you more vulnerable to financial problems. I can't emphasise enough how bad it is for your financial well-being to borrow money to pay for living expenses. In particular, you should definitely avoid long-term credit card and store card debt.

If you have succumbed to the temptation of credit card or store card debt – and you want to pay it off – read Chapter 9 on getting out of debt.

NEVER BORROW FOR LONGER THAN YOU HAVE TO

Making sure that you pay the lowest rate of interest is one way to keep the cost of borrowing down. Paying your debts back quickly is another. Compound interest (see Appendix 1) really works against you when borrowing money. The difference between paying back €1,000 at 15% APR over one year and – say – three years is a staggering €300 in interest!

BUILD UP A GOOD FINANCIAL/CREDIT RATING HISTORY

It is vital at all times to be aware that defaulting on loans or credit cards is registered with the Irish Credit Bureau (ICB) and will greatly affect your ability to borrow or borrow at attractive interest rates. Never let unauthorised arrears build up on any loan. If your circumstances change during the term of a loan, inform the lender and come to an agreed and realistic repayment schedule. (See Chapter 16, 'If I have trouble making my mortgage repayments, what should I do?' for details of whom to contact to avoid money lenders if you are in dire circumstances.)

WHY RATES DIFFER SO WIDELY

Financial institutions set their charges according to the level of risk involved and prevailing market conditions.

As far as they are concerned, loans fall into two categories:

Secured loans. Where, if the borrower fails to make the repayments, there is a physical asset – such as a house or even an insurance policy – that can be 'seized' and sold to meet the outstanding debt. Because of this secured loans should cost considerably less.

Unsecured loans. Where, if the borrower fails to make the repayments, the lender has no security and thus risks never getting paid (though this is rare). Such loans cost considerably more.

THE FIRST RULE OF BORROWING

The first rule of borrowing for less is, therefore, to take out a secured rather than an unsecured loan. This isn't always practicable – but where it is, you'll save a substantial amount of money.

Secured loans

Secured loans include:

- mortgage on your property
- secured loan (which is like a second or extra mortgage) on your property
- asset-backed finance (used, for instance, for major purchases such as cars).

Unsecured loans

Unsecured loans include:

- bank overdrafts
- credit union loans
- personal or term loans – including car loans
- credit cards
- store cards
- hire-purchase
- money lenders.

MONEY DOCTOR WEALTH WARNING

Interest rates have not always been so low

We have enjoyed relatively low interest rate stability up to recently. Things were very different less than a decade ago. Indeed, in the early 1990s mortgage rates went up to 15% at one point, and some people were paying over 30% a year on their credit card debt.

We saw in 2008 that interest rates rose by nearly 2%. Therefore, don't borrow so much that a change in interest rates (or a change in your personal circumstances) would leave you in crisis.

While rates plummeted to 1% ECB rate during 2009, and have remained there for 18 months, there is still every chance that within 12 months rates will be on the rise again. Nevertheless, consider carefully further borrowings.

CHOOSING THE BEST LOAN FOR YOUR NEEDS

With the possible exception of borrowing to fund a major holiday or a special event such as a wedding, you should try to make sure that the useful life of whatever you're using your loan for will be longer than the time it takes you to repay it. Remember, the rate of interest you're charged is only part of the equation. The other part is the length of time it will take you to repay the loan. For instance, you might think it was sensible to take out some extra money on your mortgage to buy a car since mortgages are, undoubtedly, the least expensive way to borrow. If, however, your mortgage still has 15 years to run then you'll be paying for your car over all that time. Under the circumstances, you should opt for an alternative method or else ensure that you overpay your mortgage in order to clear that part of the debt sooner.

THE MONEY DOCTOR BEST LOAN GUIDE

Here are the ten most usual ways of borrowing money ranked in order – starting with the least expensive first and ending with the most expensive last.

1. **Loans from family, friends and employers.** Often family members, friends and employers will make interest-free or low-interest loans. My advice is always to regularise such loans with a written agreement so that there is no room for misunderstanding or bad feeling at a later date.

2. **Mortgages and secured loans.** Since the demise of tracker mortgages interest rates have increased, but are still low in relative terms. However, because of funding difficulties, most lenders will no longer consider equity releases or top-up mortgages to finance other non-property purchases. If you are fortunate enough to have a sympathetic lender and have sufficient equity in your property, this can still be an inexpensive way to finance a major purchase. However, bear in mind that if you say, buy a car and add it to your mortgage what you should do is increase your monthly repayments so that that bit of your debt is paid off in less time. Otherwise, you could be paying for your car over the whole term of your mortgage. If you do this, however, ensure that your extra payments 'reduce the capital' (loan) rather than credit your repayment account.

3. **Asset finance and leasing.** I am a big believer in asset finance and leasing. Although not as cheap as a mortgage, this can be an economical way to fund major purchases and it has the benefit of being very tax-efficient if you are self-employed or running a business. You should ask an authorised financial adviser with access to all providers to find you the best possible rate. Leasing is also very quick and you can receive your cheque within 48 hours of your application.

4. **Overdrafts.** If you have a bank current account you can ask your manager for an overdraft facility. Once approved, you will be able to spend money up to this amount. There won't be a set re-payment period but there may well be an annual arrangement charge. Authorised

overdrafts are usually fairly competitive (though you shouldn't be afraid to negotiate). Exceeding your overdraft limit, however, can lead to heavy charges and the embarrassment of bounced cheques – for this reason unauthorised overdrafts should be avoided. Bear in mind, too, that most banks expect your current account to be in credit for 30 days a year and will charge you extra if it isn't.

5   **Credit union loans.** We are fortunate in Ireland to have a network of local credit unions willing to lend money to its members at a competitive rate of interest. To qualify for a loan you must first join the credit union and then – normally – save a regular amount with them for a set period of time. Because credit unions are non-profit making they tend to offer much better value for money. Not all credit union rates are the same and while it is worth shopping around, you can only open a credit union account in the nearest office to where you live or where you work.

6   **Personal or term loans.** The cost of personal or term loans can vary enormously. Essentially, when you borrow the money you agree to a set repayment period or 'term'. The rate of interest charged is normally variable and you should always pay close attention to your statements to check that it hasn't risen out of line with market rates. Where a rate is fixed in advance – giving you the security of knowing what your repayments will be – it is likely to be higher.

Where a loan is provided by a dealer or retailer, check the conditions closely. Sometimes you may be offered a low or zero rate for an agreed period that will rise dramatically in cost after the set term. Also, the cost of providing this credit will be built into the price of whatever you are buying.

7   **Credit cards.** Used properly, a credit card will give you as much as 45 days interest-free credit. On a certain day every month your bill will be calculated for the previous 30 days and sent to you for payment by the end of the following month. If your cut-off date is – say – the 17th of the month, all charges between 17 December and 17 January would have to be paid for by the end of February. If you can't pay the full amount then you are given the option of paying a reduced amount. This could be less than 5% of the total outstanding. The catch is that you will be charged an extremely high rate of interest – possibly

approaching 20% a year. Credit cards are an extremely expensive way to borrow and credit card companies are very aggressive in their marketing methods. If you are going to use a credit card then don't fall into the trap of making the minimum payment each month. A relatively small balance could take you years to clear.

Note: if your income is high enough your bank may offer you a 'gold' credit card with a built-in overdraft facility at a preferential rate. Your credit card balance will be settled each month using the overdraft. This can be a cost-effective way to borrow and is worth investigating.

8 **Store cards.** I am afraid I am not at all enthusiastic about store cards. They work in the same way as credit cards except – of course – you can only use them in the store (or chain of stores) that issues the card. Their single advantage is that having such a card may entitle you to an extra discount on first purchase and again during any sales. Their huge disadvantage is that the rate of interest charged on outstanding balances almost always makes normal credit cards look cheap by comparison. My strong advice – unless you are very disciplined with money – is not to use store cards.

9 **Hire-purchase.** Hire-purchase allows you to buy specific goods over an agreed period of time. In other words, it is a bit like a personal or term loan. The difference is that the rates charged for hire-purchase are normally somewhat higher and you might be better looking at alternatives such as a personal loan or a lease. Remember, too, that with hire-purchase you don't own whatever you are buying until you have made your last payment. This is not the case with, for example, a personal loan. However, if you have paid over half the term in the HP agreement, you can return the goods (e.g. a car) with the loan scrapped at that point.

10 **Money lenders.** Whether licensed or unlicensed, money lenders are always about the most expensive way to borrow and the rates they charge are outrageous. When they are trading illegally there is the added risk of violence or intimidation if you don't pay what they say you owe them. You should avoid them like the plague! Incidentally, the definition of a money lender – and licensed at that – is an entity or someone who charges you a minimum of 23% interest a year! A list of

licensed money lenders is available from The Central Bank.

(See Chapter 16 'If I have trouble making my mortgage repayments, what should I do?' for details of whom to contact to avoid money lenders if you are in dire circumstances.)

THE MONEY DOCTOR SAYS...

- Think carefully before you borrow money. Is it sensible to take out a loan for whatever you are planning to buy? Don't borrow money to pay for 'lifestyle' items. No loan should ever last for longer than the thing you are spending the money on!

- Shop around for the most competitive rate. There is a huge difference and you can save yourself – literally – thousands of euros by making sure you have the cheapest possible loan.

- Read any credit agreement very carefully and seek clarification of any sections you don't fully understand.

- Don't allow your short-term borrowing to become long term by mistake.

- Don't be blindly loyal to any particular lender. Go where the best rate is.

- If in doubt, seek expert help.

PART 4

COMPLETE GUIDE TO INSURANCE

Life insurance…home insurance…pet insurance…medical insurance…product warranty insurance…travel insurance…income protection insurance…there is no shortage of different insurance policies to choose from.

In principle, so much choice is a wonderful thing. It allows you to protect yourself, your family and your possessions from a whole range of risks – at one end catastrophic, at the other mildly irritating.

In practice, of course, so much choice can be confusing and can easily lead to you:

- *not taking out cover you should really have*
- *taking out cover that you don't actually need*
- *taking out the wrong amount of cover (too much or, more worryingly, too little)*
- *paying more than you have to.*

I am afraid the problem is often compounded by the fact that many people end up receiving poor or heavily biased advice.

Anyway, this section of the book has a single purpose: making sure that you have the appropriate cover for your needs and that you aren't paying more for it than is necessary. It is divided into two chapters. In the first, we will consider cover for people, and in the second, cover for things.

11
PROTECTING YOURSELF AND YOUR FAMILY

HOW TO BUY THE MEDICAL, INCOME AND LIFE INSURANCE YOU ACTUALLY NEED – AT THE LOWEST POSSIBLE PRICE

First-class medical protection, critical illness cover and life insurance are available at a remarkably low price providing you know how to buy it.

In this chapter you'll discover how to:

- make sure you aren't sold cover you don't need

- decide what cover it is sensible for you to take out

- find out who you can trust to advise you

- make sure you get your cover at the lowest possible price.

American filmmaker Woody Allen quipped that his 'idea of hell is to be stuck in a lift with a life insurance salesman'. Mr Allen is by no means alone in his distrust of both life insurance and the people who sell it. Why should this be? I'm sure it is partly because no one likes to think about anything bad happening to them, and partly because – in order to draw attention to a very real need – life insurance salespeople are forced to bring up uncomfortable subjects with their prospective clients.

However, although it is not something you may rush to tackle, making certain that you have adequate life – and health – insurance will bring you *genuine* peace of mind.

YOU KNOW YOU SHOULD...

It isn't pleasant to dwell on being ill, having an accident or – worst of all – dying. Nevertheless, you owe it to yourself – and those you care for – to spend a little time making sure you are **protected** should the worst happen. This means being:

- *protected* by PHI (permanent health insurance) if you are too unwell to earn an income
- *protected* by private medical insurance if you need medical attention
- *protected* by life cover if you, or your partner, should die.

For a relatively small amount of money you can take out a range of insurance policies designed to:

- provide for you, or your dependants, if you, or your partner, should die
- give you a lump sum or a regular income if you find you have a serious illness, are incapacitated or cannot work
- meet all your private medical bills in the event of an accident or illness.

There are, of course, plenty of facts and figures available proving just how likely it is for someone of any age to fall ill or die. Sadly, such statistics are borne out by everyone's personal experience. The truth is we all know of instances where families have had to face poor medical care and/or financial hardship as the result of a tragedy. We all know, too, that spending the small sum required to purchase appropriate cover makes sound sense.

SPEND TIME, NOT MONEY

The odd thing about the different types of insurance dealt with in this chapter is that none of them is expensive when you consider the protection they offer. The secret is to identify exactly what cover you *really* need and not to get sold an inappropriate or overpriced policy. It is also important to review your needs on a regular basis. What you require today, and what you'll require in even two or three years time could differ dramatically.

The best way to start is by considering what risks you face and deciding what action you should take. Here are three questions that everyone should ask themselves, regardless of their age, gender, health or financial circumstances.

Question 1: What would your financial position be if you were unable to work – due to an accident or illness – for more than a short period of time?

Obviously, your employer and the state will both be obliged to help you out. However, if you have a mortgage, other debts and/or a family to support, your legal entitlements are unlikely to meet anything like your normal monthly outgoings. If you do have a family then your spouse will have to balance work, caring for you and – possibly – caring for children. Is this feasible or – more to the point – desirable? How long will your savings last you under these circumstances? Do you have other assets you could sell?

Unless you have substantial savings and/or low outgoings then income protection cover (sometimes known as permanent health insurance) and/or critical illness insurance could both make sound sense.

Question 2: Do you have anyone dependent on you for either financial support or care? Are you dependent on someone else financially? Do you have children – or other family members – who would have to be cared for if you were to die?

If you are single and don't have any dependants then the reason to take out life insurance is in order to settle your debts and/or leave a bequest. If, on the other hand, there is someone depending on you – either for money or for care – then life cover has to be a priority.

If you are supporting anyone (or if your financial contribution is necessary to the running of your household) then you need to take out cover so that you don't leave those you love facing a financial crisis.

If you are caring for anyone – children, perhaps, or an ageing relative – then you should take out cover so that there is plenty of money for someone else to take over this role.

Question 3: Does it matter to you how quickly you receive non-urgent medical treatment? If you need medical care would you rather choose who looks after you, where you are treated and in what circumstances? How important is a private room in hospital to you?

We are fortunate enough to enjoy free basic health care in Ireland. However, if you are self-employed or if you have responsibilities which mean that it is important for you to be able to choose the time and place of any medical treatment, then you should consider private medical insurance.

INCOME PROTECTION COVER

If you are of working age then the chances of you being off work for a prolonged period of time due to illness or an accident are substantially greater than the chances of you dying.

It is for this reason that **income protection cover** is so valuable. As its name suggests, it is designed to replace your income if a disability or serious illness prevents you from working. If you are in a company pension scheme – or if you have arranged your own pension – you should check to see what cover you have already since it is sometimes included.

Incidentally, most policies only pay out after the policyholder has been off work for a minimum of 13 weeks *unless* hospitalised. Also, if you want to reduce the cost you can opt for a policy that doesn't pay out until you have been off work for 26 weeks.

THE MONEY DOCTOR SAYS...

As with anything *you should shop around* for all your insurance cover. Costs vary dramatically. Remember, too, that an Authorised Advisor, regulated by the Central Bank of Ireland, can explain all the policies to you and can steer you to the best for your needs.

MONEY DOCTOR WEALTH WARNING

Don't be sold something you don't need

I don't believe it is advisable to buy insurance from anyone who isn't qualified to inform you about every single option available to you. Salespeople who are tied to one company – or even a small selection of companies – are clearly not going to offer you the same quality of advice as someone who has a detailed knowledge of the entire market. For further advice on this crucial area see Chapter 4.

CRITICAL OR SERIOUS ILLNESS INSURANCE

Horrible as it is to think about, imagine being diagnosed with a serious illness. I am talking about something like cancer, heart disease or multiple sclerosis. Naturally, under the circumstances, you might need special care and/or want to make life changes. This is where **critical** or **serious illness insurance** comes in. (The name of this insurance cover is changing to **specified illness cover**.) Providing you survive for two weeks after your diagnosis you will receive a lump sum of tax-free money to spend however you wish. Clearly, such a sum would allow you to seek specialist treatment, pay off your debts or in some other way ensure that you didn't have any financial problems.

It is important to remember that this cover provides you with a lump sum – not an income.

LIFE COVER

There are several different types of **life cover** – but they are all designed to do one thing. For a relatively low monthly payment they provide a lump sum if the insured person dies. The lump sum is tax-free and may go into the insured's estate or may be directly payable to a nominated person (such as his or her spouse). Some of the uses to which this lump sum might be put include:

- paying off a mortgage
- paying off other debts
- being invested to provide a replacement income
- being invested to provide money for childcare or the care of someone else such as an ageing relative.

In the case of more expensive life cover the policy can have a cash-in value after a period of time has elapsed. The cost of life cover will be determined by your age, gender, and lifestyle. If you are a non-smoker and don't drink heavily you will save quite a bit of money.

Below are details of the different types of cover available so that you can decide which is most appropriate to your requirements.

Term insurance

As its name implies, **term insurance** is available for a pre-agreed period of time – usually a minimum of ten years. It is mandatory when you take out most interest-only home loans.

It is particularly useful for people with a temporary need. For instance, if you have young children you and your spouse might take out a 20-year plan giving you protection until your family has grown up and left home. By the same token, you might take out a policy that would pay off the exact amount of your mortgage.

Term insurance is the least expensive form of life cover and you can opt for:

Level term. The amount of cover remains the same (level) for the agreed period. For instance, you might take out €50,000 of cover for ten years. The cost will remain fixed for the same period, too.

Decreasing term. The amount of cover drops (decreases) every year. For instance, you might take out €50,000 of cover that drops to €48,000 in the second year, €45,000 in the third year and so forth. Such policies are almost always taken out in conjunction with mortgages in order to pay off the outstanding debt should the insured die. Note this sort of cover can't be extended or increased in value once you have taken it out.

Convertible term. Although the cover is for a set period of time, a convertible policy will allow you to extend your insurance for a further period regardless of your health. This is a very useful feature because it means that if you suffer some health problem you won't be denied life cover because of it. In fact, if you extend the policy, the insurance company will charge you the same premium as if you were perfectly healthy. Convertible term cover is normally not much more expensive than level term cover and – therefore – is usually the better option.

Whole of life assurance

There are two benefits to taking out a **whole of life** assurance plan. Firstly, providing you carry on making your monthly payments, the plan is guaranteed to pay out. In other words, you are covered for the whole of your life. Secondly, there can be an investment element to the cover. So if you decide to cancel the plan you'll receive back a lump sum.

There are various features you can opt for with whole of life cover. You can vary the balance between actual life cover and the investment element, for instance. Also you can decide to end the cover at a particular point – when you retire, for instance. Some whole of life policies are designed to meet inheritance tax liabilities.

Whole of life cover is more expensive than term cover.

PRIVATE MEDICAL INSURANCE

This type of insurance is designed to meet some or all of your medical bills if you opt to go for private treatment.

Only three companies provide this cover in Ireland. VHI (Voluntary Health Insurance), Quinn Healthcare and Hibernian Aviva Health. Between them they offer a wide range of plans with an array of options, conditions and limits. The basic decisions you have to make are:

- Do you want a choice of consultant?
- Do you want a choice of hospital?
- Do you want private or just semi-private hospital accommodation?
- Do you want outpatient cover?

Discounts can be available if you join through a 'group' – your employer, for instance, or a credit union.

As with all insurance, it is well worth getting expert help in deciding which option is best for your needs.

WHICH TYPES OF COVER SHOULD YOU CHOOSE?

Is it better to take out income protection or critical illness insurance? Should you opt for term life or whole of life cover? If term cover – which sort? If whole of life – what investment element should you include? Do you need private medical insurance, or is it a luxury you can do without?

Although these are personal decisions that only you can make, *a professional Authorised Advisor will be able to guide you*. You can trust these advisers to give you the best possible advice because they are bound – by law – to do so and can be prosecuted for 'mis-selling'.

Keep the following points in mind when making your decision:

- If you have a limited budget, I would opt – first and foremost – for either income protection or specified illness cover. Depending on your circumstances you might take out both.
- If you are on a tight budget, then take out decreasing term insurance to cover your mortgage.
- If you have joint financial responsibilities – for instance, if you are married – and you have limited resources, it is more important to cover the main income earner.
- Covering a husband and wife together on the same policy often doesn't cost that much more than covering just one person.
- If you are self-employed, private medical cover is not really a luxury but more of a necessity and the premiums are tax deductible for everyone.

MONEY DOCTOR WEALTH WARNING

Six things every life assurance company must tell you...

The sale of life assurance is strictly regulated and your life assurance company must provide you with six important items of information before you sign on the dotted line. These are:

1   The cost. Not just the monthly premium but also whether the cost will ever be subject to review. If the cost is fixed, this is referred to as level premiums. There are reasons why the cost could be increased. For instance, it could be because the benefit will be going up at some point in the future.

2   A description of the main purpose of the product. For instance, whether it's a savings or protection policy.

3   Full details of all the charges and any commission that is going to be made to a broker or salesperson.

4   If there is an investment element to the policy, you should be given examples of the expected return, together with details of any future tax liability. Any guarantees should also be explained.

5   You should be told what will happen if you cancel (or 'surrender') the policy early. What will this do to the projected value?

6   Background information about the insurer and anyone else involved such as the broker or intermediary.

Note: by law they must also give you a 'cooling-off' period. This is time in which you can change your mind about the policy you have purchased and cancel it, without cost or penalty.

MONEY DOCTOR WEALTH WARNING

You must be truthful

When you complete an application for life cover – in fact, for any sort of insurance – the onus is upon you to advise the insurer of any facts which may affect the risk they are undertaking. Indeed, you'll be asked to sign a declaration to the effect that you haven't withheld any relevant information. If you lie – or even if you fail to reveal something that may be important – your policy may end up being invalid. Clearly, it would be a complete waste of your money if – when you came to claim – the insurer were not legally bound to pay up. In the case of life cover you must provide information about your medical history and also about any risks (such as dangerous sports) that might have some bearing on your life expectancy.

HOW MUCH LIFE COVER DO YOU NEED?

One of the most difficult problems regarding life cover is deciding quite how much you need. If you wanted to replace your income then you will require close to between 10 and 15 times your annual *after-tax* earnings.

> So, if you take home €1,000 a month you should aim to have a minimum of €120,000 cover, which is €1,000 (your salary) x 12 (number of months in the year) x 10 (minimum advisable level of cover).

Remember, it is possible to keep the cost of life cover down by going for a 'term' policy. Bear in mind too that it's better to have some cover than no cover at all.

Life cover tax tip

If you're worried that you may have to pay inheritance tax (see Chapter 29 for further information about this), then one solution is to set up your life assurance policy so that it is not counted as part of your estate when you die. This is done by 'writing the policy under trust' – which is as simple as completing a form your insurer or agent will provide. Incidentally, if you do this, not only will the proceeds from your life cover escape inheritance tax, but also the money will be paid to your chosen beneficiaries relatively quickly – usually in a matter of weeks. It doesn't cost anything to put your life assurance under trust, and you can change the beneficiary (or beneficiaries) at any time.

KEEPING THE COST DOWN

There are two ways to keep the cost of your insurance down to an absolute minimum:

1   Always get independent professional assistance from someone who is authorised to look at *every option* for you. This is one purchase where shopping around and expert knowledge can save you serious money.

2   Refine your needs. By taking out the *right sort of cover* and the *right level of cover* you won't be wasting money. Arising from the huge increase in claims following last winter's floods, insurance premiums have risen substantially, so shopping around is <u>essential</u>.

THE MONEY DOCTOR SAYS...

- Don't stick your head in the sand, believing that 'it won't happen to me'. Protecting yourself and your family should be one of your key financial priorities.

- Choose an independent, professional Authorised Advisor who you feel comfortable with to advise you.

- Don't get sold cover you don't need.

- Review your needs regularly – every two or three years – to make sure you have adequate protection.

- This is a fiercely competitive market. Having an expert shop around for you could mean big savings.

12
PROTECTING YOUR POSSESSIONS

INSIDER TIPS ON HOW TO KEEP THE COST OF YOUR GENERAL INSURANCE TO A BARE MINIMUM

With the cost of general insurance only going one way it is important to make sure that you are getting value for money. In this chapter you'll discover:

- details of all the different types of cover you should consider
- how to ensure that you aren't paying more than you have to
- other buying tips.

THE IMPORTANCE OF PROPER COVER

The temptation, when insurance premiums rise, is to reduce the amount of cover you have or – where cover isn't obligatory – to cancel the policy completely.

There are two reasons why it is important to make sure that you have adequate 'general' insurance.

Firstly, if you have borrowed money in order to pay for something, you should always ensure that there is sufficient insurance to re-pay the debt in case disaster strikes. To quote just one real case history:

> Frank borrowed €15,000 to buy a car and only took out the cheapest motor insurance he could buy – third party, fire and theft . The car was involved in an accident and completely destroyed. Because Frank didn't have comprehensive insurance he is now saddled with paying off the original car loan plus paying for a replacement car.

Secondly, if you under-insure then you always risk receiving less of a pay-out when you come to claim. This is particularly true when it comes to home insurance. Again, let me quote a real case history:

> John and Moira didn't have a mortgage on their house and although they had buildings and contents protection they hadn't bothered to check the amount of cover for many years. Unfortunately, an electrical fault resulted

in the house being burned down (thankfully, no one was hurt). When they came to claim, because they were under-insured, the insurance company would only pay three-quarters of the price of re-building.

Shopping around for insurance is no one's idea of fun. On the other hand, the cost of not taking out adequate insurance can be huge. And if you invest even a small amount of time reading this chapter and acting on it, you will keep the cost to a bare minimum.

THE DIFFERENT TYPES OF 'GENERAL' INSURANCE

So what is 'general' insurance anyway? It is a catch-all expression encompassing some of the following areas:

- home and other forms of property insurance
- motor insurance
- public liability
- insurance for your other possessions such as boats, caravans and mobile telephones
- pet insurance
- travel insurance
- credit insurance
- professional indemnity insurance
- other risk insurance (e.g. Golfsure – for that round of drinks after a hole in one!)

DON'T JUST RELY ON BROKERS

General insurance is the one area where I would suggest that you shouldn't rely solely on brokers to get you the best deal. In many areas there are now 'direct' operations that can undercut brokers substantially. To find details of these direct operations look in your *Golden Pages* and keep an eye out for companies advertising in the national press. Remember, too, that some insurance companies tend to rely on customer inertia when it comes to renewal. So, having won your custom, they may push the cost of cover up in the second year hoping that you won't be bothered to check elsewhere. Telephoning around and filling in extra paperwork is a nuisance, but think of it this way: if it takes you – say – three hours work to save €200 then you are effectively paying yourself nearly €70 an hour after tax.

HOME INSURANCE

Home insurance is divided into 'buildings' cover and 'contents' cover.

Buildings cover

Buildings cover is obligatory if you have a mortgage and you may find that your lender automatically provides this protection (or at the very least a quotation) for you. The insurance will protect the structure of your home (the building itself, outbuildings, fixtures and fittings and so forth) against fire, storm damage, flood, subsidence, and other similar accidents. Most policies also include public liability cover so that if something happens to someone on your property (for instance, if they have an accident) you are protected. The main thing to watch for with buildings cover is that you have sufficient protection. The cost is worked out on the value of your home and is linked entirely to the re-building cost. So where your home is located, how old it is, its size and the materials from which it is constructed will all influence the premium. If you would like help deciding how much cover to take out then the Society of Chartered Surveyors (5 Wilton Place, Dublin 2) produces an annual guide. Not all buildings policies will cover you for the same things so you should check the small print. One way of keeping the cost down is to make sure you have smoke alarms fitted; another is to join your local neighbourhood watch scheme.

Contents cover

Contents cover is even less standard than buildings cover. The sort of protection you'll receive can vary enormously and when comparing prices you need to bear this in mind. For instance, are you being offered new for old cover, which means that if you claim you'll receive the exact cost of replacement with no reduction on account of the age of your possessions? Also, how much of the loss will you be expected to pay for yourself (known as an excess)? And to what extent are valuables – such as jewellery or cash – actually covered? You'll find that there are all sorts of 'extras' that may or may not be included – from employer's liability to theft of bicycles and from liability to third parties to personal liability. Tedious as it is, the only way to know what you are actually getting is to read the small print. Happily, there are a number of ways in which you can keep the cost of your contents cover down:

- Fit an approved alarm system.
- Fit approved locks to doors and windows.
- Join your neighbourhood watch scheme.

Do note that discounts are sometimes offered to people who are at home most of the day – for instance, if you are retired.

MOTOR INSURANCE

With such high insurance premiums you may be tempted to try and reduce the cost by any means possible. For instance, city-based car owners usually pay higher premiums than their rural counterparts and some are tempted to pretend that their car actually 'lives' in the country. Remember, if you ever come to claim, many insurance companies now send out an investigator to make independent inquiries and a false statement could result in being taken to court for fraud.

Motor insurance is more expensive if you:

- don't have a full licence
- have a history of motor offences
- are under 25 years old
- have made claims in the past
- have a criminal record.

Obviously, you can't make yourself any older than you actually are, but if you don't have a full licence it is well worth putting in the effort to pass the test. By the same token, don't rush to put in a minor claim as it may result in higher premiums. Also, remember that fines may not be the only cost of speeding.

INSIDER TIPS ON BUYING OTHER GENERAL INSURANCE

In my opinion many types of general insurance do not offer value for money. I am particularly suspicious of:

Extended warranties. These cover you against faults developing in your electrical and mechanical goods. Often the retailer makes more money from these insurance policies (by way of commission) than on the sale of the actual product. As legislation offers you 12 months' protection anyway (and as, in general, such goods are much better made nowadays) I am suspicious of such policies.

Mobile telephone insurance. This protects you against loss of or damage to your phone. This is often expensive in relation to the actual cost of replacing your telephone. Furthermore, many people end up buying this cover without meaning to because they don't pay proper attention when completing the contract.

Credit card insurance. There are two types of cover offered by credit card companies. The first protects you against fraud and the second against you being unable to make your repayments due to an accident, illness or redundancy. Both types of cover are expensive and in most cases I would advise against them.

Pet insurance. This protects you against having to pay vet bills if your pet is ill or involved in an accident. Again, I would strongly suggest examining the value for money offered by such policies.

One more point is in relation to buying travel insurance. This is often sold by travel agents at highly inflated prices since they earn good rates of commission on every policy sold. Travel insurance is important – but there are many different sources of cover. If you are a regular traveller, you may like to consider an annual policy. Also, if you have a credit card, a certain amount of cover may be included in with your annual fee.

THE MONEY DOCTOR SAYS...

- Check the small print! All insurance policies are not equal.
- It may not be much fun shopping around but it helps if you think of the saving in terms of effort and reward. Three hours spent saving €200 is worth virtually €70 an hour after tax to you.
- Don't get sucked into buying cover you don't really need.
- Don't be tempted to under-insure, it could leave you exposed.

PART 5

A-Z OF PROPERTY PURCHASE

I don't think it would be an overstatement to say that property – and, in particular, owning it – was something of a national obsession. It is easy to understand why: home ownership offers security and the potential to make a capital gain. Indeed, in the ten years up to 2006 residential property prices had grown at an average rate of 12% per annum. Sadly the downturn has taken hold, but there are still opportunities in the property market.

Only the fortunate few can afford to buy a home outright. For the rest of us, saving up until we had the full cost of the apartment or house we wanted to buy would be impractical. Leave aside the fact that it would probably take decades, we would need to live somewhere else in the meantime. The solution is to take out a mortgage or home loan. Such loans are 'secured' against the value of the property being purchased and – because this means the lender faces much less risk – they are normally the least expensive type of borrowing you can undertake.

From a financial perspective, mortgages are the most important consideration when buying a property, which is why the longest chapter in this section is devoted to them. They are not, however, the only thing you need to think about if you own – or are thinking of owning – a property. Just as important are issues such as whether it is better to rent or buy, investing in property, property-related costs, tax and a host of other related topics, all subjects that are covered extensively in what follows.

13
MORTGAGES

HOW TO SECURE THE BEST-VALUE MORTGAGE IN IRELAND

The number of active lenders in the mortgage market has decreased sharply in the last two years and so has the range of products and options. This chapter explains:

- how to make sure you've got the mortgage that suits you best
- how to make sure you are paying the lowest possible price
- who to trust for mortgage advice.

In addition, we look at how mortgages work, re-mortgaging, tax relief and just about every other property-related question you can think of.

TAKING ADVANTAGE OF THE MORTGAGE REVOLUTION

Please put any pre-conceptions you have about buying a home or arranging a mortgage to one side. The truth is:

- Your home is *not* necessarily your most important investment.
- Your home is definitely *not* your most expensive purchase.
- You *don't* have to take 25 years to pay back your mortgage.

Also, and this is crucial to keeping the cost of buying your home or investment property to a bare minimum:

- The interest rate your mortgage lender charges you makes a huge difference to the cost of buying your home.
- The type of mortgage you have also makes a huge difference to the cost of buying your home.

Changes in the mortgage market in the last two years have meant that for the foreseeable future you may be tied to the lender from whom you originally got your mortgage. For this reason it is essential that you do careful research before selecting a particular lender or product. *Independent advice from an Authorised Mortgage Adviser will stand you in good stead over the whole term of your mortgage.*

Not necessarily your most important investment. Definitely not your most expensive purchase.

Received wisdom has it that the most important investment most of us will probably ever make is in our home. There is no doubt that owning your home is a significant part of being financially secure:

- The cost is not dissimilar to renting a home – making it a good financial decision.

- You aren't at the mercy of unscrupulous, unpleasant, greedy or inefficient landlords.

- With luck you'll see the value of your property rise in the longer term– giving you a tax-free gain.

Nevertheless, although it makes sense to buy your own home, you shouldn't be fooled into thinking that it is the 'be all and end all' of investments. It is arguable, in fact, that building up your other investments – especially a pension plan – is substantially more important. Furthermore, the stock market has – traditionally – always produced a better return than property. I'm not trying to put you off buying your own home – far from it – but don't forget it is only one part of establishing your personal wealth.

It is also worth remembering that your home won't automatically be your most expensive purchase. Depending on interest rates, that honour could easily go to your mortgage. If you buy a house for €200,000 and take out a traditional, repayment mortgage for €160,000 (80% of the purchase price) and pay it back over 25 years at an average rate of 6%, the total cost of buying your home (including interest) will be €309,265.09. That's €109,265.09 more than the actual cost of your home. Which is why it is crucial you choose the least expensive mortgage option available to you.

INTEREST: ALL THE DIFFERENCE IN THE WORLD

The rate of interest you are charged on your mortgage makes a huge difference to the total cost of your home as the table opposite indicates:

Cost of €100,000 25-year repayment mortgage: interest payable

Annual interest rate (%)	Cost per month (€)	Total interest over term (€)
3.75	514.13	54,239
4	527.84	58,350
4.25	541.74	65,251
4.5	555.83	66,750
4.75	570.12	71,034
5	584.59	75,377
5.25	599.25	79,773
5.5	614.09	84,225
5.75	629.11	88,730
6	644.30	93,290
6.25	659.67	97,900
6.5	675.21	102,561
6.75	690.91	107,224
7	706.78	112,033

The difference between paying – say – 5.5% and 6.5% (which doesn't sound like much) actually equates to €18,336 of interest over the 25-year term and increases repayments by €161.12 per month. Put another way, think how much extra you would have to earn after tax to end up with €18,336 in your pocket. Paying more mortgage interest than you have to can seriously damage your wealth. Shopping around makes excellent sense.

TWO MORTGAGE OPTIONS: REPAYMENT VERSUS INTEREST ONLY

Although there is a whole range of mortgages to choose from, they all fall into one of two categories:

- repayment (annuity) mortgages
- interest-only mortgages

Repayment/annuity mortgage

The first option is a **repayment** (or **annuity**) mortgage. With this type of mortgage your monthly repayments are divided into two parts. The first is the interest you owe on the total amount borrowed. The second is repayment of part of the capital you have borrowed. The big advantage of this mortgage is that you are guaranteed to have paid off your whole loan at the end of the term. However, in the early years almost all your monthly repayments will be in interest. Let me give you an example:

> Sheila takes out a €200,000 mortgage over 25 years at an interest rate of 5.6%. Her monthly capital and interest payments are €1,240.15. At the end of the first year she will have paid a total of €14,881.80 but will still owe over €196,000 to her lender. In year ten she will have paid €148,817 and will still owe €150,795. Put another way, in the first ten years roughly two-thirds (66%) of what she pays to her lender will be interest, and only one-third (33%) will be capital.

MONEY DOCTOR WEALTH CHECK

Save extra interest

When choosing a repayment mortgage, make sure the interest is calculated **daily** or at least **monthly** ('monthly rest'). Why? Because over the term of your mortgage this will save you a tidy sum of money. The real thing to avoid is something called the 'annual rest system', which will cost you the most. Some lenders may still have customers on their books who are on this system and it can add about 0.35% to your interest rate. If you are in this position, go back to your lender and ask them to change you to a monthly calculation.

Interest-only mortgages

The other sort of mortgage on offer is an **interest-only mortgage**. With this type of mortgage you pay only the interest for the agreed period. With **investment mortgages** you pay interest only on the amount borrowed *and* at the same time you would set up a savings plan, which – it would be hoped – will pay off the capital at the end of the term. Your monthly repayments will, therefore, consist of interest on the loan and a contribution to a savings plan. This is ideal for certain types of loans e.g. commercial loans where the interest remains constant and the tax relief can be maximised (because the capital is not being repaid, you are receiving the most tax relief on the interest in the first year right through to the end of the term).

In the case of both a home and an investment property there are certain circumstances where you might not bother with the savings element, as I'll explain in a moment.

Around 20 years ago interest-only home loans got a bad name because many borrowers were advised to take out endowment policies (see below for an explanation) to re-pay the capital at the end of the term. Unfortunately, some of these policies failed to produce a sufficient return to do so. In other words, borrowers found that after 25 years they still owed money to their lenders.

Despite past problems with endowment mortgages, interest-only home loans can make sound financial sense. For instance, if you are self-employed, the tax benefits of a pension-linked interest-only mortgage can be very substantial, in particular when taken out for commercial property.

Here is a quick summary of the three main types of interest-only mortgage options available:

Endowment mortgages. There are various types of endowment policy available: these are investments offered by life insurance companies. The money you pay to the life insurance company is partly used to provide you with life cover (so that if you die the mortgage itself can be repaid) and partly invested in the stock market. If the money is invested well, then obviously your original loan will be repaid and you might even be left with a tax-free sum. However, if the performance of the endowment policy is not good, then you could be left with insufficient cash to repay your original loan. There is no tax relief on endowment policy premiums.

Pension-linked mortgages. The difference between this and an endowment mortgage is that the life insurance company (after taking out money to pay for life cover) invests your cash into a pension fund. This has very definite tax benefits for anyone who is self-employed or on an extremely high income. Ordinarily, the pension fund is designed to mature on your retirement age at double the original amount being borrowed. Twenty-five per cent of this pension fund is available at maturity for encashment, tax-free, and even though you will have to pay tax on the rest of the fund you should have sufficient money to pay off the rest of the mortgage.

New rules on self-direct trusts or SSAPs (small self-administered pension schemes) now allow pension funds to borrow on properties. Indeed, there are all sorts of other tax benefits available to those who buy property as part of their pension fund. Some of this is covered elsewhere in the chapters on retirement planning and tax. However, as it is such a complicated area you will need to take specialist advice if you wish to take advantage of the new rules.

Interest-only mortgages. It was possible to borrow money to purchase property at very competitive rates of interest without any obligation to re-pay the capital before the end of the term. For instance, if you took out a 20-year interest-only mortgage all you have to pay each month is the agreed rate of interest. The capital sum isn't due until 20 years have passed. This could suit you for all sorts of reasons. Perhaps you are expecting to receive a lump sum – such as an inheritance – before the 20 years are up. Maybe you intend to re-sell the property during this period. Possibly you have other investments that could be cashed in to repay the loan. Possibly you will win the Lotto! Do note that you will have to take out level term life cover that covers the entire amount borrowed for the full term in association with an interest-only mortgage, so that the loan can be repaid in the event of your death. While the credit crunch rages all around us at the moment, most lenders now only allow interest-only facilities up to the first three years.

FIXED OR VARIABLE RATE?

As if you didn't have enough choice already, another decision you must make when mortgage shopping can be whether to opt for a fixed or variable rate. A **fixed rate** means that the amount of interest you pay is pre-set for an agreed period of time. This offers you the benefit of certainty. Even if interest rates rise your repayments will stay the same. On the other hand if interest rates fall you won't benefit. You incur a penalty should you wish to pay off or part pay off your mortgage while on a fixed rate of interest. Generally, this sum is set at between three and six months' interest on the amount being repaid.

A **variable rate**, on the other hand, will move with the market. This is fine while interest rates are low but if they begin to rise you could be adversely affected. There is generally no penalty if you wish to pay off all or part of the loan before the end of the mortgage term.

Tracker mortgages *were* the real deal, and today are costing Ireland's lenders a fortune to maintain. The interest rate tracked the ECB rate (currently 1%) and the lender agreed a margin (or profit) that had to be maintained for the entire term of the mortgage; only if the ECB rate moves does your tracker rate move. Today there are some lucky mortgagers paying 0.5% over the ECB rate (1.5%) as they would have negotiated their loan based on only having to borrow less than 50% of the value of their home.

THE MONEY DOCTOR SAYS...

Unless you are self-employed, on a high-income or have some other source of funds coming to you in the future, the Money Doctor normally recommends that you take out a repayment or annuity mortgage when buying your main home. This said, there are some interesting variations now available allowing you to combine an interest-only mortgage with a repayment mortgage. The idea is to give you lower monthly payments at the beginning of your mortgage, rising as (hopefully) your income increases and/or your other expenses fall.

A WORD ABOUT 'CURRENT ACCOUNT' MORTGAGES

Also known as an offset mortgage, this means that funds on current and savings accounts are offset against your mortgage balance for interest calculation purposes. This way, you save the interest on that amount which is offset. Over the course of the mortgage term, the savings can be substantial if you are disciplined.

Only one lender in Ireland offers this product and it is well worth enquiring from that lender or your financial adviser.

WHY YOU SHOULD TRY TO MAKE MORTGAGE OVERPAYMENTS

Something I have become very keen on in recent years is the idea of overpaying your mortgage each month. This can't be done with all mortgages (for instance, you can't do it where you are on a fixed rate) but where it is possible and your income allows, it brings real benefits. With interest rates low at the moment and potentially likely to stay low for the next few years, it may be also important to remember that if your return/yield is far greater than the cost of the money (the mortgage rate), then investing your surplus monies elsewhere may be more beneficial. Consider these two examples, though, where overpayment can also be beneficial:

Mary takes out a repayment mortgage for €250,000 with a term of 25 years at 5.5%. Her minimum monthly repayment is €1535.22. However, she decides that she can afford to pay an extra €235 a month. As a result, her mortgage will be paid off six years earlier and she will save €57,070 in interest.

John also takes out a repayment mortgage for €320,000 with a term of 30 years at 5.75%. His minimum monthly repayment is €1867.43. He 'overpays' by €320 a month and as a result his mortgage will be paid off nine years earlier and he will save €120,429.31 in interest!

In both instances, by taking out a current account mortgage they could save even more interest. This is because any money on deposit in their current account is offset against their mortgage debt.

THE MONEY DOCTOR SAYS...

With so many mortgage choices available, many borrowers worry that they are making the right decision for their needs. This is where a really good independent financial adviser offering a full choice of lenders can help. He or she will be able to guide you to the least expensive, most appropriate mortgage for your needs. See below for further advice on choosing an adviser.

HOW THE RIGHT PROFESSIONAL ADVISER WILL SAVE YOU MONEY

It goes without saying that you should shop around for the best possible mortgage deal as so much of your hard-earned cash is at stake. Two things to watch out for:

1   You may not always be comparing like with like. There is a great deal of difference between a ten-year fixed rate mortgage and a current account repayment mortgage. Each will cost a different amount and each is designed to meet different needs.

2   You may not be offered a full range of options. A bank or building society – for instance – might only have three or four types of mortgage to offer you. Many mortgage advisers deal with less than five lenders.

There are 11 mortgage lenders in Ireland at this point in time, eight mainstream, one specialist and three lenders operating 'LifeLoans' for the over 65s. To get the best possible deal you should always deal with an adviser who is **authorised** by the Central Bank of Ireland to act on behalf of the majority of these lenders.

Please remember, too, that even if you are a customer with a particular financial institution, your authorised financial adviser may still be able to negotiate a better deal on your behalf. This is because a professional will know what the best deal available actually is, while the lender will know that the adviser has other options should the lender fall short of the client's requirement.

MONEY DOCTOR WEALTH CHECK

The latest information...

If you want the latest financial information – everything from interest rates to tax-saving tips – then log on to the Money Doctor website at www.moneydoctor.ie.

THE MONEY DOCTOR SAYS...

- Don't be complacent. Even a small difference in the rate you pay can make a huge difference to the cost of your mortgage. No lender deserves your loyalty. Go to where the best deal is.

- Don't trust any adviser who isn't authorised to act for all the financial institutions offering home loans in Ireland, or at the very least use an adviser who can tell you where the best deals can be obtained, irrespective of the agencies held. There are 11 lenders and anyone who can't tell you about all of them isn't going to get you the best deal.

- Do not panic if your home is worth less than your mortgage. As long as your income can meet the monthly mortgage repayment, the loss will only crystalise upon sale of the home. Always obtain professional advice for strategies.

- Remember, authorised financial advisers should be independent and, in most cases, you will pay a fee for their services, plus they will definitely find you the best package for your needs.

14
SUB–PRIME LENDING

Firstly, let me define **prime lending**. This is where a lender is able to gain full financial information about the prospective borrower and is able to apply the usual full prudent criteria. This minimises the risk of the loan going bad, and even if it does, there will be adequate collateral between asset and income to repay the loan. This type of loan justifies for the lender keeping the interest rate as low as possible.

Mention the words '**sub-prime mortgage**' and most people will run for the hills. Everyone has heard the stories about sky-high interest rates and bailiffs knocking at the door. Of course, the financial disaster that hit the US sector in the summer of 2007 hasn't helped the product's reputation. Every newspaper and TV station across the world told the story of the fall of this sector and the subsequent devastation of the international stock markets. They were scathingly referred to as NINJA mortgages – *No Income, No Job or Assets* – because of the way they were marketed in the US. They were mis-sold in their millions, packaged up and sold on or securitised to other institutions, thus releasing further capital to feed this frenzied lending. Once the housing market there started to falter and values started to drop the bubble burst, leaving many of the large lending institutions holding billions of dollars worth of mortgages on properties that they couldn't even give away.

This one financial product managed to rock the global financial markets and cause countless blue chip companies to close down. However, despite all the media coverage, there remains a lot of confusion about what has happened and how exactly a sub-prime loan **should** work and, to a large extent, has worked in the Irish context.

Sub-prime mortgages, now euphemistically called **specialist mortgages**, are home loans that are given to people with poor credit histories, at higher interest rates than standard mortgages. They can also apply to self-employed people with insufficient trading history to qualify for a prime mortgage and who can only self-certify their annual income. The interest rate varies depending on the amount of risk associated with your financial status. Applicants who are considered high risk are charged well above the standard mortgage rate.

The problem lies in the fact that people with an unstable financial background end up with even more debt that is charged at higher than average interest rates – a dangerous combination. It is not just first-time buyers that apply to these lenders; many existing homeowners go down this route when they want to remortgage their property to pay off other unmanageable debts such as credit cards.

Let me give you an example: David and Jenny have a mortgage with a regular bank. They have four different credit cards that are all maxed to the limit. They also have a personal loan each, a car loan and a holiday loan. They have already remortgaged their home on two occasions. They are sinking quickly under the weight of these loans and decide that they need to consolidate all of their debt and pay off the entire sum by remortgaging their home for the third time. When they apply to their mortgage lender, their request is turned down.

They see an advertisement from a sub-prime lender who promises to listen to their money worries and accept all applications no matter what their financial status may be. David and Jenny switch mortgage providers and pay off their credit card debt and personal loans. They feel a great sense of relief with this debt eliminated and before long they apply for new credit cards and rack up some more high-interest debt. Meanwhile, their sub-prime mortgage lender has slapped them with a whopping interest rate that is double their original rate. With a larger loan and new higher rate, their monthly repayment amount is almost two and a half times what it was previously. And, they have all of that new credit card debt.

More importantly, all of their debt is secured on their home. Once again, they find themselves up to their oxters in loan repayments that they can't meet. The sub-prime lender operates in a high-risk environment and does not have a sympathetic ear. The lender owns the deeds to their house and repossesses their home.

Although the sub-prime mortgage market is just eight years old in Ireland, it has been operating in America for far longer. The sector took off there in the mid-1990s and since 1998 over 25% of all mortgage applicants in America have received sub-prime home loans. Many believed this was a pressure cooker on the brink of explosion and they were proven correct. Following a series of hikes that saw interest rates jump from 1% to 5.25% between 2005 and 2007, the number of householders defaulting on their mortgage repayments soared. Weekly repossession figures have now hit staggering proportions. Users of eBay will see well-maintained family homes in good suburban locations for sale due to foreclosure by the banks for as little as $60,000, but in the end selling for a fraction of this.

Few were surprised when the housing market in America showed signs of collapsing at the end of 2006 and in the first six months of 2007, several major sub-prime mortgage corporations were forced to declare bankruptcy and some even shut down. That decline has continued right through to the present day. Not surprisingly, stock prices for many leading institutions in the industry collapsed as investors and lenders ran scared. Freddie Mac and Fanny Mae became household names for all the wrong reasons.

Thankfully, with every grey cloud comes a silver lining. The financial disaster has managed to highlight the dangers associated with borrowing from sub-prime lenders. Industry experts have called for tighter regulations to be enforced on a market which has become renowned for its spurious lending practices. The brokers in this industry have been accused of steering borrowers towards unaffordable loans. However, borrowers have also been criticised for over-stating their incomes on loan applications and entering into loan agreements they could not meet in the first place.

Despite the high risk attached to the industry, it was only in 2008 that this area came under the supervision of the Financial Regulator, following the introduction of enabling legislation in late 2007. Prior to that, the sector would claim that it voluntarily observed the standards laid down for other lenders and, in fairness, it must be said that in comparison with their US counterparts they operated in a responsible manner in the main.

SELF-CERTIFICATION

One of the primary concerns in this type of lending is the issue of self-certification, which enables self-employed people to prove their income without having to meet the normal qualifying criteria. The customer does not have to provide documents such as accounts and pay slips. The lender issues the loans based on the person's own stated income and recent bank statements as proof of that income.

The lenders who used to operate in this sector used to allow self-certification up to fixed income levels, but only a substantially smaller percentage of the value of the home than the prime lenders. Eventually their lending criteria became much more stringent and now this type of lending is no longer available. Court Orders for home repossessions by sub-prime lenders, which have received a lot of publicity in the papers of late, are the result of loans granted five to six years ago when interest rates were substantially lower and the economic outlook was universally brighter than it is today.

THE LENDERS

GE Money became the first company in Ireland to introduce the sub-prime mortgage in 2002. During its heyday in mid-2007 there were six lenders operating in the sector, with others in the wings waiting to launch their products. Rationalisation, the high-risk factor of some of these loans and the inability of some of the lenders to keep raising capital to fund their operations has meant that this number has now reduced to one operator in the market – Start Mortgages.

INTEREST RATES

The interest rates on sub-prime mortgages vary considerably depending on the current European Central Bank rate and the risk profile of the borrower. Applicants with no outstanding loans, a clean credit history and borrowing less than 60% of the value of the property, will usually receive a competitive interest rate that is just one or two percentage points higher than the mainstream lenders' rates.

However, customers with a poor credit rating, unpaid loans or those who have had court judgments registered against them for failing to repay debts will incur a far higher rate. There are other factors which will incur higher interest rates. For example, interest rates climb in line with the loan to value ratios. So, those who want to borrow over 70% of the property value will receive a more expensive rate.

CHARGES

While people with an unstable financial background are often drawn to a fixed rate mortgage, it is not always the best option. Hefty **redemption fees** are often charged when homeowners repay their fixed rate loans earlier than the agreed date. The amount payable is normally calculated based on the mortgage's interest rate. The rate of a sub-prime mortgage is frequently about double that of a standard mortgage, so therefore redemption fees on these loans are particularly expensive. For example, you could be charged a redemption fee of up to six months' interest.

Some sub-prime mortgage lenders often ask their customers to take out an **indemnity bond**. This is a type of insurance policy that works in favour of the lender. It aims to cover any shortfall that might arise between the amount owing and the value of your home if you default. An indemnity bond is usually required when you are borrowing more than a certain percentage of the purchase price – e.g. 75%. Standard mortgage holders are rarely, if ever, asked to buy this cover but sub-prime lenders will sometimes request that it be purchased.

The days of **arrangement fees** are long gone in the mainstream mortgage industry but these are still common practice amongst sub-prime lenders. **Start Mortgages** (the Irish subsidiary of British Kensington Mortgages) has an arrangement fee of 0.5% of the value of the mortgage, subject to a maximum fee of €1,800.

HOW TO AVOID THE SUB-PRIME MARKET

It's all too easy to stick your head in the sand like an ostrich, but avoiding money problems will land you with a bad credit rating. Once you get a bad name, mainstream lenders will avoid you like the plague. People with good credit ratings get the best rates and that means they pay less than those with a poor rating. All it takes is a few late or missed repayments and your reputation will suffer.

In case you think that it is possible to hide the fact that you have missed a few repayments, think again. Lenders check the credit ratings of applicants by contacting the **Irish Credit Bureau (ICB)** which holds the personal finance history of all borrowers.

Almost all of the lenders in Ireland send information about borrowers and their repayments to the **ICB**. According to the bureau, it holds information about borrowers and their loans for five years after the loan is closed. Lenders send details about people who have taken out mortgages, car loans, personal loans, leasing/hire-purchase agreements and credit cards. This information is held in an individual credit report that is kept by the **ICB**. The bureau reflects a full picture of your credit history, good and bad.

Your report contains the following details: the names of lenders and account numbers of loans you currently hold and previously held within the last five years; details of repayments made and missed for each month on all of the loans; information pertaining to any failure to clear a loan or loans that were settled for less than you owed; legal actions taken against you by a lender.

When you apply for a loan, the **ICB** report is checked and if your credit history is poor it is likely that the application will be unsuccessful even if you have the income to repay it.

If you want to check your rating, contact the ICB to receive a full report within a few days of the request. This will cost you €6 and you can get details of the application process over the phone from the Irish Credit Bureau at ICB House, Newstead, Clonskeagh Road, Dublin 14, Ireland, Tel. (01) 260 0388, Fax (01) 260 0390 or online from www.icb.ie.

THE MONEY DOCTOR SAYS...

- The Central Bank of Ireland is at pains to stress the importance of shopping around for the best rate and product. There is a wide variety of choice and rates in the market for borrowers. Just because a loan is being offered to you does not mean it is the only loan available or the best product to suit your needs. Consumers with financial problems should check out all the options and think hard about whether or not borrowing more money is the best solution, particularly if the interest rate is very high.

- As the Regulator says, waiting until you can afford what you want is painless compared with finding yourself trapped with a loan you cannot afford to repay. It can be tempting to take out a loan with lower monthly repayments. But, because it has a longer life term, you end up paying far more in interest. So weigh up what suits you best and how much you can really afford to borrow.

MONEY DOCTOR WEALTH WARNING

• Sub-prime lending should be the last resort. If you do find yourself in this unfortunate position, remember that in the current climate, even if you maintain an impeccable payment record with a sub-prime lender and any adverse Credit Bureau rating has expired, you may find it difficult to get back into mainline borrowing in the short to medium term. Meanwhile with only one *specialist lender* left in the Irish market, your options have diminished.

15
LOANS FOR THE OVER-60S

Everybody dreams of growing old gracefully in the comfort of their own home or, at worst, in a private, luxury nursing home. The notion of sitting in a dreary state nursing home is not one that many people relish. Unfortunately, by the time we reach retirement age we tend to be somewhat lacking in money. When you consider that the state pension in 2010 is €230.30 per week and that private nursing home fees can cost up to €1,000 per week, while the price of home help care is potentially even more expensive, it is no wonder that a small number of financial institutions and private equity companies are now targeting the elderly with what they believe is the perfect solution to this problem.

Add to this the Irish demographics – by the year 2011, it is estimated that persons aged 65 and over will represent 14.1% of the Republic's population. The percentage in 2002 was 11.13% out of a population of 3,917,203. Over 33% of those aged over 70 years of age live alone. The National Council on Ageing and Older People says that all demographic projections anticipate significant growth in the number of older people in Ireland over the next ten years. The 2011 Census will show the accuracy of these estimates.

As Irish property prices soared over the last two decades, many retirees have been left with a substantial nest egg. Releasing equity in a home when you are asset-rich but cash-poor can seem like the ideal way of boosting your quality of life. In recent years, two types of equity-release products have come on the market and both are aimed at older people. As with all financial products, these schemes will not suit everybody and people should seek family and also independent advice before signing on the dotted line.

THE LIFETIME MORTGAGE

The first product, known as a **lifetime mortgage**, allows you to borrow money against the value of your home. Sound familiar? Well, it works just like a regular equity-release product, except that no repayments are required. The loan is usually paid off from the proceeds when the home is eventually sold following the owner's death or when he or she moves out of the home for longer than six months – for example into long-term care. If there are joint borrowers and one owner dies, the mortgage must be paid off when the remaining borrower sells the home.

The financial institutions normally lend between 10% and 45% of your home's value. The older you are, the higher the percentage you can borrow. Depending on certain criteria such as your age, financial situation and the lender itself, customers can draw down the loan in two ways – as a lump sum or in instalments. Sometimes, people do both by dividing the loan, taking a lump sum and instalments.

Borrowers can end a lifetime mortgage by choosing to pay off their mortgage at any time. This can be done by selling the home and using the proceeds of the sale to pay off the loan or by using any other money they may have to repay the debt. Borrowers should be aware, however, that some lenders charge an early repayment fee if the loan is a fixed rate mortgage.

The interest rate on a lifetime mortgage

Because no regular repayments are made, the interest rate can be 1% or 2% higher than on standard mortgages. Also, because no repayments are made, the interest is compounded, that is, interest is added to the loan balance each month. As the loan balance grows, so does the monthly interest and the total debt can grow very quickly.

> Let me give you an example: Johnny and Rosie are both 65 years old. They own a house that is valued at €500,000. They decide to take out a lifetime mortgage of €100,000 with a compound interest rate fixed at 6%. After five years, the amount owed has grown to €134,907; after 10 years they owe €192,029; and by the time they are 80 years old they owe the grand total of €245,570.

Depending on the lender, lifetime mortgages are available with fixed or variable interest rates, the latter changing in line with changes in standard mortgage variable rates.

There is a big risk associated with this type of loan. By the time the homeowner dies, the interest and repayment due may be so high that the proceeds from the property's sale will barely cover the amount owed and little will be left for the beneficiaries of the will. The home may appreciate in value over the term of the loan which will offset some of the debt but this is never guaranteed.

> **MONEY DOCTOR WEALTH WARNING**
>
> There can be some downsides to taking out a lifetime mortgage. The lender can request that you sell your home and pay off the mortgage if you do any of the following:
>
> - Move out of your home for six months or more (unless your mortgage is in joint names and the other owner is still living there).
> - You don't insure your home.
> - Your home is not maintained to the standard that is set by your lender to keep its value. Although these conditions are standard in such a contract, it would appear that they are rarely – if ever – enforced.
> - Also, when you receive a lump sum or income through an equity-release scheme, it can affect your right to state benefits such as the means-tested state pension.

HOME REVERSION SCHEMES

Lifetime mortgages are not your only option if you want to take advantage of the growing value of your home. The second type of equity-release product is known as **home reversion**. It allows you to sell part of your home to a property investment company. The big advantage of this product is that you are allowed to remain living in the home until you die. You live in your own home for the rest of your life and use the cash received from the sale to enjoy your retirement in style.

Unlike a lifetime mortgage, you are not borrowing against the value of your home but are actually selling part of it. Applicants must have already paid off their existing mortgage in full to qualify for the scheme. With home reversion schemes you must take the money as a lump sum, and cannot take it in instalments.

HOME REVERSION FIXED AND VARIABLE SHARE AGREEMENTS

There are two options available if you enter a contract with a home reversion company. Under a **fixed-share contract**, the company pays you a lump sum in return for a fixed share of your home. The percentage they own and the percentage you keep is fixed from the start and cannot change, no matter how long you live or what your property may be worth in the future.

With a **variable-share contract** you get a bigger lump sum when you first sell your share. However, nothing in life comes for free. In return for the bigger lump sum, the percentage of your home that the company owns automatically increases each year without you receiving any further payments. So, the percentage you own will reduce as time passes. The longer you live, the less of your property you own.

> Let me give you a second example: Gerry is 65 years old and sells 25% of his home. By the time he is 80, the company owns 50%.

How it works

The home reversion company normally buys between 10% and 90% of the property, depending on the person's age and the value of the home.

Now, everyone knows that there is no such thing as a free lunch. This sounds like a dream product but it comes with a hefty price tag! The price paid by the investment company for a chunk of your home is significantly less than the market value of the share of the home that is sold. This is because the person remains living in the house and the home reversion company may have to wait several years before they can cash in their share. The difference between the market value and the lump sum you receive for the share you sell is the real cost of this product. You'd want to live well into your golden years to get good value from the scheme.

> Here's a third example: Dorothy is 65 and owns a house worth €500,000. The estimated market share of 50% of her home is €250,000. According to the Central Bank of Ireland, she can expect to receive €112,450 from a home reversion company.
>
> If Dorothy were 10 years older, however, she would receive €146,580. The older you are when you start the scheme, the bigger the lump sum you receive for selling the same share. This is because the company expects they will be able to cash in their share sooner for the obvious reason.

As soon as the homeowner dies or moves into a nursing home, the house is sold and the proceeds are divided between the property investment company and the homeowner or their estate, depending on the percentage owned by each.

There is no back-tracking once you enter a home reversion contract. If you sell a portion of your home and decide a year or two later that you want to end the agreement, the only option is to negotiate with the company to buy back the share you sold. You can also gain consent from the company to sell your home on the open market. This would allow you to cash in the value of the percentage of your home you still own.

When you die, your family or other beneficiaries may be given the option to buy back the percentage that the home reversion company owns. If the value of your home has increased due to inflation, it may be difficult for them to raise enough money to do this.

LIFETIME MORTGAGES AND HOME REVERSION SCHEME COSTS

Like most financial products, these schemes come with significant costs. Depending on the type of scheme you choose, you may have to pay some added costs such as a valuation fee, legal fees and costs for transferring ownership or arranging your mortgage. Some companies have a fixed 'set-up' fee to cover legal and valuation fees. A budget of €1,500 to €3,000 should cover these costs.

At your initial meeting with the particular institution you choose, you should be given a detailed breakdown of all costs. These details should be available on the lender's website. For all equity release schemes you must keep your home in a good state of repair and take out insurance noting the interest by the lender or home reversion company.

Maintenance costs can be high and usually increase over time. The lender or home reversion company can inspect your home from time to time, and has the right to carry out any necessary repairs that it believes are necessary. The company usually adds any repair costs to the amount you owe, so compound interest would be charged on those extra costs.

You should also bear in mind that some schemes may restrict you from making certain renovations, for example installing a stair lift, as they may reduce the market value of the property.

Lifetime mortgages

Bank of Ireland sells a lifetime mortgage known as **LifeLoan**. Applicants must be at least 65 years old and have paid off their mortgage in full. The product enables them to borrow between 20% and 30% of the value of their home.

LifeLoan customers can borrow up to €400,000 at a fixed annual interest rate of 5.59% APR for 15 years. The minimum amount that a homeowner can borrow is €20,000. The LifeLoan interest rate is expensive compared with current standard mortgage rates. If the homeowner lives a long time and the property only increases slowly in value, the rolled-up interest plus the capital could eventually exceed the value of the home.

This product has a number of provisions that have been criticised by the Law Society. Bank of Ireland demands that you to make a will and give the bank the names of your executor, beneficiaries and next of kin.

At the end of the term customers are offered a choice of either a new fixed rate or a variable rate. Penalties may apply if the loan is repaid early but, unlike most fixed rate mortgages, there are no penalties if the borrower dies, sells or moves out early.

Unfortunately as of 12 November 2010, Bank of Ireland temporarily withdrew their Lifeloan product from the market. They do hope to reinstate the product in the not too distant future. The only current operator, therefore, in the over-60s loan market is Seniors Money.

Seniors Money also offers an interest-only lifetime loan to those aged 60+. The total amount that can be borrowed is €200,000 and is calculated on a sliding scale based on the age of the borrower and the value of the property.

For example, at age 60 you can borrow 15% of your house value, rising to 45% at age 90. However, this is subject to an overall **maximum** loan amount, currently €200,000.

Interest is calculated and charged to the loan monthly at a current Standard Variable Rate (at time of going to press this is 4.5% – APR 4.7%). All terms and conditions are generally the same as with the Bank of Ireland product.

As with all of these types of loans it is imperative that the borrowers discuss the implications with other family members and also seek independent legal and financial advice.

Reversion schemes

Sixty Plus Finance – the trading name of Residential Reversions Limited – offers a home reversion scheme. The company buys a percentage of the value of the house; the amount it will offer to buy depends on the value of the property and the age of the homeowner. Essentially, when the homeowner dies, the property is sold and the percentage bought by Sixty Plus Finance is repaid. However, the minimum amount it will pay a 65-year-old is €50,000 and the maximum amount is €500,000.

If a house is worth between €500,000 and €1m, the maximum amount the company will buy is 60% of the value of the property. Sixty Plus Finance will buy a maximum of 40% of a property worth between €1m and €1.5m. If the scheme ends within four years, or if house price inflation is exceptional, the company will provide additional cash benefits.

So, whatever you decide, ensure you have the best of family, legal and tax advice before you embark on that little bit of comfort in your twilight years. And remember, you deserve it!

16
PROPERTY QUESTIONS

ANSWERS TO YOUR PROPERTY AND MORTGAGE QUESTIONS

This chapter contains detailed answers to all your property and mortgage questions, including:

- Should I buy or rent my home?
- How much can I borrow on my income?
- What is 'APR'?
- Is it worth switching my mortgage to get a lower rate?
- Help! I'm self-employed. How do I get a mortgage?
- What will it cost for me to buy my home?
- What tax relief will I receive on my home loan?
- Does it make sense to buy a second property as an investment?
- What are the benefits of owning a home in a designated area?
- What's the story with local authority loans?
- What other state housing grants might be available to me?
- Is it worth repaying my mortgage early?
- What different types of home insurance will I need?
- If I have trouble making my mortgage repayments what should I do?

SHOULD I BUY OR RENT?

Ireland is one of the few countries in Europe where buying one's home is the norm. Broadly speaking, at present the cost of buying a home is the same as – or in many cases less than – renting the same property. This is linked to supply and demand, of course, and varies from region to region as well as from property to property. We were in a low-interest environment until 2006 – and this favoured house purchase – as did the availability of mortgage interest relief. Interest rates rose betweeen 2006 and 2008, and while they are now back to historically low levels, consumers are more reluctant to borrow, and the relatively meagre tax relief for first-time borrowers only is not an attraction in itself.

If a future government were to introduce greater tenant rights the situation might change, but at the moment – if you can raise the sufficient deposit – buying makes better long-term sense. After all, when you give up a rental property you receive nothing back. Whereas when you have paid off your mortgage you will own your home and may have seen a nice, tax-free capital gain as well.

House prices in Ireland rose at an unprecedented rate in the ten years to 2006 and most informed opinion then was that as long as we continued in a low-interest environment and our economy remained healthy, a sharp fall in house prices seemed unlikely. However, things have changed dramatically over the last 3 years and prices are down 35% from the 2006 peak. Renting is cheaper but as property values fall, you may pick up a bargain from foreclosures or 'distressed sales', while the introduction of more rental purchase schemes may be an interesting development over the next few years.

HOW MUCH CAN I BORROW?

You should always put down as much of a deposit as possible when buying your home. You will need a minimum of 8% of the purchase price (that is to say €24,000 if you are buying a €300,000 property) but it is preferable to have more. Why? Because it makes you less vulnerable to moves in interest rates and property values, plus your authorised mortgage intermediary will be able to negotiate a lower interest rate with a lender if you have over 20% deposit – the less the percentage you have to borrow, the better the interest rate.

Depending on what you earn, lenders may give you a mortgage of between three and five times your income. For example:

- If you earn €60,000 a year you may be able to borrow up to €300,000 over 35 years.
- If you and your partner earn a combined income of €80,000 you may be able to borrow between €300,000 and €360,000 over 35 years.

Your ability to repay a mortgage will be based on your net disposable income (gross income less tax, levies, PRSI and any existing loan repayments) and will be stress-tested to allow for future rises in interest rates.

For first-time home buyers a 100% mortgage package was available with most lenders, even though it was subject to very stringent income guidelines. Now it has been withdrawn owing to the continuing economic troubles.

WHAT IS APR?

The initials 'APR' stand for **annual percentage rate** and it is the way in which the cost of your loan is expressed. What makes it different from a straight interest rate is that it takes into account not just the interest rate but also the timing of any interest payments, capital repayments and other charges, arrangement fees and so forth. The APR must, by law, reflect the actual rate of interest charged over the full period of the loan.

IS IT WORTH SWITCHING MY MORTGAGE TO GET A LOWER RATE?

The short answer is: **it depends if you can find a new lender willing to allow you to switch**. If the loan to value of your mortgage is less than 60% there are two things to consider:

- How much can you save by switching lender?
- What is switching lender going to cost you?

The first question is relatively easy to answer. The second question will depend on a variety of factors including:

- whether you are on a fixed interest rate – in which case there may be a penalty for switching
- how much it is going to cost you by way of legal and other costs.

If you can save 0.25% a year interest – or more – it could well be worth the switch. If in doubt, consult an authorised mortgage intermediary or accountant and ask them to do the figures for you.

HELP! I'M SELF-EMPLOYED

Most financial institutions are pleased to lend to someone who is self-employed – though if you have less than three years' sets of accounts it may be harder. This is another instance where a professional authorised mortgage intermediary will help. He or she will know which lenders are keen for your business and willing to offer you the lowest rates.

Note: it is no longer possible to get a mortgage in Ireland without a statement from your accountant to the effect that your tax affairs are completely up to date.

WHAT WILL IT COST FOR ME TO BUY MY HOME?

There are various expenses in buying a home:

Survey fees. No lender will let you have a mortgage without a proper survey and valuation. The price of this will vary but is likely to be in the region of €130. You may like to ask an architect or some other type of professional property adviser to survey the building for you to check its condition and the likely cost of repairs. The fee for this will be linked to the amount of work required and could run to several hundred euros or more for a large house.

Legal fees. This is primarily the cost of employing a solicitor to look after the whole transaction for you. The normal cost is in the region of 1% of the total price plus VAT at 21% and outlay. So for a €200,000 house you will have to find in the region of €2,400. Your lender may also charge you a certain amount to cover their legal fees if it is a commercial transaction. Negotiation over legal fees is possible and you should ask for a reduction, especially if you are a first-time buyer.

Land registry fees. On a €200,000 property these would be up to €750. The fee is to cover registering the property in your name.

Stamp duty. You have to pay two lots of stamp duty. Firstly, on the value of the house. If you are a first-time buyer then the duty is waived. Otherwise, it will be from between 3 and 9% (on a sliding scale) depending on the price. There is also stamp duty at 0.1% on your mortgage if it is over €254,000.

Stamp duty*

Residential property consideration	Standard	First-time buyer	Investors
Up to €125,000	Exempt	Exempt	Exempt
Next €875,500	7%	Exempt	7%
Balance	9%	Exempt	9%
Commercial stamp duty rates	For any property over €150,000, stamp duty is chargeable at 9%		

*No stamp duty payable by owner-occupiers or first-time buyers on purchase of homes up to 125 square metres. On new houses/apartments above this limit, duty is charged on site value or a quarter of the value, whichever is greater.

(Source: Matrix courtesy of www.moneydoctor.ie)

Search fees. This is to check that the property has planning permission, isn't located on the site of a proposed development and so forth. Usually around €150.

Arrangement fees. Some lenders charge application and arrangement fees. These could amount to between €100 and €300 but generally only apply to non-home loans.

If you would like to know exactly what your home loan is going to cost you to buy visit my website – www.moneydoctor.ie – where you'll find a calculator that will work it out for you.

To give you a typical example, for a first-time buyer purchasing a house for €200,000 with an 80% mortgage (€160,000) the total fees will be on the order of €2,000.

WHAT TAX RELIEF WILL I RECEIVE ON MY HOME LOAN?

You will be entitled to **mortgage interest relief**, which will be given to you automatically 'at source'. From **1 January 2009**:

First-time buyers: the rate of mortgage interest relief is increased from 20% to 25% in years 1 and 2, and to 22.5% in years 3, 4 and 5. The relief remains unchanged at 20% for years 6 and 7 of the mortgage. First-time buyers relief ends after year 7.

Non-first-time buyers: the rate of mortgage interest relief is reduced from 20% to 15%.

With effect from **1 May 2009** the number of tax years in respect of which mortgage interest relief may be claimed is 7 years for first-time and non-first-time buyers.

MEASURES IN FINANCE ACT 2010

- Mortgages taken out **between 1 January 2004 and 31 December 2011** will continue to qualify for mortgage relief at current levels up to the end of 2017.

- For mortgages taken out **between 1 January 2012 and 31 January 2012**, there will be a 15% rate of relief for first-time buyers and a 10% rate for non-first-time buyers. The maximum amounts of interest that will qualify for relief will be €6,000 for married or widowed people and €3,000 for single people. These ceilings will be the same for first-time buyers and non-first-time buyers.

- Mortgages taken out on or **after 1 January 2013** will not qualify for mortgage interest relief.

- Mortgage interest relief will be abolished completely **after 31 December 2017**.

DOES IT MAKE SENSE TO BUY A SECOND PROPERTY AS AN INVESTMENT?

Buying property and renting it out has become an increasingly popular investment over the last few years. There are various reasons for this including:

- tax incentives – you can claim 75% any loan interest you pay on borrowings to acquire and/or improve the property, against any rental income you receive. Plus, if you buy certain types of property or property in particular areas you will receive additional tax breaks

- rapid increases in property values

- high yields in relation to other investments

- low cost of borrowing money.

In general, the only investors who don't make money from renting out property are those who have over-estimated the return they'll receive, haven't allowed for all the likely costs and lack the patience to wait out any market downturns. The secret to success is undoubtedly:

- Allow for periods without tenants (known as 'voids').

- Make sure you have calculated all the costs including loan repayments, redecoration, maintenance and repair.

- Don't view it as a short-term investment.

WHAT ARE THE BENEFITS OF OWNING A HOME IN A DESIGNATED AREA?

If you buy, build or restore a house in particular areas of the country – called 'designated' areas – you are entitled to tax relief on part of the expense. This tax relief is quite generous and well worth claiming.

WHAT'S THE STORY WITH LOCAL AUTHORITY LOANS?

County councils and city corporations both provide financial support to anyone on relatively low incomes so that they can afford to buy their own home, but you can be waiting a long time to be facilitated.

If you cannot get a loan from a building society or bank, you may be eligible for a local authority mortgage. The amount borrowed can be up to 97% of the cost of the house subject to a maximum loan of €165,000 and subject to repayments which cannot exceed 35% of the household net income (i.e. income after tax and PRSI).

WHAT OTHER STATE HOUSING GRANTS MIGHT BE AVAILABLE TO ME?

There are various other grants available from the state including:

Affordable housing. Many new developments now include a percentage of what is referred to as 'affordable housing'. These are houses, flats or building sites that must be sold at well below market price to people who would not otherwise be able to afford to buy their own home.The affordable housing scheme allows lower-income house buyers the chance to buy newly constructed homes and apartments in areas where property prices have created an affordability gap for lower-income house buyers. There are of course conditions that preclude the buyer from making a 'quick kill'.

Improvement grants. A range of loans will be available from your local authority so that you can improve or extend your home.

Mortgage subsidy. If you are a local authority tenant and you give up your home to buy a property on the open market, you may be entitled to financial support for up to five years. The **mortgage allowance scheme** is an allowance of up to a maximum of €11,450 payable over a five-year period to local authority tenants. The allowance is paid directly to the lender and your repayments are reduced accordingly for the first five years of the mortgage. The allowance paid in any year cannot exceed the amount of the mortgage repayments.

Shared ownership. The **shared ownership scheme** is aimed at those who cannot afford to purchase an entire home in one transaction. It allows you to buy a proportion of your home initially and to increase that proportion in steps until you own the whole house. During this stage, ownership is shared between you and the local authority and you make payments on a mortgage for the part you own and pay rent to the local authority for the other part at a rate of 4.3%.

Disabled persons grant. Given to cover the cost of adapting a private home for the needs of someone who is disabled.

Thatching grant. Available towards the cost of renewing or repairing thatched roofs on houses. Thatchers are a dying breed but it is important to reward and help those who are maintaining our heritage.

Home Energy Savings Grants. A range of grants is available to improve home insulation, install renewable energy systems and upgrade existing heating systems to become more energy-efficient. Details can be found on www.seai.ie.

IS IT WORTH REPAYING MY MORTGAGE EARLY?

Should you overpay your mortgage each month? Should you use all your available cash to reduce your mortgage? Should you use a lump sum of cash to reduce or pay off your mortgage? The answer is *probably* yes if the following applies to you:

- You don't have any other – more expensive – debts. (If you do, these should be paid off first.)
- It won't leave you without some savings tucked away against a rainy day.
- There aren't other investment opportunities that might be worth more to you in cash terms.

If you were thinking of paying off some or all of your mortgage, I would strongly advise consulting an Authorised Advisor or mortgage intermediary first. He or she will be able to work out the figures for you.

WHAT DIFFERENT TYPES OF HOME INSURANCE WILL I NEED?

This is covered in greater detail in Chapter 12 on insurance. In summary, homeowners should take out the following cover:

Buildings insurance. This will be compulsory if you have a mortgage. Basically, it means that if some damage is done to the fabric of your home (by a fire or flood, for instance) then money is available to repair or rebuild as necessary.

Contents insurance. This protects you against loss of or damage to your home contents.

Mortgage repayment insurance. This cover is optional but means that if you are ill or made redundant, your mortgage repayments would be paid for you. Payments usually last for up to a year.

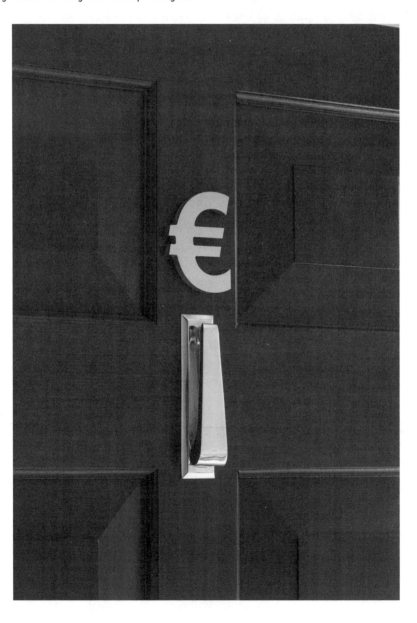

IF I HAVE TROUBLE MAKING MY MORTGAGE REPAYMENTS, WHAT SHOULD I DO?

Contact your lender immediately. The worst thing you can do is keep them in the dark about any financial problems you may be encountering. If you need help with your finances you could contact:

- Your local St Vincent de Paul Society, which runs a special advice scheme.
- The Department of Social Welfare, which also runs a free advice scheme called MABS (Money and Budgeting Advice Service). You can obtain details from your local social welfare office or public library.

THE MONEY DOCTOR SAYS...

- If you have any questions about property or mortgages not answered in this book then please do email me (jlowe@moneydoctor.ie) or a Money Doctor adviser and we will be delighted to help.

PART 6

GUARANTEED SAVINGS AND INVESTMENT SUCCESS

My favourite quote about wealth is Ernest Hemingway's, who in response to F. Scott Fitzgerald's comment that the rich are different, replied: 'Yes, they have more money.'

And getting yourself into a position where you have 'more money' is what this section of the book is all about for, as the entertainer, Sophie Tucker observed, 'I've been rich, and I've been poor: rich is better.' Not, I hasten to add, that I am suggesting you get rich for the sake of it. My interest is in making sure you have sufficient money to be free – free from the worry of not having enough and free to choose how you spend your time.

There are some widely held misconceptions about how to get rich. Some people think the only way they will manage it is by owning their own business; others feel the Lotto offers them their best chance; a third group seem to imagine it will happen all by itself.

In my experience, the only way to get rich is to take it slowly and steadily.

Set aside part of your income every month and invest it wisely and you will be amazed at how – over the years – it grows.

Many people feel that there is not much difference between savings and investment, but to my mind there is a clear distinction:

- *Saving is all about short-term goals. It's the money you tuck away on a regular basis to pay for your holidays, or in case of emergency. Because it's money that needs to be available to you it can't be tied up where you can't get your hands on it.*

- *Investment, on the other hand, is all about medium- to long-term goals. You invest to ensure yourself a more prosperous and secure future. You may invest a lump sum, or on a regular basis, but the real thing is (barring an unforeseen crisis) you should be able to leave your money to work for you undisturbed for a reasonable period of time.*

Accordingly, this section is divided into two chapters. In the first you'll discover the best possible way to save your money with a view to building your own emergency fund. In the second, you'll learn how to invest your money in such a way as to build your wealth. Between the two you'll have all the tools you need to make your money grow, and grow and grow…

17
SAVING FOR A RAINY DAY

THE QUICKEST, MOST EFFICIENT WAY TO BUILD UP AN EMERGENCY FUND

One of your key financial objectives should be to have some easily accessible cash savings to pay for larger expenses or simply in case of a 'rainy day'. In this chapter you will discover:

- why it is so important to have cash savings
- how much savings you should build up
- the best way to make your savings grow.

GOOD, OLD-FASHIONED SAVINGS

We are lucky enough to live in a country where the state will provide a safety net for widow(er)s, those who are seriously ill or disabled, pensioners and anyone in dire financial straits. However, the amount on offer is relatively meagre and won't cover most of the day-to-day financial crises ordinary people face. For instance, the state isn't going to help you with an unexpected bill for repairs to your home or car. Nor will they pay all your regular bills if you find yourself without an income for any reason. The fact is you should have a bit of cash tucked away – good, old-fashioned savings – just in case you ever need it. You should probably also have some extra cash to hand so that you can take advantage of an unexpected investment opportunity, for capital expenditure or just in case you see something you want to buy.

Saving up money to create a safety net requires a degree of commitment. It is in our nature, after all, to spend rather than to save. But if you can motivate yourself to tuck a little bit away each month I promise you'll never regret it!

SAVING MADE SIMPLE

It is one thing to think 'I must build up my savings' but often quite another thing to actually do so. Saving can only be achieved by conscious effort.

Ideally, you should open your savings account somewhere convenient and arrange to make regular payments into it. For instance, you might set up a standing order to transfer a regular amount each month from your bank current account to a deposit account. Some employers offer 'payroll deduction' schemes where the money goes straight from your salary to a savings account. Also, if you are entitled to receive a child allowance from the state you could consider saving all of this on an automatic basis. The real thing to remember is that a savings plan should be regular, and sacrosanct.

HOW MUCH IS ENOUGH?

Just how much savings you should aim to accumulate will be determined by your personal circumstances.

- A single person in his or her 20s without any responsibilities and low overheads probably only needs to have enough cash to cover – say – three months' worth of expenditure.
- A couple with children, a mortgage and a car to run should probably aim to build up as much as six months' expenditure.

If you aren't already lucky enough to have a lump sum available to form your safety net, then the best way to build it up is to establish a pattern of regular saving each week or each month. Remember, something is better than nothing – even if it is a relatively small amount, it will soon add up.

YOUR SAVINGS STRATEGY

If you have – say – six months' worth of expenditure saved up and you don't need instant access to all of it, my advice is to keep about a third where it is readily available and the rest where you can access it by giving notice. This strategy will allow you to earn extra interest.

Incidentally, if you are in a permanent relationship then ideally you should both have access to the emergency fund. In the event of some problem affecting one of you, the other may need to use this money.

EMERGENCY FUND: THREE BASIC REQUIREMENTS

An emergency fund should meet three basic requirements:

1 It should provide you with total security. Your savings must not be at risk.
2 It must earn as much interest as possible under the circumstances.

3   It must provide you with the level of access you need.

For these reasons the number of options available to you are limited pretty much to those listed below.

Deposit accounts

If you leave money on **deposit** with a bank, building society or credit union they will pay you interest. How much interest you earn can vary according to:

- how much money you have on deposit
- the length of notice you have to give before you can make a withdrawal (notice accounts/fixed rate accounts)
- the commitment to saving regularly (check out Regular Saver Accounts).

Rates can vary substantially and change all the time. Shop around and don't be afraid to move your money to where it can be earning more for you. Remember, currently the Deposit Protection Scheme will guarantee €100,000 of your savings. In addition, that portion of deposits in excess of €100,000 held with the six Irish-owned banks and not covered by the Deposit Protection Scheme is covered to an unlimited amount by the Eligible Liabilities Guarantee Scheme (ELGS). This scheme is due to expire on 31 December 2010 and its continuance will be reviewed by the EU.

An Post accounts

An Post offers a good range of savings products, all of which offer competitive returns and some of which are tax free. If you want to build up an emergency fund the two most appropriate accounts to consider are the **Instalment Savings** scheme or the **Instant Access** deposit account. An Post's Instalment Savings scheme requires you to make regular monthly payments for at least one year of between €25 and €500. In exchange, you will enjoy tax-free growth. An Post's Instant Access deposit account is very similar to a bank or building society deposit account. The interest rate isn't high, but it is competitive and you do have instant access. Once you've built up your emergency fund you may like to consider transferring your money into either an An Post **savings bond** or An Post **savings certificates**. Both are designed for medium- to long-term growth (at least three years), but you can get your money quickly if you need to. In addition, it's worth keeping in mind that the interest earned on savings bonds and certificates is tax free.

Membership of a credit union

As a member of a credit union you will earn an attractive return on the 'shares' you hold. This return is in the form of a dividend and will vary from year to year and from union to union. However, it is usually well above the rate offered by ordinary deposit accounts.

Note that if your local credit union offers a **Special Term Share** account, the return should be tax free, providing the amount of interest you've earned is less than €476 a year.

SAVINGS AND TAX

On deposit accounts, deposit interest retention tax (**DIRT**) is levied at source on your interest at a standard rate of 25%. However, if you are not liable for income tax, or you or your spouse are over 65 years of age or you are permanently incapacitated then you are entitled to claim back any DIRT deducted from your interest. You can make a back claim for DIRT tax for up to four years. Send a DE1 form to your deposit taker to reclaim the tax. The institutions will then pay you a gross return. Otherwise, use the 'old system' for back claims.

MONEY DOCTOR WEALTH CHECK

How to reclaim DIRT

Nothing could be easier than reclaiming DIRT. All you do is complete a short form available from any larger post office, bank, building society or tax office. You'll need to attach evidence of the DIRT that you have paid. This is done by asking the financial institution (or institutions) concerned to provide you with a special certificate. The DE1 leaflet is available at www.revenue.ie/leaflet/dde1.pdf for those who wish to claim exemption from paying DIRT.

THE MONEY DOCTOR SAYS...

- Saving on a regular basis may not always be easy but it will bring you real peace of mind.

- You should have an emergency fund in place sufficient to cover all your bills for between three and six months.

- As with everything: shop around. You could earn a considerably greater return by moving your money to where the best rates are.

- Watch out for Regular Saver Accounts – you save from €100 to €1000 per month up to 12 months at very attractive rates. E-mail me for details of these deposit takers and their interest rates and terms.

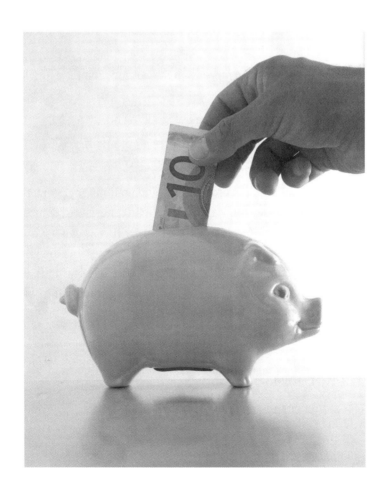

18
INVESTMENT STRATEGIES YOU CAN COUNT ON

HOW TO MAKE YOUR MONEY GROW AND GROW AND GROW

Every investor faces the same conflict: how to balance risk and reward. Should you accept a lower return in exchange for peace of mind? Or should you attempt to make your money grow more quickly and face the possibility of losses? In fact, the best solution to the dilemma is: neither. As this chapter will demonstrate, the optimum way to build up your wealth is to:

- Set clear objectives. Know where you are going and what you want to achieve.
- Diversify. Invest your money in more than one area to combine growth and security.
- Be consistent. Don't chop and change but stick to your strategy.
- Stay on top of it. Keep an eye on performance all the time.
- Avoid unnecessary expenses and charges.

In addition to outlining a proven method of making your money grow, the chapter summarises all the major investment vehicles you should consider, providing you with 'insider' tips in relation to:

- pooled investments
- stocks and shares
- property
- tax-efficient investment.

BASIC INVESTMENT PLANNING

As discussed in earlier chapters your primary investment priorities should be to:

- build up an emergency fund

- start a pension plan
- buy your own home.

What you should do next will depend on your circumstances. Whether you have a lump sum to invest or simply plan to save on a regular basis, your objectives will basically revolve around the following questions:

- How much money is involved?
- How long can you tie your money up for?
- What type of return are you looking for?
- What risks are you willing to accept?
- To what extent is tax an issue?

Let's look at each of these in turn.

How much money is involved?

If you are saving regularly, then you have a choice between investing in a specially designed longer-term plan or building up 'blocks' of capital and investing each one somewhere different.

If you have a lump sum – or as you build up 'blocks' of capital – then the choice of investments available to you opens up. For instance, with some capital available, property investment becomes an option, as does buying publicly quoted shares.

You must have a clear idea in your mind about how much you plan to invest and in what form. If you are saving on a regular basis, consider how long this will be for. Bear in mind that regular savings products have advantages and disadvantages. On the one hand, they tie you in and there can be strict penalties for early encashment or withdrawal. On the other, they force you to be disciplined and take away the tricky decision of how to invest your money. You should also think about the cost of such plans.

How long can you tie your money up for?

Is there a date you need your money back? In other words, are you investing for something specific or just to build your overall wealth?

Investments have varying degrees of accessibility or **liquidity**. An investment that allows you to get at your money immediately is considered 'highly liquid'. Cash in a deposit account or publicly quoted shares, for instance, are both liquid. Property and pension plans are not.

How long you stay with any particular investment will partly be determined by the investment vehicle itself (a ten-year savings plan is – unless you break the terms – a ten-year savings plan) and partly by events (there may be a good reason to sell your investment).

What type of return are you looking for?

Returns vary enormously. The graph below shows how, up to 2004, €1,000 would have grown over almost 20 years had you invested it in different ways.

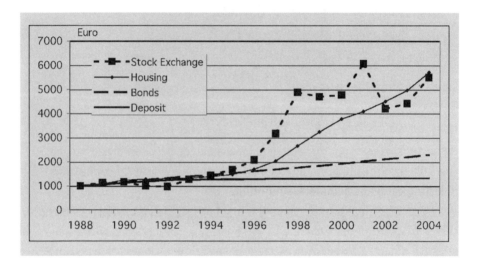

What risks are you willing to accept?

In general, *the higher the return, the greater the risk*. The highest possible returns are to be made from investments such as **commodities** and **spread betting** – but in both cases you can actually lose substantially more than your original investment. The lowest returns are to be made from investments such as bank deposit accounts and An Post savings plans – where your money can be considered 100% secure.

In formulating your overall investment strategy, you need to consider your approach to risk. Are you willing to accept some risk in order to boost your return? How much?

To what extent is tax an issue?

If you are a higher-rate taxpayer – or expect to be – then you need to consider to what extent tax saving is an issue for you. Bear in mind that there are a number of highly tax-effective investment options available – though all carry above-average risk. Remember, too, that capital gains are taxed at a much lower level than income – which may make this a more attractive option for you (see Chapter 28).

A proven investment strategy

The saying 'don't put all your eggs in one basket' is extremely relevant when it comes to building wealth. In fact, it forms the basis of the only investment strategy I believe can be relied upon: diversification. If your investment strategy is too safe, then you won't enjoy decent growth. If your investment strategy is too daring, then you risk losing everything you have been working towards. The solution? To diversify your investments so that your money is spread across a range of areas. Which leaves you two simple decisions:

1   In which areas should you invest your money?

2   How much should you invest in each area?

As already mentioned, you should start by diversifying into the three most important areas of investment – your emergency fund, your pension and buying your own home. Having done this, I would suggest putting your money into the following five areas:

1   Pooled investments.

2   A 'basket' of directly held stocks and shares.

3   Investment property.

4   Higher risk and tax-efficient investments such as BES schemes.

5   Alternative investments such as art, antiques, gold and other precious metals.

Within each area there is much scope for choice, allowing you to vary the amount you invest, the length of your investment, the degree of risk and so forth. You must decide for yourself what mix of investments best suits your needs.

The information on the next pages will give you a feel for the various opportunities available. Your next step will depend largely on how active a role you want to play. One option is to investigate each area thoroughly yourself. Another option is to allow an Authorised Advisor to handle it all for you. My own suggestion would be to go for a combination of the two. Educate yourself, keep yourself informed but let an expert guide and support you.

When long-term means long-term

One of the biggest mistakes investors make is that they forget their own financial objectives. If you are investing for long-term, capital growth – a good, solid gain over, say, 20 years – then if you change your strategy half way through you must resign yourself to a poor return and even losses. This is true regardless of the investment vehicle you are using.

If a change of strategy is unavoidable, then try and give yourself as long as possible to enact it.

There are various areas where investors seem particularly prone to chopping and changing. Long-term savings plans – such as endowments – is one. The stock market is another. In every case (leaving aside some sort of personal financial crisis) the usual reason is despondency over perceived lack of growth or falling values. If you have chosen your investments well you shouldn't be worrying about the effect of a few lean years or an unexpected dip in values. If you are concerned that you have made a bad investment decision in the first place do take professional advice before acting. The biggest losses come when an investor panics.

POOLED INVESTMENTS

A **pooled investment** – sometimes known as an investment fund – is a way for individual investors to diversify without necessarily needing much money. Your money – along with the money of all the other participants – is pooled and then invested. Each pooled investment fund has different, specified objectives. For instance, one might invest in the largest Irish companies, another in UK companies, a third in US gilts and a fourth in Korean property. In each case the fund managers will indicate the type of risk involved. They will also provide you – on a regular basis – with written reports or statements explaining how your money is performing.

Since it would be impossible for all but the richest of private investors to mimic what these pooled investments do, they are an excellent way to spread your risk. A typical fund will be invested in a minimum of 50 companies and will be managed by a professionally qualified expert.

The fund managers make their money from a combination of commission and fees:

• There is often an entry fee of up to 5% of the amount you are investing.

- There will definitely be an annual management fee – usually 1% of the amount invested.

- If you want to sell your share in a pooled investment, you may also be charged a fee.

It is sometimes suggested in the media that fund managers are rewarded too highly. My view is that if a fund is meeting its objectives, then it is only fair that the fund managers recoup their costs and earn a fee for their expertise. I wish journalists would put more effort into reporting performance figures and less into complaining about whether a manager is charging 0.85% a year or 0.93%!

A couple of other points before we look at all the options in a little bit more detail:

1   The funds described below are all medium- to long-term investment vehicles. In other words, you should be thinking about leaving your money in them for an absolute minimum of five years – and more like ten years or even longer.

2   Although past performance – as it always says in the small print – can be no guide to future performance it is still useful to know. One thing to note is who is making the actual investment decisions and how long they have been doing it for. If the individual manager of a fund has changed recently then the past performance may not be so relevant.

I include several different types of investment in this category:

- tracker bonds

- unit trusts and other managed funds

- with-profits funds

- stock market 'baskets' (or guaranteed stock market active funds).

This is because all of them are what I would describe as 'tailor-made investment vehicles'. That is to say they have been specifically designed to meet the needs of ordinary, private investors. This is in direct contrast to, say, un-tailored opportunities – such as buying a publicly quoted share or an investment property – which aren't aimed at any specific group of investors.

Tracker bonds

This is a fund that guarantees to return your initial investment *plus* a return based on a specific stock market index or indices. For example, it might give you all your money back after five years *plus* 80% of any rise in the FTSE 100.

Unit trusts

Your money is used to purchase 'units' in an investment fund. The price of the units will vary according to the underlying value of the investments. For instance, if the unit trust specialises in European technology shares then it is the value of the shares it holds which will determine the price of the units. You can sell your units at any time but you should be wary of buying and selling too quickly as charges and fees can eat up your profit.

Unit-linked funds

As above, but with the added element of a tiny bit of life insurance so that they can be set up and run by life insurance companies.

Managed funds

Again these are – in essence – unit trusts. The term is used to denote a fund which makes a wide spread of investments – thus theoretically reducing the risk – though you should not assume that this is the case.

Specialised funds

A fund that concentrates on a very specific market opportunity – such as oil shares or companies listed in an emerging market. This is obviously riskier but if the underlying investment performs well, then you will make above-average returns.

Indexed funds

This is a fund that aims to match the overall market performance. For instance, you might have a fund that plans to achieve the same return as the UK's leading 100 shares (FTSE 100).

With-profit funds

These funds are run by insurance companies and they guarantee a minimum return *plus* extra bonuses according to how the fund has performed over the longer term. These bonuses might be added annually (**annual bonus**) or when the fund is closed after the agreed period of time (**terminal bonus**). The terms, conditions, objectives and charges for these funds vary enormously.

Stock market 'baskets'

Investors or their advisers choose a number of stocks, which can range from blue chip shares (such as the big banks and retail groups) to downright risky stocks. Depending on how risk-averse you are, a percentage of your 'basket' will be conservative solid choices, while the smaller percentage will be a little bit of a gamble. Diversification is again the buzz word – the greater the spread or choice of stocks, the softer the fall if there is to be a fall.

SPECIALISED STOCK MARKET STRATEGIES

Futures, options, hedge funds, exchange traded funds, derivatives, contracts for differences (CFDs) and the like all form part of the specialised investment sectors of the stock market. Good solid advice is essential if you wish to participate in this area.

ALTERNATIVE INVESTMENTS

There is a large number of alternative investment options, all of which come with varying amounts of risk. Some, such as gold or other precious metals, are easy to buy and sell. Others, such as art, may have a limited market, making them difficult to find a buyer for when you want to dispose of them. Examples of alternative investments include:

- paintings and other art
- antique furniture and other objects
- debentures at Wimbledon
- rock memorabilia
- gold and other precious metals
- diamonds and other precious gems
- wine
- jewellery
- collectibles such as rare stamps, coins, classic cars or watches.

In general, alternative investment is 'direct' – this is to say, you purchase the actual items. Specialist knowledge is vital if this is to be a genuine investment and you should not consider alternative investments until you have a reasonably high net worth and a portfolio of more conventional investments since the risks can be high.

MONEY DOCTOR WEALTH WARNING

Think carefully before you buy an annuity

If you have a lump sum to invest and you are aged at least 65, then one option is to purchase an **annuity**. The key advantage of an annuity is that it guarantees you an income for the rest of your life. The key disadvantage is that, once purchased, you cannot get your lump sum back. Furthermore, when you die the income stops and nothing will normally be returned to your estate.

Annuities are purchased from life assurance companies, and the return is linked to your age. The younger you are, the lower the return you can expect to receive. It's possible to take out a 'joint survivor annuity' if you're married. With these, when either you or your spouse dies the income continues at a reduced rate until the death of the other. Joint survivor annuities produce a lower return – or income – than single life annuities.

At the moment annuity rates, like interest rates, are relatively low. If you were a male, aged 65, and you wanted to generate a guaranteed income of €1,000 a month, you would need to invest €190,000. However, if you were aged 75, you would only need to invest €130,000.

Annuity rates differ from insurance company to insurance company, and from day to day. It is possible to arrange for your annuity rate to be linked to inflation, and some companies will also guarantee you a minimum return if you die within five years of purchasing the annuity. Finally, you should be aware that the income from an annuity is subject to income tax.

If you've got a limited amount of capital and you're worried about supporting yourself through your retirement years, an annuity could well be the perfect solution. However, I would advise getting professional help to make sure that you purchase the best-value annuity for your needs.

A low-risk, medium-term investment option

For a low-risk, medium-term investment option, consider **guaranteed bonds**. These offer above-average returns in exchange for you locking your money in for an agreed period. Some offer limited penalty-free withdrawals or provide a regular income for the term of the bond.

INVESTING IN STOCKS AND SHARES

Direct investment in the stock market is not for everyone. The risk associated with buying individual shares is obviously much greater than when buying into a diversified portfolio of shares – which is essentially what you are doing with a pooled or investment fund. If the share price goes up – yes – you can make a small fortune. But if the price falls or the market crashes then your shares can become worth a fraction of what you paid for them.

For an investor with limited funds, buying shares is probably not a sensible option. However, once you have started to build your capital wealth you should definitely consider adding individual share holdings to your portfolio of investments:

- Over the longer term, the stock market has shown a greater return to investors than any of the alternatives including property.

- Irish investors are not limited to the Irish stock market – you may buy shares anywhere in the world.

- The charges for buying and selling shares have dropped dramatically, making it feasible to buy and sell in much smaller quantities.

- There are excellent sources of advice on which shares to buy and sell.

- Shares have widely varying degrees of risk.

- One of the big advantages to share ownership is that you literally own part of the company itself and its assets.

- Share ownership should bring you a regular income in the form of dividends plus capital appreciation (if the company is doing well).

Private investors have a choice of doing their own research and making their own decisions or seeking professional help from a stockbroker. Either way, if you are tempted to start buying and selling, you should arm yourself with as much information as possible. Remember, it is ultimately your decision what happens to your portfolio. You should always keep a close watch on what is happening to any company whose shares you have bought, the sector it operates in and the market as a whole. I would particularly recommend the internet for information purposes.

How to read the financial pages

If you do decide to buy stocks and shares, you can keep track of their performance by reading the stock market pages in your daily newspaper. Next to the name of your company you'll find the following information:

High. This is the highest price that your particular company share has reached in the past 12 months.

Low. This is the lowest price that your share has reached in the past 12 months.

Share price. This is the average price paid for your share at close of business on the previous day.

Rise or fall. This is usually represented by a (+) or (-) symbol, and it lets you know how much your share increased or fell by in the previous day's trading.

Dividend yield. The dividend yield is the relationship of a share's annual dividend to its price. The figure will be before tax. For instance, if the dividend yield was 5.8%, and if you'd purchased €100 worth of shares at the current price, you would receive an annual income of €5.80 before tax.

P/E. This stands for **price-earnings ratio**, and it is one of the methods experts use to value a share. The price-earnings ratio is calculated by dividing the company's share price by the after-tax earnings due to each share over the company's most recent financial year. A high price-earnings ratio means that the market is confident in the company's future. But, by the same token, it could mean that the shares are over-priced. A low price-earnings ratio implies a lack of market confidence in the shares but the potential for an investor to pick up a bargain.

Dividend payments

When you own shares in a company you are entitled to a share of the profits — pre-supposing there are profits to be shared. This share is referred to as a **dividend**, and it is paid twice a year. The first payment is called an 'interim dividend' and the second payment is called a 'final dividend'. Several weeks before the dividend is due to be paid the company directors will announce how much it is to be. A few weeks after this they will 'close the register of shares'.

Although you can still buy and sell the shares, if you do so while the register is closed you won't be entitled to the forthcoming dividend. During this period the company shares will be marked **XD** – which is short for ex-dividend – in the newspapers.

Shares and tax

Irish shares are liable to two different types of **tax**. First, you'll have to pay **income tax** on any profits (in other words, 'dividends') you receive. In fact, when you receive a dividend from an Irish company they will have already withheld tax at the standard rate of 25%. If the amount of tax withheld exceeds your liability for that particular year you can claim a refund. However, if you are in fact a higher-rate taxpayer, you'll have to pay the difference between the standard rate and the higher rate when completing your annual tax returns. Second, when you sell your shares, if you've made a gain, you'll be liable for **capital gains tax** at 25%.

Choosing a stockbroker

The only way to buy and sell shares is through a **registered stockbroker**. When you do this, you will either pay a flat fee or commission, depending on whether the stockbroker is also advising you and/or the size of the transaction.

If you don't need advice when buying or selling, then you will require an **execution only** service. In this instance your main concern should be to keep the costs down to a bare minimum. Online services tend to be the cheapest, but it is well worth checking with your bank and the leading stockbrokers just to make sure.

Stockbrokers will be happy to provide you with an advisory service. You'll pay a higher level of commission for this (up to an average of 1.25%) but – of course – you'll benefit from your stockbroker's knowledge of the market.

There is no official minimum value regarding the volume of shares you can purchase. However, there's the minimum level of charges, usually around €25, so it probably doesn't make much sense to buy less than €1,000 worth of shares at a time.

If you want a list of Irish stockbrokers, then contact:

The Irish Stock Exchange
28 Anglesea Street
Dublin 2
Tel. (01) 617 4200.

> **MONEY DOCTOR WEALTH CHECK**
>
> ### Why not start an investment club?
>
> If you'd like to dabble in the stock market but only have a relatively small amount of money to invest, why not start an **investment club**? An investment club is when a group of friends or work colleagues pool their resources and make buy-and-sell decisions together. My own experience of investment clubs is that they regularly out-perform the stock market because those involved take a real and detailed interest in every investment decision. However, you need time and patience.

Bonds

A **bond** is a long-term, fixed interest investment. Bonds are issued by public companies and also by governments as a way of raising money and are, in effect, loans by you to a company or the government. Government bonds are usually referred to as **gilt-edged** securities or, for short, 'gilts' (see below). Bonds have a face value and term – expressed as a **maturity date**.

> For instance, if you had purchased a 15-year €100 bond in a Dutch health insurer in 2002 for a face value of €99.10 – the discount is 90c – at a yield of 6.375% (the **coupon**) you would receive an annual income of €6.38 until the bond reaches its maturity date in 2017 if it is not 'called in' beforehand. On maturity, you are guaranteed to receive €100.
>
> What if you want to cash in your bond sooner? There is a thriving market for second-hand bonds. For instance, the example I mentioned above is currently worth €122.37 with a yield of 3.925%. The second-hand value of a bond will be linked to the underlying security, the rate of interest, and the length of time until it matures.

Gilts

Gilts are the name given to government stock. Governments over the years use 'stock' (rather like an IOU) to raise money to fund their spending. They offer investors a fixed rate of interest for a set period of time in exchange for the use of their savings. The interest is paid without DIRT being deducted – making them very tax-efficient for some non-taxpayers. As interest rates in general fall, government stock tends to rise in value. Gilts are a totally secure and inexpensive way to invest. The returns are usually above average and the cost of buying stock is low – normally a one-off charge of 1%.

PROPERTY

It is easy to understand why so many private investors are attracted to residential and even commercial property:

- Property values have risen and fallen dramatically over the last 30 years.
- It is possible to fund up to 75% of the purchase price with relatively inexpensive loans.
- Rental income from property can cover all the expenses – interest, maintenance, tax and so forth.
- Your investment is in bricks and mortar – something solid – that you can actually see.
- If you make a gain when you sell the property, you will pay substantially less tax – because it is not 'income' but a capital gain and thus taxed at a lower level – currently 25%.

Looking at how property prices have increased over the last 20 years, if you had borrowed €180,000 to buy a €200,000 property some 20 years ago, you would have seen your €20,000 deposit turn into €341,200 profit!

Furthermore, it is possible to take out interest-only mortgages for three to five years that ensure your rent more than covers the cost of the loan and other overheads.

Clearly, property prices rise and fall, so you would be unwise to assume that this is a one-way bet. If the market does fall, you may find it hard to sell the property and take out your money as we have witnessed during 2009. Also, the supply of property to rent has risen so much that in some areas it is now harder to find and keep tenants.

On the other hand, as the old saying goes, 'they aren't making any more of it', and as planning restrictions become tighter there is every reason to believe that property will continue to be a highly attractive investment. The golden rule, in my opinion, is to pick a location and type of property that is always easy to rent.

MONEY DOCTOR WEALTH CHECK

Tax treatment of rental income

Basically, your rental income will be treated the same way as if it was income you had earned by self-employment. You will be allowed all your expenses including:

- wear and tear on furniture, currently an eighth of the cost for each of the following eight years
- any charges made by a management company or letting agent
- maintenance, repairs, insurance, ground rent, rates and so forth
- the cost of any other goods or services you supply to your tenants (such as cleaning).

With regard to relief on interest payable on loans borrowed to purchase, improve or repair a rented property this is allowable (only 75% of the interest) except – roughly – from the period 23 April 1998 to 1 January 2002. If you bought rental property during this period, you should seek professional advice or contact the Revenue Commissioners to clarify your position. **Do note that not all your property expenses will be allowable for tax relief in the year in which they are incurred. For instance, the cost of 'wear and tear' will be spread over several years.** For more information about tax treatment of property see Chapter 26.

TAX-EFFICIENT INVESTMENT OPTIONS

Financial experts often comment that 'you should never let the tax-saving tail wag the investment dog'. In other words, you shouldn't invest in anything simply to enjoy the tax savings but should always consider the underlying value of the opportunity.

When it comes to **property investment** there are a number of tax incentives designed to make certain types of property more attractive. Basically, these can be summarised as:

- **Capital allowances** when you buy, repair and improve certain sorts of industrial buildings.
- A range of allowances available to owner-occupiers and investors in

various urban, town and rural renewal schemes – including **Section 23** (allowable against all rental income and not just for the property itself) and **Section 50** (student accommodation property) investments. We are now in the last throes of these reliefs.

- It is also possible to get substantial tax rebates by investing in **BES (Business Expansion Scheme)** schemes. These schemes require you to lock into a five-year, higher-risk investment and are only suitable for those with a relatively high income and/or substantial other assets.

THE MONEY DOCTOR SAYS...

- Don't put all your eggs in one basket. Divide your savings and investments into different parts so that if one area doesn't perform as hoped your overall financial objectives can still be met.

- Remember, the stock market has outperformed all other investments over the long term. You can take advantage of this by investing in a pooled fund such as a unit trust or by investing directly in shares.

- You must keep reviewing your investment decisions even if you get a professional to help and advise you.

- Investment is for the long term – anything from five years upwards. Don't allow short-term rises and falls to distract you from your long-term strategy.

MONEY DOCTOR WEALTH WARNING

As with everything, if you get professional help, make sure that they are unbiased and don't only represent one or two firms. Some so-called experts will sell you their solution without listening to your objectives. Choose an Authorised Advisor as described in Chapter 4.

MONEY DOCTOR WEALTH CHECK

If you want more information about investment options...

I regularly update the www.moneydoctor.ie website with details of investment opportunities as well as general advice and information. Or you can always write to me at jlowe@moneydoctor.ie.

PART 7

PLANNING FOR A RICHER RETIREMENT

Until twenty or thirty years ago the word 'retirement' was associated with a certain age. Women, if they worked, retired at 60 and men at 65. Life expectancy was shorter and money was scarcer.

Today, retirement has taken on a whole different meaning. With a bit of careful planning it is now common for people to give up work and 'retire' from their late 40s onwards. There is also a strong trend towards second and even third careers.

So when we talk of retiring – yes – we mean giving up work, but we also mean having enough money to do what we want.

Thankfully, successive governments have encouraged the trends I am describing and have rewarded those who save for their retirement with very, very, very tasty tax breaks. Also, there are some relatively new pension structures that offer incredible flexibility.

Anyway, in this section you will learn how it is possible to ensure that when you retire (whenever it may be), you have sufficient wealth to lead a comfortable life. Specifically, you will discover how to:

- *decide what sort of pension you will need*
- *assess your current pension prospects*
- *understand all the various options open to you*
- *arrange a pension that will ensure a comfortable retirement for you*
- *retire early and*
- *find someone you can trust to steer you through the pensions minefield.*

I must emphasise that no one should be complacent about retirement planning. Even if you have a pension, you must review it on a regular basis. You could be a long time retired, anything from 20 to 40 years, so you need to get it right.

19
RETIREMENT BASICS

HOW TO TAKE ADVANTAGE OF THE PENSION OPTIONS OPEN TO YOU

In this chapter we will look at why pension planning is so important and also learn about what I call 'retirement basics' – such as understanding what your existing entitlement (if any) is – together with general planning advice.

WHY YOU SHOULD MAKE PENSION PLANNING YOUR NUMBER ONE PRIORITY

The only people who don't have to worry about retirement planning are those lucky enough to belong to a really first-class pension scheme (one with generous, cast-iron benefits) or who are so rich that money will never be a problem.

For the rest of us, pension planning should be a top priority – more of a priority, in fact, than almost any other financial decision we take. Frankly, it doesn't matter if you haven't bought your own home or invested a single penny of your money providing you have a good pension plan. I say this because, thanks to longer life expectancy, many people will spend anything from 20 to 40 years in retirement.

Typically, as we get older and progress in our careers we earn more money. However, on retirement we are no longer able to earn an income and must rely on either our savings or state benefits. Our earnings are therefore usually at their highest just before we retire. And unless we have made proper provision they will be at their lowest just after we retire. This can result in a massive drop in lifestyle at the point of retirement.

This is where the concept of **income equalisation** comes in – that is, reducing your disposable income when you are earning good money to help increase your income when you are not able to earn. We reduce our disposable income now by putting money into a pension scheme that can be used to increase our retirement income. It is still likely that when we retire our income will fall, but with this type of planning the transition will be far less of a shock to the system.

> ## MONEY DOCTOR WEALTH WARNING
>
> ### *Is your company or government pension going to let you down?*
>
> Are you in a company or government pension scheme – outside the state pension which you would be entitled to at age 66? You should check on a regular basis, certainly every other year, that it is actually going to meet your needs on retirement. A growing number of pension schemes are producing disappointing returns and you should not be complacent. Very few company schemes provide enough money to ensure a comfortable old-age income. Get expert help too, because whereas companies are obliged to give you details of your benefits (and losses), you might not necessarily understand them. You can't rely on whoever is operating the scheme to provide you with the information you need.

IT IS NEVER TOO EARLY OR LATE TO BEGIN

Given that it is not impossible that your retirement may turn out to be a longer period than that of your working life, it isn't surprising that pension experts stress the importance of starting to plan early.

Nevertheless, if the number of men and women in their 40s, 50s and even their 60s consulting the Money Doctor on pension planning is anything to go by, a huge percentage of the population don't start thinking about their retirement until it isn't that far away.

Obviously, the later you leave it, the more of your income you will have to devote to building up a decent pension fund and the less well off you can expect to be once you stop work. But just because it is never too late to begin, it doesn't mean you should go to the wire. Every single day counts.

START BY TAKING STOCK

The first step towards a comfortable retirement is to take stock of where you are now in pension terms:

- Are you part of one or more companies or occupational pension schemes already?

- Are you entitled to a state pension by virtue of your employment?

- Are you entitled to a non-contributory old age pension?

- Could you live on a quarter of the average industrial wage – because that is roughly what the state pension will give you!

- Have you started a pension plan in the past?

If you answer 'yes' to any of these questions then you need to find out what your existing pension is going to be worth to you.

You also need to consider what other assets you have. Will your home be paid for by the time you retire? Have you any other savings or investments? By the same token, are there any other debts that you will need to discharge before retirement?

WHERE DO YOU GO FOR THE ANSWERS TO ALL THESE QUESTIONS?

The easiest thing to do is to get a qualified professional to do the work for you, in other words, either an accountant (if they specialise in this area) or an Authorised Advisor. The alternative is to approach all the relevant parties yourself. That is to say:

- your current employer and any past employers

- the managers of any pension scheme you may have started in the past

- the Department of Community, Family & Social Affairs (check your telephone directory for the relevant department or Chapter 5)

- the Pensions Board (Verschoyle House, Mount Street, Dublin 2).

If you are unhappy with any aspect of the way a non-government pension scheme has been administered, then you should contact the:

Pensions Ombudsman
36 Upper Mount Street
Dublin 2.

THE MONEY DOCTOR SAYS...

If you are self-employed or you are not in an employer-sponsored pension scheme then, unless you take action, you'll have to rely on the state. You can guess how well off that will leave you.

HOW MUCH WILL YOU NEED WHEN YOU RETIRE?

The whole concept of retirement has been turned on its head in recent years. As a population we are:

- giving up work sooner – often in our late 40s or 50s
- living longer and healthier lives
- leading more active lives in retirement.

We also expect a much higher standard of living. As a result we need more money in retirement than our predecessors. Here are some things you will need to consider:

- Will you need a lump sum on retirement to pay off debts or to invest for a regular income?
- Will you still have unavoidable expenses (such as children's education) to pay for?
- How much of an income will you need? Could you manage on half of what you earn now? Could you manage on a quarter?

What changes would you have to make in your lifestyle if the only money you had coming in after retirement was the state pension?

Do you have anyone else to provide for? Your spouse, for instance? What will happen if you die before they do?

Our civil servants receive an index-linked income of up to half of their final pay, a tax-free sum of up to one-and-a-half year's salary, and a half-pension for their spouses after they die. Only a very tiny percentage of private-sector schemes offer this type of benefit.

What's more, if you work in the private sector and wanted to receive the same sort of benefit from the age of 65, you would have to put about 15% of your income into a pension fund from the age of 20 and even 40% when aged over 60.

THE GOOD NEWS

There are three excellent reasons why you shouldn't despair, regardless of whether or not you have any sort of pension in place already:

1 The government realises that it is vital to encourage you to save for your

retirement so they will give you *huge* tax incentives to do so. For every €1 invested in a pension, you will receive 20c or 41c back depending on your tax margin and excluding levies.

2 Good planning at any age can optimise your retirement income.

3 By taking action now, you can alter your position dramatically. It is only people who continue to ignore the risks they are running who face the possibility (one might say certainty) of an impoverished retirement.

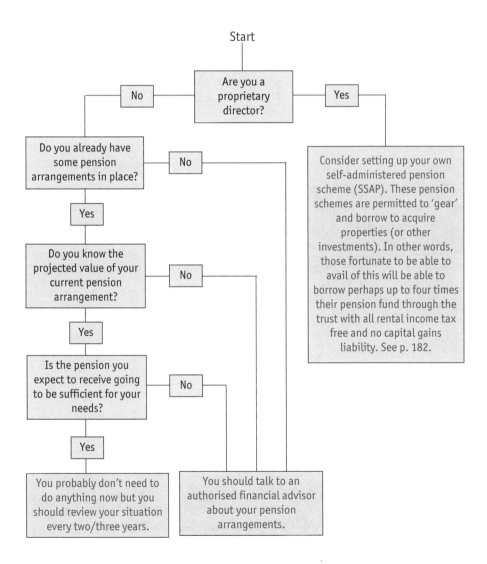

Start

Are you a proprietary director?

No

Yes

Do you already have some pension arrangements in place?

No

Yes

Consider setting up your own self-administered pension scheme (SSAP). These pension schemes are permitted to 'gear' and borrow to acquire properties (or other investments). In other words, those fortunate to be able to avail of this will be able to borrow perhaps up to four times their pension fund through the trust with all rental income tax free and no capital gains liability. See p. 182.

Do you know the projected value of your current pension arrangement?

No

Yes

Is the pension you expect to receive going to be sufficient for your needs?

No

Yes

You probably don't need to do anything now but you should review your situation every two/three years.

You should talk to an authorised financial advisor about your pension arrangements.

WHAT TO DO IF YOU WORK IN THE PRIVATE SECTOR

If you work for someone else you will be in one of two situations:

- either you will be in a company or occupational scheme or
- you won't be in any scheme at all.

If you are in a company or occupational pension scheme, then you will need to ascertain how good the scheme is, the sort of pension you can expect, what other benefits you may be entitled to and whether it is possible to increase your pension by making **additional voluntary contributions** (AVCs). If, on taking expert advice, the existing pension scheme doesn't appear to be that good, then concentrate on those AVCs.

Don't forget any schemes you may have been in during your previous employment.

If you aren't in your employer's scheme (and all employers are now obliged to operate a scheme under recent legislation – **personal retirement savings accounts** or PRSAs – or at least have a direct debit provision from your salary to such an investment) then you should consider joining. If you have no pension arrangements at all (and you don't want to do something through your employer) then you need to start a scheme of your own.

Your own pension scheme might be a personal pension plan or the more recently introduced PRSAs. I'll be looking at these options in greater detail in the next chapter.

WHAT TO DO IF YOU WORK FOR YOURSELF

If you work for yourself, you are going to have to provide your own pension. The big advantage of this is that you can design a pension plan that matches your needs perfectly:

- It will be flexible, allowing you to invest on a regular basis or with lump sums.
- You'll have the choice of investing your money in an established fund or starting your own if you are a company owner, proprietary director (i.e. have at least a 5% shareholding in your company) or a senior company employee (e.g. a small self-administered pension scheme – SSAPs) or self-directed trusts.

- If you own your own company you could even consider setting up a company scheme.

THE MONEY DOCTOR SAYS...

- You are probably, to quote a line from the TV programme *Black Adder*, 'perfectly happy to wear cotton without understanding how the weaving process works'. By the same token, you shouldn't feel that you need to understand pensions legislation in its entirety to make your retirement plans!

- Action is imperative. If you have a really good pension plan, allowing you to retire early, you don't need any other investments (not even a house).

- The sooner you act, the better it will be, but it is never too late to start. Extra tax benefits may apply the older you are.

20
PENSIONS MADE EASY

STEP-BY-STEP INSTRUCTIONS ON HOW TO MAKE YOUR RETIREMENT DREAMS COME TRUE

This chapter contains detailed instructions on retirement planning – all the information, advice and tips you need to make your own decisions about what you need and want.

A QUICK GUIDE TO PENSION SCHEMES

One of my teenage daughter's favourite expressions is 'too much information'. This may be the reaction many of you have when trying to understand the pension system. Nor is it any wonder when you consider how complicated the various options are. Opening a book on the subject at random (a book aimed at ordinary consumers, by the way), my eyes fell immediately on the following sentence:

> Where a 5% Director chooses the New Retirement Options, they must first ensure that the total fund accumulated would not result in a situation where the maximum benefits would be excluded had they gone down the traditional annuity purchase route.

My own view is that you should inform yourself, in the same way that you would inform yourself before making any major purchase, but that unless you find the topic fascinating don't waste your time grappling with the minutiae. Instead, let an independent and authorised expert advise you. Here, then, is my quick guide to pension schemes.

LET'S BEGIN AT THE VERY BEGINNING...

Basically, a pension scheme, or a retirement plan, or whatever you want to call it, is a way of saving money specifically for **your retirement**. What differentiates it from an ordinary savings plan is that you will receive substantial help from the Revenue and, in exchange, access to your savings will be restricted. How restricted? Well, it will vary but typically you won't be able to touch any of the money you have saved until you reach a minimum age (this will vary according to the scheme and even the sort of job you have) and even then you won't be able to get your hands on all of it as a tax-free lump sum.

There are three basic employment categories and the pension options can be defined as follows:

- employee
- self-employed
- directors.

Employee

Occupational pension schemes. Money invested in these schemes is locked away until you actually retire. At this point there will be restrictions on how you take the benefits. For instance, you'll only be allowed a limited amount as a lump sum – tax free – and the rest will have to be taken as an income.

Defined benefits. This is the Rolls Royce of schemes and extremely valuable. It can be either a contributory or non-contributory scheme – invariably, the employer will make contributions to the scheme. With this type of pension the employer guarantees you a certain percentage of your final salary, as a pension for life, for every year you have been working for them. Depending on the particular scheme, this can be up to 66% of the annual average of your last three years' income. You can also elect to take part of your benefits as a tax-free lump sum of up to one-and-a-half times your salary. The beauty of defined benefit schemes is that, irrespective of fund performance, you are guaranteed to receive the promised pension. It is the trustees of the scheme who have to worry about how they are going to fund what could be a very expensive company cost. More and more employers are opting out of the defined benefit pension because of cost, a trend exacerbated by the poor pension fund performances of the late 1990s and first part of the new century. Defined benefit schemes undoubtedly provide the best pension benefits. However, you should note that benefits are based on how long you have been working for that company. If you have a relatively short number of years' service, you can still top up your pension benefits by making some contributions through additional voluntary contributions (AVCs).

Defined contributions. Your pension is based on the growth of your monthly contributions (again the employer will usually also make contributions to your pension) up to maturity on retirement age. Unfortunately, there is no guarantee of how much you will receive on retirement as values may fall as well as rise. Your fund is purely down to how fund managers perform and how much you have invested. It is vital therefore that you be fully briefed and communicated with on a regular basis so that you can take corrective action if necessary. That corrective action may be an AVC.

Additional voluntary contributions (AVCs). Depending on your own existing pension contributions and your age, you could put up to 40% of your annual income into an AVC. You can offset the entire 40% against your income tax liability, making this procedure a very tax-efficient one. Furthermore, most employers will deduct your AVCs directly from your wages. If they do this you will also benefit from PRSI relief on your AVC. There is also greater flexibility about how and when you take the benefits and you won't have to pay for setting up a scheme of your own. If your employer's pension scheme has a good investment performance or guaranteed benefits, then putting more money into it via an AVC can make excellent financial sense.

Check with an Authorised Advisor for specific details, as there are so many regulations and you want to ensure you're making the right decision.

No occupational pension scheme is available to you. If your employer does not offer an occupational pension scheme, you have the same options as someone who is self-employed (see below). The one exception is that your employer is required, by law, to provide you with a payroll deduction facility to a nominated PRSA provider.

Self-employed

Personal Retirement Savings Accounts (PRSA)/personal pensions – with the recent introduction of PRSAs, pensions became more accessible and less expensive to start. PRSAs have maximum charges of 5% of each premium paid plus 1% a year of the accumulated fund. The affordable pension is here to stay. Benefits include:

- it's low cost
- generous tax relief at your marginal rate. Depending on your age this can be on contributions of up to 40% of your income
- it's easy to understand – you decide how much you want to invest and where you want the money invested

- it's portable in that you can bring the pension with you from employment to employment together with flexibility in being able to adjust your annual contributions depending on your circumstances, and flexible about how you use the fund on retirement

- when you retire, you can have up to 25% of the fund as a tax-free lump sum (useful for paying off a mortgage) and

- it's suitable for people who work for themselves, have no company scheme or change their employment frequently.

In theory, a PRSA is a simplified version of a personal pension plan. In practice, the rules governing PRSAs are just as complicated. You should seek independent advice.

Directors

If you are a director, you can avail of a **director's executive pension** (if you have 5% or more shareholding in your company). In fact, the advantages offered by company schemes are so good that if you are self-employed (a sole trader), it may be worth your while to form a limited company in order to take advantage of them yourself. If you do own your own company, then setting up a company pension scheme will probably be the best route for you. The main reason for this is that the limits for which the Revenue will give tax relief on pension contributions are significantly higher for a company investing in a company pension scheme than for an individual investing in a corresponding PRSA or personal pension.

Company schemes can be arranged to benefit as many employees as you want, just you, or selected members of your staff, as you prefer. Note that this route is particularly good for anyone who has left it late in life to plan for his or her retirement.

- As there is no benefit in kind on contributions to a company pension scheme, your company will be able to put substantial tax-free money into your pension.

- There is greater flexibility with regard to your retirement date.

- You have more control over where your contributions are invested.

- You can take a portion of your fund tax-free – so tax breaks on the way in and the way out!

MORE ON **PRSA**S/PERSONAL PENSIONS

Small self-administered pension schemes (SSAP) or self-directed trusts

Under most pension arrangements it is left up to fund managers to determine what the pension funds actually invest in. However, if you want more direct control on the actual assets that make up your pension fund you can always set up an SSAP. Here you appoint a **pensioner trustee** to run your pension but you dictate what it invests in. For example, if you want to invest in shares you can pick the individual shares as opposed to just a managed fund.

Recent legislative changes have also brought in for the first time a provision which allows pension funds to borrow for **property acquisition**. This effectively means that you could borrow within your pension fund to buy an investment property (at arm's length – not your own company's offices, your holiday hot spot or your granny's flat) and both the rental income contributions and your own monthly contributions will be paid into your pension fund tax-free, while all along your fund (i.e. your property) should be appreciating as you are making those contributions. There is also the added benefit that no capital gains liability is incurred and your estate keeps the asset (i.e. your property) after you die.

I think that for the company executive, the SSAPs/self-directed trusts will grow considerably over the coming years as a result of the introduction of that one provision, allowing pension funds to borrow or gear perhaps up to four times the fund value to buy investment property. SSAPs are not just confined to property. Shares, investments and even complex financial instruments (e.g. hedge funds) can be incorporated into SSAPs. Email me for a free brochure on self-directed trusts at jlowe@moneydoctor.ie

BIG TAX RELIEF – THE REVENUE COMMISSIONERS ARE ON YOUR SIDE

I have made repeated mention of the huge tax incentives offered to those who invest in a pension. These include:

- Tax relief at your marginal rate of tax. So if you are paying tax at 41% when you put €100 into your pension fund it will only cost you €59. Put another way, pension funds almost double the value of your savings before the money has been invested in anything.

- Investments grow tax-free. If you put money into your own company scheme it is a legitimate business expense for tax purposes.

- It can be possible to save PRSI (including the health levy of 2%), which represents a further saving of 9% on the annual premiums for those paying at the top tax rate, or a total saving of 50% when income tax is included. Put another way, if a gross premium of €5,000 were paid for 20 years, the value of the premiums would be €100,000 at the end of the period. Thanks to the tax element, the net cost **from after-tax income** is €50,000. To achieve the same return on investing, the net income would need an annual compound return of 7%! This is the value of the government's contribution and it is given **for free**.

- While it is in a pension fund, no income tax or capital gains tax is payable on your investment.

- All pension schemes allow you to take out a certain portion of your fund tax free when you come to retire.

- PRSI is not payable once you are 66, excluding the 2% health levy portion, which ceases to be payable at age 70.

There are limits on the amount you can invest into a pension fund and still get the tax relief. Check with your Authorised Advisor for details.

WHAT HAPPENS TO YOUR PENSION CONTRIBUTIONS?

If you are part of an occupational pension scheme, then your money will be invested by the scheme's managers. If it is a big scheme, they may invest it directly themselves. Most companies, however, use the services of professional fund managers who invest in everything from stocks and shares to property and commodities. Performance will be determined by how well the scheme is managed and if you are in a 'defined contribution' scheme, you need to pay close attention to this. For employer-sponsored schemes (e.g. occupational pension schemes) trustees play an important role as they look after the investment decisions on advice from fund managers.

    If you set up your own personal pension plan or your own company sets up a company scheme, then you have much more control over how your contributions are invested while you have to make the investment choices. Most opt for equity funds – where your money is pooled and invested in stocks and shares. Such funds will have varying returns and different levels of risk. As you near retirement you will be less likely to place your fund in a higher-risk investment than you would if you were in your early 30s.

MONEY DOCTOR WEALTH WARNING

Don't buy a pension from someone who can't offer you choice

All the financial institutions involved in the retirement market, and I'm speaking chiefly about life insurance companies and banks, employ salespeople whose job it is to promote their own company's pension products.

One such example is that of a young solicitor who was persuaded to take out a bank assurance pension plan at a premium of more than €500 per month, based on her expectation of a certain income on retirement in keeping with her current levels of salary. After a couple of months she cancelled the policy because she wasn't asked one of the most important questions: 'Can you afford to pay this amount each month into a pension scheme?'

While it is important to aim for a similar level of income to retire on, it is equally important to be able to afford it and have a life in the meantime. Ideally, you should not choose a pension from someone who only represents one company. You should always deal with someone independent who is authorised to tell you about every single option available to you. Pension fund performance and management fees vary enormously. Buying without comparing the whole market could cost you a great deal of money.

WHAT IS IT GOING TO COST?

Almost without exception, the pension industry gets paid on **commission**. This commission comes out of your monthly payments. The amount will vary according to the type of pension scheme you join or set up. Many schemes (but not all) will involve an initial, one-off fee followed by an **annual management charge**. To give you an example, for a standard PRSA the maximum annual management charge is 1% of the accumulated fund, whilst the initial set-up fee is capped at 5% of the premiums. When you take out a pension your Authorised Advisor will explain, in full, what charges you are paying. Remember, however, the charges are one thing, but what is it going to cost to provide an income?

Having a pension is one thing, but having a pension which is going to provide you with the income you think you will need is another. One example of this was a shop-owner who sought advice on investing a lump sum. One suggestion was to look at investing this in a pension. However, he indicated that he was alright here as he had already put a pension in place. It transpired that this 45-year-old shop-owner was currently earning €50,000 a year and had just taken out a pension plan for €400 a month. He was shocked to learn that if he kept contributions at this level, and took the state contributory pension into account, he could expect to have a total after-tax retirement income of around €750 a month (in today's terms) at age 65 – a fraction of what he currently earned.

You get what you pay for. One way of looking at it is to look at what level of income you think you need and finding out how much it would cost to provide this. You may not be able to afford the cost now but at least you will know what to expect.

Below is a table showing the approximate costs of funding a total after-tax income of €1,250 a month and €2,500 a month in today's terms should you retire at 65. They assume that you will be entitled to the state contributory pension. These figures are meant as a guide only, and make a number of assumptions. You should discuss your own particular circumstances with a qualified Authorised Advisor.

	Aged 25	Aged 30	Aged 35	Aged 40	Aged 45	Aged 50	Aged 55
€1,250pm	€191pm	€255pm	€347pm	€482pm	€673pm	€1,001pm	€1,681pm
€2,400pm	€341pm	€457pm	€623pm	€864pm	€1,207pm	€1,790pm	€3,019pm

The above figures are before tax relief and assume that contributions are increased by 5% a year, inflation is 5% a year and the state pension increases by 5% a year. It also assumes that the funds the pension is invested in increase by 6% a year and that the tax rates on retirement are similar to today.

WHAT BENEFITS SHOULD YOU BE LOOKING FOR?

How do you judge a pension scheme? Here are some tips:

- If it is a defined benefit scheme, then you should judge it primarily on what percentage of your salary you'll receive once you retire. Remember, these are the only schemes where the benefit is guaranteed based on service and salary.

- Depending on the type of pension plan you have you will be given a certain portion, by way of a tax-free lump sum, of the fund's value. Establish how much.

- Death-in-service benefit. Essentially, this is life cover giving your beneficiaries a lump sum and/or income should you die before retirement age.

- Death-in-retirement benefit. This gives your beneficiaries a lump sum and/or an income if you die after you have retired.

- The minimum retirement age (for occupational pension schemes it is 60, but if you own your company you can take a well-earned rest at age 50).

- How much will your pension income increase each year after you have started claiming it? Will it increase in line with the cost of living? More than the cost of living?

- Any special benefits offered to your spouse or other dependants.

WHAT HAPPENS WHEN YOU RETIRE?

This will depend on your employment status and scheme.

For **defined benefit schemes**, you will receive a tax-free lump sum and a guaranteed annual income, usually index-linked and based on your service.

For **defined contribution** schemes, the accumulated fund on retirement is used to buy annuity income based on how much is in the fund after taking out an allowable portion by way of a tax-free lump sum.

For funds accumulated through **director schemes, AVCs, PRSAs** or **personal pensions**, the choices are greater as recent legislation brought in new options – **approved retirement funds** (ARFs) and **approved minimum retirement funds** (AMRFs) – allowing pension funds to be held outside of annuities and effectively kept within your estate when you pass on. The taxable benefits can be taken as needed. If you have an annuity, the insurance company keeps the money when you die and your dependants lose out.

THE MONEY DOCTOR SAYS ...

- The tax benefits of having a pension are enormous. For a taxpayer on the higher rate of tax, putting €100 into a pension will currently only cost €59 (less if PRSI is taken into account). This is a bargain by anyone's standards.

- If your pension incorporates life cover you may receive extra tax relief.

- Please, please take independent professional advice. I am repeating myself, I know. But only someone who is authorised to advise you on every pension available is going to guarantee you the most appropriate pension for your needs.

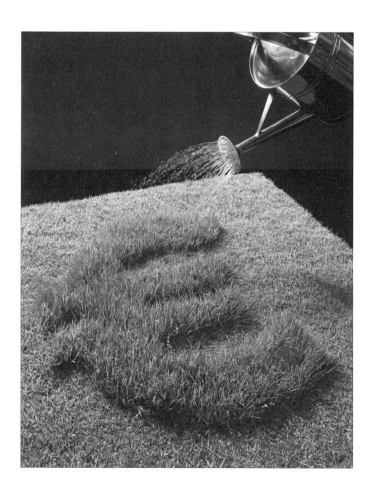

PART 8

WHY PAY MORE TAX THAN YOU HAVE TO?

Would you like to slash your 2011 tax bill quickly, easily and without having to plough through a lot of incomprehensible jargon? Then this section is for you. Because in plain English – using plenty of examples and case histories – I am going to explain how, as a taxpayer, you can:

- *make certain that you don't pay a single cent more tax this year than you have to*
- *reclaim any tax you may have overpaid in previous years*
- *plan your finances so that future tax bills are kept to a bare minimum.*

MONEY DOCTOR WEALTH CHECK

For the hottest tax tips check out www.moneydoctor.ie

Because tax rules sometimes change during the year and because the Money Doctor's team of tax advisers are always searching for new ways to save you tax, our website contains a special tax-saving section. So for the hottest tax tips visit www.moneydoctor.ie *today.*

To make it as easy as possible to find the tax-saving information you require I've divided this section up into lots of short chapters. From the list below you can check which chapters are relevant to your circumstances:

Chapter 21: *Tax basics. An overview of how the Irish tax system works – and your part in it!*

Chapter 22: *Income tax basics. The first steps towards reducing your income tax bill.*

Chapter 23: *All about income tax credits. How tax 'credits' and 'allowances' can help you save money.*

Chapter 24: *PAYE. How to make the Pay As You Earn (PAYE) tax system work in your favour.*

Chapter 25: *Income tax for the self-employed. How to reduce your income tax bill if you work for yourself.*

Chapter 26: *Tax and property. Property investor? How to ensure you keep your tax bill to a minimum.*

Chapter 27: *Tax and the company car. How motorists can drive down their tax bill.*

Chapter 28: *Capital gains tax. Lots of useful tips on how to reduce, delay and avoid capital gains tax. If you think you may be selling any of your assets (including a property) during 2011 or in the foreseeable future then you need to read this chapter.*

Chapter 29: *Capital acquisition tax. The purpose of capital acquisition tax is to tax gifts and inheritances – and the purpose of this chapter is to make sure that your gifts and inheritances aren't taxed!*

Chapter 30: *Love, marriage and lower taxes. Extra tax benefits for those who are married.*

Chapter 31: *Tax for the ex-pat. Tax planning tips for those living and working abroad.*

Chapter 32: *Special tax advice for farmers. Special tax tips for farmers and farming businesses.*

MONEY DOCTOR WEALTH CHECK

Could you take advantage of the seed capital scheme?

If you're thinking of starting your own business – and you've never been in business before – then you may be able to take advantage of something called the seed capital scheme. To be eligible you have to have been employed on a PAYE basis and you have to have capital of your own (or be able to borrow capital elsewhere) to invest in the new venture. Under these circumstances the government will give you an income tax rebate of up to €100,000 (relating to the PAYE paid in the six years preceding cessation of your employment) to help you get your new business off the ground. Because the seed capital scheme is essentially returning or rebating tax you've paid in the past, it doesn't stop you from taking advantage of other government incentives such as grants and employment incentives. Furthermore, you can claim this rebate pretty much regardless of the sort of business you are establishing.

21
TAX BASICS

GETTING TO GRIPS WITH THE TAX SYSTEM

There are really only two things you need to know about Irish tax to start beating the system. Firstly, most people are hit hardest by just three taxes and it is these that you want to concentrate on reducing or – better still – avoiding completely. They are:

- income tax
- capital gains tax (CGT)
- capital acquisition tax (CAT).

(Of course, there are many other taxes, such as stamp duty and deposit interest retention tax [DIRT], and, believe me, I am not going to ignore them. But it is the first three that will probably offer you the biggest scope for juicy savings.)

Secondly, the beauty of the Irish tax system is that it consists almost entirely of exceptions. There are, literally, hundreds of different reasons why you might not have to pay a particular tax. So, cutting your tax bill is simply a matter of either:

- studying these reasons to see which ones apply (or could be made to apply) to your own circumstances so as to save you tax
- looking at your circumstances and seeing how they might be altered to give you a tax advantage.

Let me give you a quick example. In theory, if you are single, the first €36,400 of your 2010 income should be taxed at 20%, and anything over this sum should be taxed at 41%. In practice, there is a minimum income (**income exemption limit**) you have to receive before you pay any tax at all (this could be as high as €40,000 depending on your age and circumstances) and once your income exceeds this level there are all sorts of allowances, credits and other ways to reduce the amount you actually have to part with.

How old you are, where you live, your marital status, the source of your income, any borrowings you may have, your health, the health of your family... all these factors and many, many others can be used to slash your tax bill.

It is not inconceivable that you could have an income of as high as €75,000 and not actually have to pay a single cent in tax – except for levies!

KEEPING IT LEGAL

The difference between legal tax saving – which is called **tax avoidance** – and illegal tax saving – which is called **tax evasion** – was once described as being 'the thickness of a prison wall'. It is perfectly legal to use our tax laws in any way you can to reduce the amount of tax you pay. Naturally, all the tax-saving suggestions in this book are 100% legal.

GET TO KNOW YOUR TAX LIABILITIES
AND THE REVENUE COMMISSIONERS IN THE PROCESS

Here is a list and brief description of taxes affecting individuals:

Income tax

This, as its name implies, is a tax on annual income. How much you have to pay is linked to:

- how much you earn
- your personal circumstances
- what tax credits and allowances you are entitled to.

If you are an employee you pay your income tax monthly but if you are self-employed you pay it annually. Either way, there are dozens of income tax-saving tactics available.

Capital gains tax

If you buy something at one price and either sell it later for a higher price or give it away when it is worth more than you paid for it, then you will have made a capital gain. This gain may be taxed – depending on all sorts of factors including:

- how big the gain is
- what sort of gain it is
- the rate of inflation
- allowable expenses.

It is paid annually. As with income tax there are plenty of ways in which to reduce your liability to capital gains tax. See Chapter 28.

Capital acquisition tax

This is a tax on gifts and on inheritances. The person receiving the gift or inheritance pays it. Whether tax has to be paid will depend on a variety of factors including:

- the amount of money or the value of the property involved
- the relationship between the parties involved
- the nature of the gift or inheritance.

Once again, it is paid annually and there are any number of ways in which it is possible to avoid and/or reduce this tax. See Chapter 29.

Stamp duty

If you are buying a property you will be liable for **stamp duty** – which is a one-off tax. You'll also have to pay stamp duty – at a considerably lower level – on your mortgage deed. For individuals, it is very hard to legally reduce or avoid this form of taxation. See p. 137 for matrix.

Pay Related Social Insurance (PRSI)

If you are employed or self-employed you will have to pay health, employment and training levies – which are usually all lumped together and referred to as PRSI. There is little scope for legally avoiding PRSI.

However, PRSI is no longer payable once you reach the age of 66, with the exception of the health levy portion (2%) which is no longer payable at age 70.

Value Added Tax (VAT)

This is a tax on your spending. It is charged at different rates from 0% to 21% – depending on what you are buying. Businesses and the self-employed have some opportunities for avoiding or reducing their VAT liability – individuals are limited in their options.

Do you have to fill in a tax return?

One question I frequently get asked – especially by those in retirement, regular employment, or receiving welfare payments – is whether or not they are legally obliged to complete an annual tax return. Let us start by considering who must fill out that dreaded form whether they want to or not. Into this category falls:

- anybody who works for themselves – full- or part-time
- anyone with a second income, even if it's from casual work like cleaning or baby-sitting
- all company directors
- anyone in receipt of income that hasn't already been taxed – for instance, a private pension or dividends from an overseas investment
- anyone who has made a capital gain
- anyone with rental income from a property
- anyone who has received or made a gift
- anyone who has received money of any sort that may be liable to tax here in Ireland.

The fact that you may be paying PAYE does not exclude you from having to complete a tax return. Indeed, even if you're on PAYE it may be to your advantage to complete a tax return as it could reduce your tax bill for the year.

So who *definitely* doesn't have to complete a tax return? If you fall into any of the following categories, you are off the hook:

- You have a relatively low income. See p. 199 for details.
- You have absolutely no income.
- You pay your tax through the PAYE system, and haven't received any other money that might be liable to tax.

Money Doctor Wealth Check

Take advantage of the taxperson

Many people forget that the Revenue Commissioners are there to serve you. They publish a wide range of brochures designed to assist taxpayers, and you'll also find an enormous amount of information online at their website (www.revenue.ie). Your local tax office will be delighted to answer questions for you, and you can also telephone them on their information helpline, details of which you'll find in the 'Useful Addresses' section (Appendix 7). The Revenue Commissioners also have a highly efficient on-line service called, oddly enough, the Revenue On-line Service or ROS. This internet facility allows you to file your tax returns, make payments, and access your personal revenue data any time, night or day. Registering is a simple process, and the software is easy to use and compatible with every type of computer. When completing a tax return you will also find that it saves you a vast amount of time since you won't have to wade through all the relevant sections looking for the questions you need to answer. However, it is not yet available to everyone.

22
INCOME TAX BASICS

THE FIRST STEPS TOWARDS REDUCING YOUR INCOME TAX BILL

'Income tax', claimed Will Rogers, 'has made more liars out of the American people than golf.' Being a patriotic soul I like to think that we Irish people are above such deceit. Not that we mightn't be tempted when it comes to income tax – if only because the thing is so wretchedly confusing.

The Revenue Commissioners (who appear to be allergic to plain English) hardly help by defining income tax as being the tax:

> payable on your taxable income, i.e. your total assessable income tax for a tax year, less deductions for any non-standard rate allowances (not tax credits) to which you may be entitled.

Then, as if this wasn't sufficiently obscure, they divide 'income' into several different categories which they call – unhelpfully – **schedules**. The schedules are then divided into 'cases'. And so it goes on.

Unfortunately, if you are going to make a serious attempt to reduce your income tax bill, you really need to understand how the Revenue Commissioners are actually taxing you. Therefore, the first part of this chapter is devoted to a basic, jargon-free guide to income tax. However, once the terms of engagement, as it were, have been explained we will get straight down to all the different ways in which you might cut – or even avoid altogether – your income tax liability.

WHAT SORT OF INCOME DO YOU HAVE?

In order to differentiate between the different types of income people receive, the Revenue Commissioners classify income under a number of different headings or 'schedules'. Since accountants and other financial professionals refer to these schedules all the time, it's quite useful to know what they are:

> **Schedule C** relates to organisations like banks that have deducted income tax from certain payments. You almost certainly won't have to worry about this.

Schedule D is divided into five separate classes referred to as 'cases'.

– Case I relates to profit from a trade.

– Case II relates to profits from a profession.

– Case III refers to interest not taxed at source, and all foreign income.

– Case IV refers to taxed interest income not falling under any case schedule.

– Case V refers to rental income from properties in Ireland.

Schedule E basically covers all the money earned from regular employment, and is technically defined as 'income from offices or employments, together with pensions, benefits in kind, and certain lump sum payments arising from an office or employment'.

Schedule F covers dividends and other distributions from Irish-resident companies.

Whenever you deal with the Revenue Commissioners in relation to income tax you'll find that they make reference to the above schedules and cases. It is always worth checking that they have your income correctly classified as – if they don't – it could help to reduce your tax bill.

A QUICK EXPLANATION OF INCOME TAX RATES

For many years, income tax has been levied at a different rate according to the amount of income involved. There are currently two different rates in Ireland – **20%** and **41%**. Which rate of tax you'll pay will depend on your circumstances and income. For instance, for 2010 if you are a single person the **first €36,400** of your income will be taxed at **20%** and the balance would be taxed at **41%**. It is worth remembering that these tax rates can change from year to year.

The table overleaf shows the different tax bands and rates for 2010. As you will see, taxpayers are divided into four different groups. These are:

• single people and widow(er)s

• one-parent families

• married couples where only one spouse is working

• married couples – where both spouses are working.

Rates of income tax

Single/widowed without dependent children	36,400 @ 20% Balance @ 41%
Single/widowed qualifying for one-parent family tax credit	40,400 @ 20% Balance @ 41%
Married couple (one spouse with income)	45,400 @ 20% Balance @ 41%
Married couple (both spouses with income)	45,400 @ 20% (with increase of 27,400 max.) Balance @ 41%

Income Levy

An income levy was introduced in the budget of October 2008 and increased in the supplementary budget of April 2009. The exemption threshold is €15,028.

Rates

€15,028–€75,036	2%
€75,037–€174,980	4%
€174,981+	6%

Some good news for anyone on a low income

If your income falls below a certain level, you are completely exempt from income tax. The chart below sets out the maximum amount of income you can receive – according to your circumstances – this year without paying a single cent in tax. It's worth noting that if you earn income over the amounts set out below, you will be eligible for something called 'marginal relief', which is explained below.

Low income exemption limits

Single/widowed	Exemption limits for 2010
65 or over	€20,000
Married	
65 or over	€40,000

Additions to exemptions limit for dependent children (€)

1st and 2nd child (per child)	€575
Each subsequent child	€830
Marginal relief tax rate	40% of the amount by which the total income exceeds the exemption limit.

Taking advantage of marginal relief

Supposing you are on a relatively low income, but you earn slightly more than the amount necessary to avoid tax completely? Recognising that it would be unfair to tax you too heavily, something called **marginal relief** exists. Any individual/married couple whose total income from all sources is slightly over the exemption limit may qualify for marginal relief but it will only be granted if it is more beneficial to the claimant than their tax credits. It restricts the tax payable to 40% of the difference between your income and the appropriate exemption limit. The exemption limits vary depending on age, marital status and the number of qualifying dependent children. As this is quite complicated, let me explain it with an example:

Marginal relief advantageous

Over 65 married with two children

	€		€
Total income	40,000	Total income	40,000
Tax @ 20%	8,000	Less: Exemption	40,000
Less: Tax credits	5,830	Excess	nil
Tax due	2,170	Tax @ 40%	nil

PERSONAL CREDITS AND TAX ALLOWANCES

Although you are liable to pay income tax at the rates outlined, you are entitled to claim all sorts of **personal tax credits** and **allowances** which will help you to reduce this bill by a fairly substantial amount. You'll find a complete guide to all the income tax credits and allowances in the next chapter.

PRSI – another form of income tax

The initials PRSI stand for **pay related social insurance**. Because it is calculated as a percentage of your income it is effectively a form of income tax. In fact, PRSI incorporates two other taxes: the health levy, and the employment and training levies.

The purpose of PRSI is to raise money to provide all sorts of social welfare benefits – these range from invalidity pensions to redundancy pay, and from a bereavement grant to a maternity benefit. Your ability to claim social welfare benefits is linked to your having paid your PRSI. It is, therefore, worth remembering the following points:

- How much PRSI you have to pay will depend on your job. There are three key categories: private sector employees, public sector employees, and the self-employed.

- Your entitlement to benefits is normally based on your contributions made two years before the benefit year in which you claim! In other words, what you paid in 2008 will determine what you can claim in 2010.

- The level of PRSI you have to pay is calculated as a percentage of your gross income, less any payments to an approved pension scheme or certain other health schemes.

- If you earn less than €127 a week, you don't have to pay any PRSI at all. If you earn less than €500 in a particular week, you won't have to pay the health levy.

- You can volunteer to pay PRSI, or pay it at a higher level, if this is to your advantage.

The PRSI health levy rates are set every year in the Budget. It's worth noting that the employee and employer normally share PRSI contribution costs. Most employees, of course, pay their PRSI through the PAYE tax system.

A summary of the benefits to which you are entitled under PRSI is to be found in Chapter 5. It is, perhaps, worth mentioning here that to claim a **social insurance benefit** it is necessary to have a minimum number of PRSI contributions. Confusingly, the word 'contribution' means not just the PRSI you've paid, but also your PRSI credits. PRSI credits are awarded to someone who would normally have been making a contribution but for various reasons did not do so. For instance, you would receive PRSI credits during any weeks when you received a disability benefit or unemployment benefit. You also receive credits when you first start working.

If there was an Olympic category for the 'most complicated tax in the world', then PRSI would probably win a gold. If you need help with your PRSI then I would suggest either talking to an accountant or else contacting the Department of Social & Family Affairs or – alternatively – the Revenue Commissioners.

23
ALL ABOUT INCOME TAX CREDITS

HOW TAX 'CREDITS' AND 'ALLOWANCES' CAN HELP YOU SAVE MONEY

Depending on your circumstances, you can reduce your income tax bill by claiming certain **tax credits** and **allowances**. A great deal of confusion exists over the difference between 'credits' and 'allowances'. The key points to remember are:

- A tax credit is money off your actual tax bill. So, if you have a tax bill of €1,000 and tax credits of €800, you only pay €200 in tax.

- A tax allowance reduces the amount of income on which tax is payable. How much it will be worth to you will depend on the rate of tax you pay. For instance, if you pay income tax at 20% then a €1,000 tax allowance will save you €200 of tax.

The old system of tax allowances has largely been replaced by tax credits.

Every year you are sent an annual **tax certificate** referred to, somewhat long-windedly, as the 'notification of determination of Tax Credits and standard rate cut-off point', which sets out full details of all your tax credits together with the income level at which you will start to pay the higher rate tax.

HOW TAX CREDITS WORK IN PRACTICE

Before going into detail about all the different personal tax credits that exist, let's just look at how they work in practice. In 2010, John O'Brien, a single taxpayer on PAYE, pays tax at 20% on the first €36,400 of income and 41% on anything above this sum. His tax credits amount to some €3,660. I've shown on the next page how his tax credits reduce his tax liability on an assumed income of €40,000.

Income	€40,000	
Tax €36,400 @ 20 %		€7,280
Tax €3,600* @ 41%		€1,476
Total tax before tax credits		€8,756
Deduct tax credits		
Single tax credit	€1,830	
PAYE tax credit	€1,830	€3,660
Tax payable		€5,096
*€40,000 less €36,400		

CHECK YOUR TAX CREDITS EVERY YEAR

Do remember to check that you're claiming all your tax credits every year. It's also worth bearing in mind that you can go back to the Revenue Commissioners and claim tax credits that you failed to take advantage of for the previous four tax years.

A COMPLETE GUIDE TO PERSONAL TAX CREDITS AND ALLOWANCES FOR 2011

Over the next few pages you'll find brief details of all the different tax credits and allowances for which you may be eligible.

Single person's credit

You can claim this if you're single; if you're married but decide to opt for single/separate assessment or if you're separated and you and your former partner have not opted for joint assessment. It is worth €1,830 for 2011.

Married person's credit

This is double the single credit, and it's granted to married couples who have opted to be assessed together. It can also be claimed by separated couples where one partner is maintaining the other and is not entitled to claim tax relief on the maintenance being paid. For more details on tax relief for separated and divorced couples see Chapters 34 and 35. The married person's credit is worth €3,660.

One-parent family credit

If you're a parent (or guardian) and, for whatever reason, you are not entitled to the married person's credit, then you're entitled to a personal credit of €1,830.

Widowed parent credit

A special credit is granted to widowed parents for the first five years following the year of bereavement. For the year 2010 the credit is: €4,000 in the first year; €3,500 in the second year; €3,000 in the third year; €2,500 in the fourth year; and €2,000 in the fifth year.

Special age credits

If you are over 65 – or if your spouse is over 65 – then you receive an extra credit. If you're single or widowed this is worth €325. For a married couple it is worth €650.

The home carer's credit

If you care for someone who's elderly (defined as being over 65) or incapacitated, you may be eligible to claim an additional credit of up to €900. The home carer credit is only available to married couples where one spouse cares for one or more dependent people. You can't claim if you are looking after your own spouse. The maximum income of the home carer to claim maximum relief is €5,080. A reduced tax credit applies where the income is between €5,080 and €6,750.

A new childminding relief was introduced in 2006. Where an individual minds up to three children (other than their own children) in the minder's own home, no tax will be payable on the childminding earnings received provided the amount is less than €15,000 per annum. If the childminding income exceeds this amount, the total amount will be taxable, as normal, under self-assessment. An individual will be obliged to return their childminding income in their annual tax return.

Incapacitated child credit

If you are looking after an incapacitated child, then you're entitled to claim a tax credit of €3,660. Note that the child must be under the age of 18 or, if over the age of 18, must have been incapacitated before reaching 21 years of age or whilst still receiving full-time education.

Dependent relative credit

If you can prove that you maintain, at your own expense, a relative who cannot live independently (or a widowed mother whether incapacitated or not), you can claim a tax credit of €80 per year provided the relative's income does not exceed €13,837 per year.

Incapacitated person's allowance

An allowance of €50,000 is available to any taxpayer who is incapacitated and has to employ someone to look after them. The same allowance is available to any taxpayer who is employing someone to look after an incapacitated spouse. In fact, the allowance is available where a family employs a carer to look after a totally incapacitated person. Clearly, to take advantage of this allowance you need to have an income, and because it's an allowance (as opposed to a tax credit) the value of the benefit will be determined by your marginal – or top – rate of tax.

Blind person's credit

If you are blind, you can claim a tax credit of €1,830. If both you and your spouse are blind then you may both claim, bringing the total credit up to €3,660. An additional allowance of €825 is available to any blind person who uses a guide dog. This allowance is at marginal rate (up to 41%).

PAYE credit

If you pay tax by the PAYE system you're entitled to a PAYE credit of €1,830. If you're married, and both you and your spouse are on PAYE, then there is a doubled credit. However, you should bear in mind that you cannot claim the PAYE credit if you are the director of a company and control, either directly or indirectly, 15% or more of the shares. You can't claim it, either, if you employ your spouse (either as an individual or as a partner in a firm).

Medical insurance

If you take out medical insurance, the premium you pay will already have been discounted by the standard rate of tax (currently 20%). The insurance company will receive this tax relief directly from the government so there is no need for you to make a separate claim. It is worth noting that you can enjoy this tax relief even if you don't pay tax!

Permanent health insurance

If you are worried about a drop in your income as a result of an accident or illness, and you take out permanent health insurance to protect you against this eventuality, your contributions will be tax deductible. Do note, however, that the amount of relief you can claim must not be more than 10% of your total income for the year of assessment. Do remember that any benefit you claim under a permanent health insurance policy will be liable to income tax.

Medical expenses relief

If you have to spend money on medical care, or non-routine dental treatment, then you can claim tax relief at the standard tax rate. You should note that:

- You can claim for yourself, your spouse or any other person for who you claim tax allowances.

- The allowance can be shared among a number of people so that if, for example, several children are paying for their parent to receive treatment, each can claim.

- You may even be able to claim the cost of travelling to and from the hospital or other treatment centre.

- When it comes to medical expenses most things are eligible for tax relief, from an ordinary visit to a doctor to hearing aids, and from physiotherapy to the cost of gluten-free food for cœliacs.

- Note that all expenses in relation to maternity care are fully allowable.

There are a few exceptions you should be aware of including routine dental treatment, having your eyes tested, and the purchase of spectacles or contact lenses.

- For nursing home expenses, relief is available at your marginal rate of tax.

Rent relief

If you're single and are a tenant paying rent for private rental accommodation, then you can claim a tax credit of €400. A married couple can claim €800 and a widowed person can also claim €800. If you are aged 55 or over then the amount of the credit increases to €800 for a single person and €1,600 for a married couple or a widowed person.

Relief for long-term unemployed people

If you have been unemployed for at least 12 months, and you then return to work, you will receive an additional personal allowance as well as a child tax allowance if, of course, you have one or more children. The allowance lasts for three years, and the amounts are set out below:

	Personal tax allowance	Child tax allowance (for each qualifying child)
Year 1	€3,810	€1,270
Year 2	€2,540	€850
Year 3	€1,270	€425

Third-level college fees

The government give a very generous €3,175 of tax relief in respect of tuition fees paid either for yourself or for a dependent relative. The relief applies to tuition fees for full- and part-time undergraduate courses, a wide range of training courses, and many postgraduate courses. This relief is given at the standard rate and cannot be recouped by grants or scholarships. Whilst you can claim relief up to €5,000, the relief itself may not exceed the liability of the taxpayer.

Charitable donations

If you are self-employed (but not if you pay tax through the PAYE system) tax relief is available for any donations or gifts (minimum €250) made to charities or a wide range of not-for-profit organisations.

Trade union subscriptions

A tax credit at the standard rate of tax (20%) of €70 is available for trade union subscriptions.

Loan interest relief

If you're paying interest on a loan, you may be able to claim tax relief. Various types of loan are eligible, including:

- mortgages in relation to your main home
- bridging loans
- loans taken out for business purposes

- loans borrowed to pay death duties
- borrowings used to acquire shares in your own business.

With regard to mortgage interest relief, this is now granted 'at source' which, in plain English, means that your lender will claim it on your behalf and reduce your monthly payments accordingly. You should be aware that mortgage interest relief is available on money borrowed for the purchase, repair, development or improvement of your sole or main residence situated in Ireland or in the UK. You can also claim the relief if you have to borrow money to 'purchase a residence for a former or separated spouse or a dependent relative where the accommodation is being provided by you rent-free'. The amount of relief you can claim will be determined by your personal circumstances. Only first-time mortgage holders can claim tax relief for the first seven years of the mortgage, up to a limit of €20,000 for married couples or widow(er)s or €10,000 for a single person.

Amount of relief available

2008 – First-time buyers and non-first-time buyers: mortgage relief is due at the standard rate of 20% subject to the upper limits in the following chart.
2009 – First-time buyers: From **1 January 2009** the rate of mortgage interest relief is increased from 20% to 25% in years 1 and 2, and to 22.5% in years 3, 4 and 5. The relief remains unchanged at 20% for years 6 and 7 of the mortgage. First-time buyers relief ends after year 7.
Non-first-time buyers: the rate of mortgage relief is reduced from 20% to 15%.

With effect from **1 May 2009** the number of tax years in respect of which mortgage interest relief may be claimed is 7 years for first-time and non-first-time buyers.

Relief available for loan interest on secured and non-secured loans for the tax years 2008 and 2009

Personal circumstances	Single	Married/Widowed
First-time buyers	€10,000	€20,000
All others	€3,000	€6,000

Note: Amounts shown in the above table are the ceiling amounts for the years 2008 and 2009

Relief on deeds of covenant

If you make a legal commitment – known as a deed of covenant – to pay money for a period of time to someone who is aged 65 or over, or permanently incapacitated (providing the latter isn't to a son or daughter under 18) you will be able to claim the tax relief.

Pension contributions

If you're making payments into an approved personal pension scheme (here the word 'approved' refers to Revenue Commissioners' approval!), then income tax relief will be available to you at your marginal (top) rate of tax. The amount of relief is restricted to a percentage of your income. Unused allowances in any one year can be carried forward to the next. The percentage of your income that you're allowed to put, tax free, into a pension scheme increases as you get older. For 2010 it works as follows:

- If you're under the age of 30 you can put up to 15% of your income into your pension scheme tax free.
- If you're aged between 30 and 39 you can put 20%.
- If you're aged between 40 and 49 you can put 25%.
- If you're aged 50 and over you can put 30%.
- If you're aged 55 and over you can put 35%
- If you're aged 60 and over you can put 40%.

However, there is a cap of €150,000 on the income taken into account.

Service charges

Most of the service charges in relation to your home are eligible for tax relief at standard rate. This includes:

- charges imposed by your local authority for water, rubbish collection and/or sewage disposal
- any money you pay to an independent contractor for refuse collection
- the cost of water when arranged through a group water scheme.

If you're on PAYE, then it should be possible to arrange for your local authority to inform your tax office when they receive payment, so that it can be taken into account when calculating your income tax. If you're not on PAYE – or if your payments aren't being made to a local authority – then you'll have to keep your receipts and make a separate claim.

Investment relief

Two different forms of tax incentive are available to investors. The first is 'relief for investment in corporate trades' – known generally as BES. The second is a relief for investment in the film industry – known as Section 35 Investments. Note that BES relief was extended in the 2007 Budget to 2013, and that film industry relief will cease on 31 December 2012.

Seafarer's allowance

If you are a seafarer and you're away on a voyage for at least 161 days in a tax year, then you are eligible for a special allowance of €6,350. Do note, however, that this allowance can only be offset against seafaring employment.

24
PAYE

HOW TO MAKE THE PAY AS YOU EARN (PAYE) TAX SYSTEM WORK IN YOUR FAVOUR

Just because you're in salaried employment and have your income tax is deducted automatically using the **pay as you earn** (PAYE) system doesn't mean there aren't plenty of things you can do to keep your tax bill to a bare minimum. So, in addition to explaining how PAYE operates, this chapter also examines some of the tax-saving opportunities open to those who pay tax by this method.

THE INS AND OUTS OF **PAYE**

It is easy to understand why the Revenue Commissioners like the PAYE system. It allows them to collect tax as it falls due rather than once a year. But it does have two advantages for the taxpayer as well. Firstly, your employer and the Revenue Commissioners handle all the administration involved with your tax bill. If you were self-employed this could cost you thousands of euros a year. Secondly, you don't have to worry about being faced with a tax bill every year.

PAYE is operated by employers in conjunction with the Revenue Commissioners. The system is simplicity itself:

- Your employer provides your details to the Revenue Commissioners.
- Before the beginning of each tax year (usually in December), the Revenue Commissioners issue a 'Notification of Determination of Tax Credits and Standard Rate Cut-off Point'. This sets out any tax credits due to you, details your rate or rates of tax, and incorporates something called your **standard rate cut-off point** which I'll explain further in a moment.
- Using the information supplied by the Revenue Commissioners, your employer calculates how much tax to deduct from your salary.

So what is the standard rate cut-off point? Basically it's the amount of money you can earn at the standard rate – currently 20%. This is determined by your personal circumstances – whether you are married, single or widowed. You may also have allowances that are allowed at the higher rate of tax, such as a contribution to an approved pension scheme. Where this is the case, your standard rate cut-off rate will be higher.

The formula for working out PAYE is:

- The standard rate of tax (currently 20%) is applied to your gross pay up to the standard rate cut-off point for the period in question.
- Any income over and above that amount in the pay period is taxed at the higher rate (currently 41%).
- The tax payable at this point is referred to as the **gross tax payable**.
- Any tax credits you're entitled to are then deducted from the gross tax payable to arrive at the **net tax payable**.

This is probably best explained with a couple of real-life examples.

> John earns €53,000 per annum and, being married, takes all the tax credits available as he pays all the bills, the mortgage and the little luxuries. This means that approx. €28,000 is tax free and the balance is at 20% equating to €5,000 tax liability together with PRSI of approx. €4,000 means that John's net income is approx. €44,000.
>
> Patricia, his wife, earns €26,000 and, as she has no credits, has to pay PRSI plus levies and the higher tax rate of 41% on her entire salary. Therefore, her net income is approx. €13,000 or half of her salary.

MONEY DOCTOR WEALTH CHECK

It is in your interest to keep the taxperson up to date…

If the Revenue Commissioners don't have all your personal information, they may make a mistake regarding all the different sorts of tax credits and allowances to which you are entitled. You can use the information in the previous chapter to compile a list of credits and allowances that you believe you can claim, and you should then complete a **Form 12A** 'Application for a Certificate of Tax Credits and Standard Rate Cut-off Point' and send it to your tax office. This form is available on request or can be downloaded from www.revenue.ie When you receive your 'Notification of Determination of Tax Credits and Standard Rate Cut-off Point' double-check that it lists all the tax reliefs you wish to claim.

EMERGENCY TAX

If your employer doesn't have the information needed in order to calculate the correct amount of tax to deduct (a 'Notification of Determination of Tax Credits and Standard Rate Cut-off Point') you will automatically be put onto PAYE **emergency tax**. As emergency tax only incorporates minimal tax credits, it is important, from your point of view, to contact your local tax office to resolve the situation.

GETTING YOUR TAX BACK! PAYE REFUNDS

There are various circumstances under which you may be entitled to a PAYE tax refund. For instance:

- If you become unemployed: in this situation you should write to your Inspector of Taxes and ask for a **Form P50**. You should complete and return this, along with Parts 2 and 3 of your **Form P45** (the form your last employer should have given to you prior to you leaving).

- If the Revenue Commissioners have made an error and overtaxed you due to some factor of which they were unaware.

After the end of the tax year (31 December), your employer should give you a **Form P60**, which sets out the amount you earned in that year together with any tax that has been deducted. Check this form in order to make sure that all the allowances, deductions and credits to which you are entitled have been claimed. If you believe there is an error you should advise your employer and your local Inspector of Taxes in order to request a refund.

MONEY DOCTOR WEALTH CHECK

Double-check you are claiming everything

Below is a list of all the tax credits and allowances you may be entitled to (full details are to be found in the previous chapter). Why not take a moment or two to check through it now to make doubly sure that you aren't paying a cent more tax than you have to?

Tax credit	2010 (€)
Single person	1,830
Married person	3,660

Widowed person (w/o dependent children)	2,430
Widowed person (qualifying for one-parent family tax credit)	1,830
Widowed person (in year of bereavement)	3,660
One-parent family (widowed person)	1,830
One-parent family (other person)	1,830
Age tax credit (65 years plus & single/widowed)	325
Age tax credit (65 years plus & married)	650
Home carer's credit (max.)	900
Incapacitated child (max.)	3,660
Dependent relative (max.)	80
Employee's tax credit	1,830

MAKING SURE YOUR EXPENSES ARE TAX FREE

One of the areas in which the Revenue Commissioners are extremely strict is that of **expenses** paid to employees. What they don't want is a situation where employers are disguising a benefit (effectively extra salary) in the guise of a legitimate expense. The Revenue Commissioners' guidance rules say that any expense 'must have been wholly, exclusively and necessarily incurred for the purpose of performing the duties of your employment'. (What is interesting is that if you're self-employed, the 'necessarily' criterion doesn't apply.)

So what is, and isn't, allowable? If you have to buy special equipment or clothing, for instance, it is unlikely that the Revenue will argue with your claim. By the same token, they are unlikely to take issue if you use a company-owned computer at home or claim part of your telephone bill when used for work calls. In general, what you can get away with – I mean, legitimately claim, of course, slip of the pen – will very much depend on the nature of your employment. For instance, if you work in a publishing company, any books you buy will almost certainly be allowable, as might trips to the theatre or cinema. If you're an engineer, this is unlikely to be the case!

If the Revenue Commissioners believe that you are making a claim for something that is not wholly, exclusively and necessarily incurred for the purpose of performing the duties of your employment, they will tax it! This tax is called **benefit in kind**. Your employer will be required to value the benefit and to stop tax and PRSI at source through the PAYE system. So, for example, if your employer were to send you away on a one-week holiday to recuperate

, you would pay tax on the cost of that holiday as if you had
extra salary.

travelling expenses

a journey in your own car for business purposes, the money paid
to you by your employer will not be taxable as a benefit in kind providing it
does not exceed something referred to as the **civil service mileage rate**. If
you are going to claim motoring expenses from your employer, you should
keep a track of the journeys you make and the mileage actually incurred.

Sadly, you cannot claim for journeys between your home and work.

The amount you can claim under the civil service mileage rate rules varies
according to whether or not you use your car in the normal course of your
duties, or only occasionally. The current rates are set out in the table below:

Civil Service kilometre rates from 5 March 2009

Official Motor Travel in Calendar Year	Engine capacity up to 1,200cc (Cent/km)	Engine capacity 1,200cc to 1,500cc (Cent/km)	Engine capacity 1,501 cc and over (Cent/km)
Up to 6,437 km	39.12	46.25	59.07
6,438 and over	21.22	23.62	28.46

A chance to claim more

Some trade unions and professional bodies have negotiated special, higher,
flat-rate motoring allowances for their members. For instance, **teachers,
nurses, journalists** and **building workers** may all claim their special flat rate
allowance tax free – without the Revenue Commissioners questioning it. It's
worth checking with your own trade union or professional body to see if such
an arrangement is in place.

OTHER TAX-FREE AND TAX-EFFICIENT PERKS

Below is a list of tax-free or tax-efficient benefits that it's possible for an
employee to receive.

Daily and overnight allowances

If you're working away from home your employer can pay you a daily and/or
an overnight allowance to cover the cost of any expenses you may incur, such

as lunch, an evening meal, accommodation, and so forth. The amount you can receive tax free depends on your salary level. The more you earn, the more you can receive tax free. However, the longer you stay away the less you can receive. The current rates are set out in the chart below.

The Civil Service Subsistence Allowances have recently undergone a revision per Department of Finance Circular 27/2002. The revised rates, effective from 5 March 2009, are as follows:

Civil Service domestic subsistence rates from 1 July 2008

	Overnight Rates			Day rates	
Class of Allowances	Normal Rate	Reduced Rate	Detention Rate	10 hours or more	5–10 hours
A Class	€108.99	€100.48	€54.48	€33.61	€13.71
B Class	€107.69	€92.11	€53.87	€33.61	€13.71

Class	Salary
A	Excess €59,956
B	€31,159–€59,956

Free or inexpensive accommodation

If your job necessitates it, your employer can offer you **rent-free** or **subsidised accommodation** without any tax being incurred. Naturally, your residence has to be in part of your employer's business premises and there has to be a clear work-related reason for your needing to live there.

Staff entertainment

Your employer is allowed to entertain you at a reasonable cost without you incurring any benefit in kind.

Communal transport to your place of work

For instance, if your employer provides a **company bus** or **shared taxi** to bring you or from your place of employment, this is tax free.

Presents!

Your employer can give you **non-cash personal gifts** providing it isn't for some reason connected with your work. However, it could be because you are retiring.

Meals

Meals, whether free or subsidised, are entirely tax free if they're provided in a staff canteen. However, the facility has to be open to all the employees.

Lump sum payments

Lump sum payments for special reasons – such as redundancy, on account of an injury or disability, or relating to your pension scheme – may be totally exempt from tax depending on the amount and circumstances. Details relating to redundancy payments may be found in Chapter 33.

Educational fees

Any scholarship income or bursaries paid by your employer will be completely free of tax providing that the course is relevant to your employment.

Injury or disability payments

Payment made on account of an injury or disability will also usually be 100% tax free.

Work tools

Equipment, tools, or working clothes, or anything else required to fulfil your employment will not be taxed.

Pension scheme payments

If your employer contributes to an approved or statutory pension scheme, then those contributions are also tax free. For more details on this, see Chapter 20.

Life cover

The cost of providing you with life assurance cover is also tax free provided the amount of cover is no more than eight times your salary.

€250 bonus!

You are entitled to receive an annual, non-cash benefit of up to a value of

€250 without paying a cent in tax. Many employers provide this in the form of a gift voucher, which gives the employee flexibility as to how to use it.

Health insurance

If your employer pays the cost of permanent health insurance for you, this is tax free.

Medical cover

Your employer can also pay for your VHI or other medical expenses insurance without you being taxed on the benefit unless you're a higher rate taxpayer (when you will have to pay tax at 41%).

Season tickets

Bus, train and Luas passes are tax free. Furthermore, the only condition is that they are monthly or annual transport passes, so they don't necessarily have to be used for work purposes.

Childcare

Crèche and childcare facilities, provided by your employer on a free or subsidised basis, will not be taxed provided that they are not privately owned.

Relocation expenses

All your home relocation expenses will be tax free providing you are being forced to move as a requirement of your job.

Sports and recreational facilities

Sports and recreational facilities – so long as they are located on an employer's own premises – can be enjoyed tax free by workers. This, of course, can include a company gym or health spa.

Mobile telephones

Your company-provided mobile telephone is tax free providing it can be justified on the basis of business use. This rule also applies to the provision of computers, and even broadband access at home.

Car parking

A free car-parking space will not be taxed either – potentially a very valuable benefit indeed if you happen to work in a city centre.

Exam payments

A cash award given to you in recognition of obtaining a qualification of relevance to your job will also be treated as tax free providing it is roughly equivalent to the expenses incurred in studying for the exam.

Membership fees

If you need to join any professional body by reason of your employment, then your subscription will be tax free.

Health screening

If your employer insists on you having a medical check-up it will be tax free.

Long-service presents

If you work for your company for at least 20 years they can buy you a present costing no more than €50 for each year of service, and it will be completely tax free, a potentially €1,000 tax-free gift.

Has your employer offered you an opportunity to buy shares?

An increasing number of employees are being offered an opportunity to buy shares – directly or indirectly – in their employer's company. The tax treatment of the various different types of share schemes varies. Some offer an opportunity to save tax and others don't. You should also note that some employee share schemes won't cost you anything to participate in, whereas others will require you to make an investment. As this is a complicated area I would always suggest taking professional advice before participating. However, to give you a general idea of the different types of scheme work I have outlined the seven (!) main options below, together with a few guidance notes.

> **Approved profit share scheme.** This is probably the most advantageous scheme from an employee's point of view, as it allows you to receive shares tax free up to an annual limit of €12,700 provided certain conditions are met. Basically, provided you hold the shares granted to you for at least

three years, they will be entirely tax free.

Employee share ownership trusts (ESOTs). Employee share ownership trusts were created to run alongside company profit-sharing schemes and they work pretty much in the same way so far as the employee is concerned. One additional benefit, however, is that after ten years a one-off additional payment of €38,100 can be made.

Stock options. A stock option allows you the opportunity to purchase shares in your employer's company at a pre-set price, normally within a certain timeframe. The benefit arises if the price at which you can buy the shares is less than their market value. This does, of course, constitute a gain from your point of view, and such a gain would be taxable. Stock options are rarely tax efficient.

Share subscription schemes. If you purchase new shares in your employer's company and hold them for at least three years, then you will achieve a tax benefit. However, there is an upper limit on the amount of tax you can save and you will – of course – incur a risk, since the value of the shares you buy may fall during the period you hold them.

Save as you earn scheme (SAYE). Save as you earn (SAYE) is basically a scheme that allows you to purchase shares in your employer's company over a period of time, with the cost of those shares being deducted from your salary as it's paid. There is the potential for some tax savings here – though they are not enormous.

Share incentive schemes. Share incentive schemes and employee share purchase plans offer you an opportunity to buy shares in your employer's company, but do not normally attract much of a tax benefit.

The free gift of shares. If your employer gives shares to you, without charge, you will be liable to tax on the benefit of receiving them but you should escape PRSI.

All the different schemes outlined above have stringent conditions attached to them by the Revenue Commissioners, and I cannot over-emphasise the need to take professional advice.

REVENUE ON-LINE SERVICE (ROS)

Finally, a point to note is that the Revenue in mid-2006 extended their Revenue On-line Service (ROS) to be available to PAYE taxpayers. Once you have registered you can avail of a full suite of services, including viewing information on your Revenue record and submitting tax credit claims and incomes information. You can also carry out a range of transactions without the need to fully register for the service. To access the site and register go to www.ros.ie.

MONEY DOCTOR WEALTH CHECK

You should find out if you are eligible for any refund of tax already paid, e.g. bin allowances, rental relief, union fees, dental and medical expenses, etc., even going back as far as four years. This is particularly relevant to PAYE workers who sometimes overlook their entitlements. There are two main companies in Ireland offering tax refunds on a 'no refund – no fee' basis:

- **www.taxback.com** is an award-winning company that specialises in this area. To start the ball rolling, text MONEYDOCTOR to 53377 (normal SMS rates apply) and they will be in touch with you to assess your situation within 48 hours.

- **www.redoaktaxrefunds.ie** also specialises in tax refunds. Simply quote on their on-line request form the code MONEYDOCTOR to receive a special discount on their fees.

Better in your pocket than theirs!

25
INCOME TAX FOR THE SELF-EMPLOYED

HOW TO REDUCE YOUR INCOME TAX BILL IF YOU WORK FOR YOURSELF

If you are self-employed – or thinking of becoming self-employed – then this chapter is essential reading. You will find out:

- how the tax system operates in relation to your earnings
- the different ways in which you can reduce your share of the tax burden
- how to avoid the unwanted attention of the Revenue whilst simultaneously making some worthwhile tax savings.

First things first

Perhaps it would be helpful to start by explaining the basic ground rules. Let's look at what is meant by the self-assessment system and preliminary tax.

SELF-ASSESSMENT SYSTEM

If you are a director in your family company or if you're in salaried employment (in other words on PAYE) but have income from other sources, you'll have to pay tax under the self-assessment system. Self-assessment means that you have to complete your own tax return, decide how much tax you owe, and pay it to the Revenue Commissioners at the specified time. You can, of course, get a professional accountant to do all of this for you.

The latest date by which you can complete your income tax return (Form 11) for the Revenue Commissioner is 31 October following the year of assessment. In other words, your 2010 tax return must be submitted no later than 31 October 2011, or mid-November 2011 if using the Revenue Online Service (ROS).

PRELIMINARY TAX

When you submit your income tax return you must also pay something called

preliminary tax. Preliminary tax is the amount of income tax you think you're going to owe for the year in which you pay it. In other words, on 31 October 2010 your preliminary tax will be the amount of tax you think you'll owe for 2010. The amount you'll actually have to pay is the lower of either 90% of your final liability for 2010 or 100% of your liability for 2009. Let me give you an example:

> Supposing you had a good year last year, but are having a bad year this year. Last year you had to pay €10,000 tax, but this year you believe you only expect a liability of €1,000 tax. Your preliminary tax bill would, therefore, be 90% of this year's liability – or €900.
>
> Since your preliminary tax is only an estimate of the tax you owe you will, naturally, either have to pay the difference or ask for a refund. This is done at the same time. Supposing, for instance, you've paid €1,000 preliminary tax on 31 October 2009. Your final tax bill for the year, however, turned out to be €1,500. The €500 extra will fall due no later than the 31 October 2010.

In other words, on or before 31 October every year you submit a return and pay an amount on account plus the balance of the previous year's income tax. If you're owed money by the Revenue Commissioners from the previous year, then you are allowed to deduct it from the amount you're paying. This is known as **Pay and File.**

THE MYSTERY FACTOR!

As if this isn't all complicated enough, there is an added factor that makes it all even more confusing: you can choose the dates of your financial year. The tax year, of course, runs just like the calendar year, from 1 January to 31 December. However, the Revenue Commissioners will allow you to pick your own accounting period. So while your 2010 tax return could refer to the period 1 January 2010 to 31 December 2010, it could actually refer to the 12 months ending on 2 January 2010.

A quick aside about accounting dates

It may seem like a tiny detail to you – considering the enormity of being self-employed and running your own business – but your **accounting date** can have important implications. For instance, if you run a seasonal business you're unlikely to want your accounting period to end during a busy period. Also, whilst you can choose an accounting period that gives you the longest possible time to pay your tax, if you aren't good at putting money away to meet your tax liabilities all you're doing is postponing your problem and making it worse.

As hardly anyone starts a new business on 1 January, what many self-employed people do is submit their first set of accounts for a period of less than 12 months. For instance, if you started your business on 1 July you might submit your first set of accounts to cover the period 1 July to 31 December. Your second tax return would then run from 1 January the following year.

You are actually entitled to change your accounting period any time you want. However, this can trigger an additional tax charge so you need to think carefully before you do so.

MAKE YOUR PAYMENTS ON TIME... OR ELSE

The Revenue Commissioners do not take kindly to income tax returns being submitted late. They take a similar line if you fail to pay any tax you owe on the date it is due. Indeed, if you don't submit your tax return by 31 October the Revenue Commissioners will add a surcharge to your tax bill:

- a surcharge of 5% of any tax due can be imposed if you are up to two months late
- if you are more than two months late then the surcharge can rise to 10% of the tax due
- in addition to the surcharge, you will be charged interest at the rate of roughly 1% per month on any outstanding tax.

If you are going to have trouble making a tax payment, let the Revenue Commissioners know in good time. Remember, it is almost certainly cheaper to borrow the money from a bank than to suffer heavy late payment surcharges and interest.

Revenue On-line Service (ROS)

The Revenue has a service 'Revenue On-line' known as 'ROS' which has been available to self-employed taxpayers for some time. Once registered for this service ROS enables you to view your own current position with Revenue for various taxes and levies, file tax returns and forms and make payments for these taxes online in a variety of ways.

The service is highly efficient and avoids the pitfalls of postal delays when returns are being sent close to the due date.

Furthermore, self-employed taxpayers filing their annual return (**Form 11**) through ROS are given an extra two weeks approximately after the 31 October deadline to pay and file. To qualify for the extension you must:

- File your return through ROS.
- Pay preliminary tax for the current year.
- Pay income tax balance due for previous year.
- Pay capital gains tax on gains arising from 1 January to 30 September in the current year.

To register for ROS go to www.ros.ie.

MONEY DOCTOR WEALTH WARNING

Don't get on the wrong side of the Revenue

If you are self-employed or a company director, then the last thing you want is an investigation or audit by the Revenue Commissioners. You'll be pleased to discover, therefore, that it is possible to reduce dramatically your chances of being bothered by Revenue. All you have to do is follow a few very basic rules:

1   If your return is late then this increases the Revenue's interest in you. By the same token, make sure you pay the tax you owe on time.

2   Given that the Revenue Commissioners deal with every business in the country, they have a good idea about the sort of profits that you ought to be making. If you consistently appear to be making less than the industry average, they may decide to take a closer look.

3   A low salary or low drawings may make them suspicious as well. They'll be wondering if you're earning cash and not declaring it.

4   Incomplete returns. If your tax return has not been completed correctly, you are simply asking for trouble.

5   **Discrepancies.** The Revenue Commissioners are not idiots, and if there is a discrepancy between, say, your VAT return and your annual tax return, eyebrows will be raised and questions will be asked.

6   **Erratic turnover** figures. If your company or business seems to do well one year, and not the other, your inspector may decide to look a little closer.

7   Ownership by an **offshore entity**. If the Revenue Commissioners notice that your shareholders are located in a tax haven – or if they see that you are doing a lot of business with a tax haven – this is bound to set off alarm bells.

The basic rules are **stay on top of your paperwork** and **pay your tax on time**, and you are much, much less likely to suffer the bother and expense of a Revenue investigation.

DO YOU NEED TO REGISTER FOR **VAT?**

You only have to register for **value added tax** (VAT) if your sales are in excess of certain amounts. The amounts are:

- €37,500 per year if you provide services
- €75,000 per year if you provide goods.

Once you're registered for VAT you must charge it on all your invoices but – looking on the bright side – you can reclaim any VAT you pay out on business expenses (other than those for entertainment or motoring). Once registered, you will need to keep proper VAT records and complete a return every two months.

Don't forget your PRSI

If you are self-employed and your gross income exceeds €3,174 a year, you will have to pay PRSI contributions. For more information about PRSI see Chapter 5.

AND ANOTHER THING

If you are operating your self-employed business from home, remember that it is now also a business premises and that you should advise your insurance company. In most cases, this is unlikely to affect your insurance premium – but it is important that you are covered if equipment is stolen or damaged, or if a business visitor has an accident while on your premises.

Incidentally, if you do use your home as business premises, then you can claim some of the running costs as expenses against your annual tax bill. Do bear in mind, however, that if you pay yourself 'rent' this may have capital gains tax implications when you come to sell your home. This is because although there is no capital gains tax on a principal residence there could well be a liability on a business premises.

Self-employment comes in many forms

The term 'self-employed' refers specifically to people who are:

- in business as a 'sole trader'
- in partnership with one or more other people.

Many people who work for themselves actually do so as a 'contractor' working on a regular basis for someone else. You should be aware that if you work for an employer for more than eight hours a week you are entitled to a contract of employment. Such a contract would give you all sorts of benefits such as the right to holidays, the right not to be dismissed unfairly, minimum notice and so forth. On the other hand, as a contractor, you aren't protected under employment legislation and must – of course – make your own tax arrangements.

Many self-employed people find it is worth their while to form a limited company and to trade in this way. The advantages of running a limited company include:

- limited financial risk
- ability to make more generous pension contributions to your retirement fund
- possible tax benefits.

However, don't rush into forming a company without taking legal and accounting advice.

WORKING OUT YOUR PROFITS

When you are self-employed you pay income tax on what the Revenue Commissioners refer to as **taxable profits**. Your taxable profits are your gross income (the total amount you make) less any expenses which are allowed for income tax purposes. So, if you earn a total of €20,000 a year and have expenses of €5,000, your taxable profits will be €15,000 a year.

EXPENSES

So what expenses are allowable against your profits? In some ways it is actually easier to consider what expenses the Revenue Commissioners will definitely *not* allow:

- any money you spend which is not '**wholly and exclusively**' for the purpose of your business. For example, if you buy a suit for work the Revenue Commissioners would say that it isn't 'wholly and exclusively' for business purposes. If you're considering any sort of major expenditure as part of your business, and you're not sure if it will be allowable, it's well worth checking with either the Revenue Commissioners or your accountant first
- **entertainment**. With the exception of entertaining your staff, the provision of accommodation, meals, or drink for your customers is not allowable. Indeed, if you take a client out to dinner not only will the expense be disallowed but you may also suffer benefit in kind tax yourself
- any sort of **personal expenses**
- money spent on **improving your business premises**. This said, money spent renewing or repairing your business premises is allowable.

So what *can* you claim? Let me give you an example. Imagine that you are a chef who has opened his or her own restaurant. Here are some of the expenses that you could legitimately claim against your profits:

- rent
- wages paid to employees
- interest paid on business loans
- other property expenses including electricity, gas, water, rubbish disposal and so on
- furniture
- equipment for the kitchen

- linen, tableware, glasses, and related items
- travel, stationery, telecommunications, postage and advertising
- cookery books
- buying trips overseas to source produce not only for your restaurant but – perhaps – because you plan to go into the import and wholesale business
- ingredients
- uniforms for yourself and staff
- wine
- other beverages.

You might also argue that you needed to eat in your competitors' restaurants for research purposes. The real point is: if you can show you had to spend the money to run your business, then it is almost certainly an allowable expense.

A WORD ABOUT CAPITAL EXPENDITURE

Many businesses require special plant, machinery or equipment. When you buy this, it is referred to as **capital expenditure**. Such expenditure will be allowed as a business expense. However, not all at once. Since December 2002, 12.5% of the cost is allowed as an expense each year. So if you spend, say, €1,000 on a photocopier you can claim €125 a year as a cost against your income for the following eight years. This is one of the reasons why many people who are self-employed opt to lease rather than purchase certain items.

OTHER TAX-SAVING POSSIBILITIES

There are a number of different ways in which someone who is self-employed can hope to reap a tax advantage. These include:

- claiming for business expenses that would be disallowed for someone who was employed
- by taking advantage of the special rules regarding pension plans
- by using the self-assessment system to delay the payment of tax.

26
TAX AND PROPERTY

PROPERTY INVESTOR? HOW TO ENSURE YOU KEEP YOUR TAX BILL TO A MINIMUM

From a tax perspective, property is just about the most complicated investment you can make. Which is why I have devoted this short chapter to the subject. The reason it is complicated is that:

- If you make a profit on the rent, you will have to pay income tax.
- If you make a profit when you sell the property, you will have to pay capital gains tax.
- There are all sorts of expenses you can claim against your profits and it is important to make sure you claim all of them.

The benefits of investing in property are huge, especially if you have been a property investor since the early 1980s.

THE TAX ADVANTAGES OF PROPERTY INVESTMENT

There are several generous tax advantages to be had from property investment including:

- In the current climate of low capital gains tax, should you sell the property at a profit you will only have to pay tax at a rate of 25%.
- You can currently earn up to €10,000 a year in rent tax free from the letting of a room in your own principal private residence.
- All the normal personal allowances are available to you, if you haven't already used them against other income.
- The Revenue Commissioners will allow you to set a surprisingly wide range of expenses against your rental income, thus helping to keep your income tax bill to a minimum.

A WORD OF WARNING

It is worth bearing in mind that rental income is treated in the same way as self-employed income. As a result, it may have the effect of pushing you into the higher tax bracket (in other words, 41% tax plus 5% PRSI and levy). Many people wrongly believe that they will reduce their tax liability by holding property through a limited company. This is not the case, because:

- The rate of **corporation tax** on rental income is 25%.

- Undistributed investment and rental income in a **close company** is liable to a further tax charge of 20%. (A 'close' company is one that is controlled by five or fewer shareholders or is controlled by any number of shareholders who are directors.)

- The effective corporation tax rate can be as high as 40%.

TAX INCENTIVES

Over the last few years, there have been two property tax incentives you could have availed of:

1   Capital allowances in relation to **industrial buildings.** The term 'industrial buildings' includes not just factories but nursing homes, crèche facilities, and even – in certain cases – holiday cottages.

2   Tax incentives to **designated areas.** These designated areas are to be found in run-down parts of Cork, Dublin, Galway, Limerick and Waterford. The idea is to encourage urban renewal. The best known of these tax incentives was the '**Section 23**' relief in respect of expenditure on the construction, conversion or refurbishment of residential property in certain inner-city areas.

'GENEROUS' EXPENSES

Below is a list of the expenses that can normally be deducted from your rental income for tax purposes:

- any rates you have to pay on the property

- any rent (such as ground rent) that you have to pay on the property

- interest paid on money borrowed to acquire or improve the premises. Note that since 7 April 2009 this has been restricted to 75% of the interest paid on loans relating to residential investment property. This restriction does not apply to non-residential property.

- the cost of anything you supply to your tenant that isn't covered by their rent. For instance, if you pay for the electric light in the hallways, or for the lawns to be mown, it is an allowable expense
- the cost of any maintenance, repairs, insurance or management fees
- a capital allowance of 12.5% a year on the value of any fixtures, fittings or furniture you have purchased specifically for the property. In plain English, this means that if you buy furniture for the flat you can write it off over an eight-year period.

Do note that where your costs exceed the income from your rental property, the loss you incur may only be offset against future rental income. In other words, you can't use a loss from property investment to reduce – say – the tax you pay on your monthly salary.

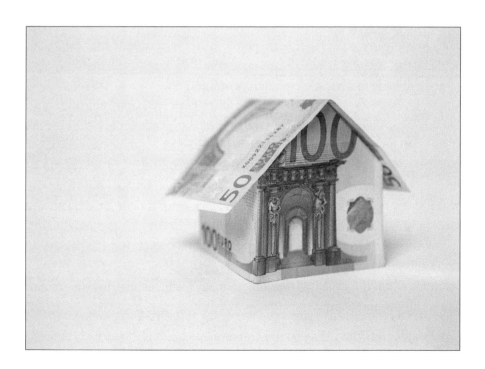

27
TAX AND THE COMPANY CAR

HOW WORKING MOTORISTS CAN DRIVE DOWN THEIR TAX BILL

There was a time, in the distant past, when being provided with a company car was a genuine perk. Not only were there major tax advantages but also there was the additional benefit of not having to purchase, maintain or run a vehicle oneself. However, as the table below shows, it may not in fact be to your advantage any more to have a company car.

Civil Service motor kilometric rates from 5 March 2009

Official Motor Travel in a calendar year	Engine capacity		
	Up to 1,200cc (cent/km)	1,200cc to 1,500cc (cent/km)	1,501 cc and over (cent/km)
Up to 6,437 km	39.12 cent	46.25 cent	59.07 cent
6,438 km and over	21.22 cent	23.62 cent	28.46 cent

Nowadays, however, company cars are liable to both PAYE and PRSI. The amount of tax you have to pay is linked to the value of the car and the amount of mileage you do. For instance, if you do less than 15,000 miles a year you will be taxed as if you had received a cash amount equivalent to 30% of the 'original market value' of the car supplied. This calculation does not change even if the car you drive is second hand. Keep in mind, though, that if you do a very high annual business mileage, the amount of tax drops substantially. For instance, if you do more than 30,000 miles a year, you only have to pay the cash equivalent of 6% of the 'original market value'. Let's look at a real-life example:

> Your company provides you with a car worth €30,000 and your business mileage is less than 15,000 a year. You will be taxed as if you had received 30% of €30,000 – in other words, €9,000 of extra salary a year. Assuming that you're paid monthly, you will be taxed on an extra €750 per month – in other words, one-twelfth of the €9,000 benefit you are considered to have received.

The cost of this can be brought down if you contribute towards the cost of the car and also pay for your own private fuel.

HOW TO SLASH THE COST OF YOUR BENEFIT IN KIND

It is possible to reduce your **benefit in kind** charge to a flat 20% providing the following conditions are met:

- You spend 70% or more of your time away from your place of work.
- Your annual business mileage is between 5,000 miles and 15,000 miles.
- Your average working week is more than 20 hours.

To have any hope of reducing your benefit in kind tax bill, it is very important that you maintain a logbook detailing all your business trips and make it available, if required, to your Inspector of Taxes.

Another clever way to cut your benefit in kind

If, for some reason, the car is not available to you for a period the amount of tax will be reduced. For instance, supposing you gave the car back to your employer for one month a year, you would reduce your tax liability by one-twelfth.

SHOULD YOU HAVE A COMPANY CAR AT ALL?

For many people, the benefit in kind tax is so high that it makes better sense to use their personal car for business and take a mileage allowance instead of a company car. One benefit of this is that if you only receive the civil service kilometric rates (see previous page), any money paid to you by your employer will be completely free of tax.

If you're entitled to a company car, and forgo it, you may also find yourself better off. As the table below shows, this will be particularly true if you do a relatively low business mileage each year.

Car costing €20,000 and over 1500 cc

Kilometres per year	40,000	30,000	20,000	10,000	5,000
Depreciation	€6,500	€5,500	€4,000	€3,000	€3,000
Petrol	€8,000	€6,000	€4,000	€2,000	€1,000
Insurance	€1,000	€1,000	€1,000	€1,000	€1,000

Road tax	€350	€350	€350	€350	€350
Service/repairs	€2,000	€1,200	€750	€300	€300
Total running costs	€17,850	€14,050	€10,100	€6,650	€5,650
Mileage claims at civil service rates*	€13,384	€10,508	€7,662	€4,816	€2,953
Net running costs	€4,496	€3,542	€2,438	€1,834	€2,697
BIK **	€1,200	€2,400	€4,800	€6,000	€6,000

* First 6,437 miles at 59.07 cent per mile and balance at 28.46 cent per mile.
** Benefit in kind calculation.

Note: Income levies apply to the benefit in kind.

Cost	Mileage	BIK %	BIK
€20,000	5,000	30	€6,000
€20,000	10,000	30	€6,000
€20,000	15,000	30	€6,000
€20,000	20,000	24	€4,800
€20,000	25,000	18	€3,600
€20,000	30,000	12	€2,400
€20,000	40,000	6	€1,200

100% TAX-FREE MOTORING!

There is one way in which you can enjoy a company car with absolutely no tax liability whatsoever. Any car included in a **car pool** will be tax free provided all of the following conditions are met:

- The car is available for use (and is actually used) by more than one employee and isn't ordinarily used by any one such employee to the exclusion of the others.
- Private use by any employee is incidental to business use.
- The car is not normally kept overnight at, or in the vicinity of, any of the employees' homes.

Finally, if you work for your own company or are self-employed, bear in mind the cost of running a 'business' car will be further reduced by capital allowances. As with other capital expenditure, you're allowed to write off the cost for tax purposes over a period of eight years. So if you purchased the car for €10,000, you can set an allowance of €1,250 per year against your tax bill.

28
CAPITAL GAINS TAX

DON'T PAY A PENNY MORE CAPITAL GAINS TAX THAN YOU HAVE TO

Just because **capital gains tax** – at a flat rate of 25% – is much cheaper than it used to be (at its peak it was 40%) it doesn't follow that you want to pay any more of it than you have to.

Capital gains tax planning is not easy even though, ironically, the rules relating to it have been much simplified. Nevertheless, there are still some useful allowances and exemptions which do make it possible to reduce, delay, and – in some instances – completely avoid this tax. As you'll discover in this chapter.

HOW THE TAX WORKS

If you buy something for one price and then sell it at a higher price or, for that matter, give it away when it is worth more than you paid for it, then the Revenue Commissioners consider that you have made a 'capital gain' and may, therefore, be liable for tax.

> ### MONEY DOCTOR WEALTH CHECK
>
> #### Indexation relief
>
> If you owned whatever you have sold prior to 31 December 2002 – good news – before 1 January 2003 something called **indexation relief** was applied to all possible gains and this has the effect of reducing tax liability. Indexation relief was, essentially, an allowance designed to take account of inflation. As such, it meant that only gains over and above the rate of inflation were liable for tax. You can still apply indexation relief to assets held prior to 31 December 2002.

BASIC CAPITAL GAINS TAX PLANNING

Below is a list of the main ways in which capital gains tax can be reduced or avoided:

- It may seem a bit dramatic, but if you **move abroad** prior to making a disposal of your assets (in other words selling them), you will not be liable for any Irish capital gains tax. The only exception to this is if you're selling Irish property or mineral/exploration rights. Obviously, you would want to be selling a fairly major asset to make it worth becoming non-resident. For further information about becoming non-resident see Chapter 31.

- The **first €1,270** made as a capital gain in each tax year is tax free.

- You do not have to pay capital gains tax from the **sale of your principal residence**, including up to one acre of land. However, if you sell your home for development, then you will be taxed on the profit attributed to the 'development value'.

- If you've **bought a home for a dependent** relative (this would include a relative who was unable to look after themselves, a widowed mother, and so forth) then any gain you make on the sale of the property would be free of tax.

- If you **give a house site** to a child who then builds his or her private residence on it, providing that site is not worth more than €254,000, no tax will be due.

- There is no capital gains tax on bonuses from **post office** or **state savings schemes**, or from the disposal of **government stocks**.

- You don't have to pay tax if you sell an asset with a '**predictable life**' of less than 50 years – for instance, if you sold a car or a horse at a profit.

- If you **hand your business** (including a farm) to a member of your family on retirement, there will be no capital gains tax liability either. This is called 'retirement relief'.

- You can dispose of a '**moveable, tangible asset**' worth €2,540 or less without paying capital gains tax.

- Capital gains tax is not applicable to any **winnings** from gambling, the lottery, or competitions.

- Any benefits from **life assurance** policies or **deferred annuities** are tax free.

- If you transfer something to your **spouse** there is no capital gains tax charge.

Incidentally, the retirement relief not only applies when you pass an asset to a member of your family. Providing you're aged over 55, and have owned the farm or business for more than five years, if you sell that farm or business for a sum that is less than €750,000 you won't have to pay capital gains tax. If you sell the asset for more than €750,000 you will pay a reduced level of capital gains tax.

ONE MORE USEFUL WAY TO REDUCE YOUR BILL

If you incur expenses relating to the item you are selling – or if you have improved it in some way – then you may be able to claim them against your tax bill.

For instance, supposing you purchased an investment property and added an extra bedroom to the attic. The cost of doing this could be deducted from the sale price, thus reducing your tax liability.

29
CAPITAL ACQUISITION TAX

DON'T ALLOW YOUR GIFTS AND INHERITANCES TO BE TAXED UNNECESSARILY

The purpose of **capital acquisition tax** is to tax gifts and inheritances – and the purpose of this chapter is to ensure that your gifts and inheritances aren't taxed unnecessarily!

There are two key ways to lessen the effect of capital acquisition tax (which operates at a flat rate of 25% on benefits taken on or after 8 April 2009):

1   Make sure that the value of what you're leaving or giving falls below the tax-free threshold that is available.

2   Make sure that what you're leaving or giving is excluded completely from the tax. As there is a long list of excluded benefits, this is not as hard as it may seem.

TAKE FULL ADVANTAGE OF THE TAX-FREE THRESHOLDS

There are all sorts of gifts and inheritances that the government feel it would be unfair to tax. Or, to be more accurate, they feel it would be unfair to tax them unless the amount involved was fairly substantial. What we are talking about here are gifts and inheritance made to members of your immediate family and other people who are close to you. The tax-free allowances that apply are referred to as **tax-free thresholds**. I am afraid the tax-free threshold system is not straightforward but I'll do my best to summarise its key features.

Essentially, there are **three different groups**. The first applies to your **closest relatives**, the second to your slightly **more distant relatives**, and the third to **everyone else**. The thresholds are personal to the recipient, not to the donor (known legally as the **disponer**). For instance, for the current year the total amount a child can receive as gifts and/or inheritances is €414,799 from a parent. So providing the amount a child inherits from either of his or her parents is beneath this figure, he or she will pay no tax on it. Where it gets complicated is in the case of – say – nieces and nephews, who may receive bequests from a number of uncles and aunts. Anyway, below are the current thresholds:

Group 1: Children. €414,799 where the recipient is a child, or a minor grandchild of the benefactor, if the parent is dead. In some cases, this threshold can also apply to a parent, niece or nephew who has worked in a family business for a period of time. The threshold is also available if a parent receives an inheritance from a child. And foster children may also receive this amount providing they were maintained by and resided with the foster parent for a successive period of five years while under the age of 18.

Group 2: Close relatives. €41,481 where the recipient is a brother, sister, niece, nephew or linear ancestor/descendant of the benefactor or where the gift is made by the child to the parent.

Group 3: Everyone else! €20,740 in all other cases.

In other words, as an individual you can receive €414,799 from a parent, a total of €41,481 from uncles and aunts, and an additional €20,740 from friends or other more distant relatives without incurring any tax.

The rates indicated apply from 1 January 2010.

FIVE COMPLETELY TAX-FREE CATEGORIES

Five different categories of gift or inheritance are excluded completely for purposes of capital acquisition tax. They are:

1 Any gift or inheritance made **between spouses.**

2 Any inheritance received from a **deceased child** which was originally given to that child by one or other of their parents.

3 Up to €**3,000 worth of gifts or cash** in any single calendar year.

4 Irish government stock when given to a **non-Irish domiciled beneficiary.** There are conditions attached to this – the main one being that the person receiving it must hold it for at least six years after receiving it. The legal definition of 'non-Irish domiciled' is complicated, but essentially it means someone who wasn't born in Ireland or who hasn't married someone born in Ireland.

5 Your family home. Again, there are certain conditions. It should be your **principal private residence** (or the recipient's principal private residence); the recipient should have been living in the home for the three years prior to the transfer; and the recipient should not have an interest in any other residential property. Furthermore, the recipient mustn't sell the home for at least six years.

As you will see from the list above, with a bit of careful planning it is possible to take the main family home and other assets out of one's estate for inheritance tax purposes.

TWO USEFUL WAYS TO AVOID CAPITAL ACQUISITION TAX

Because the government knows it would be unfair to include **farms** and **business assets** in the capital acquisitions tax net, both can be given away or bequeathed with only minimal tax liability.

The rules are written so that someone who wished to reduce or avoid capital acquisition tax could, in fact, with a little foresight transfer their assets into either a business or a farm and see them escape tax. As you can imagine, the rules governing these two tax loopholes are complex, so I will only summarise them below. It would be unwise (to say the least) to attempt to take advantage of these tax breaks without consulting a professional accountant and/or solicitor.

FARMS

With regard to farms, 'agricultural assets are valued at only 10% of their true market value when calculating a liability for capital acquisitions tax'. Farm assets, in this instance, include not just land but buildings, woodland, livestock, bloodstock, and machinery. The recipient of the farm must be a 'farmer', which means that at least 80% of his or her assets are farm assets. You must also hold onto the assets for at least ten years to avoid any clawback of tax.

A farm may, of course, also be considered a family business, and the Revenue Commissioners very generously allow them to be taxed as such for capital acquisition tax purposes, if it means a lower tax bill in the hands of the recipient.

BUSINESSES

So what are the rules regarding **business** assets? Once again, the primary condition is that the recipient must hold them for at least ten years after the transfer. The business itself must be Irish. Most businesses qualify, including property, unquoted shares, buildings, land, and even machinery. However, businesses whose 'sole or main business is dealing in land, shares, or securities' are not covered by this loophole. The transfer of a business by way of gift or inheritance is not entirely tax free under these circumstances, but the assets will be assessed at just 10% of their market value.

Incidentally, keep in mind that the person giving away or bequeathing either farm or business assets need not have owned them for very long. In the case of a gift it should be five years, but in the case of death it need be only two years.

30
LOVE, MARRIAGE AND LOWER TAXES

EXTRA TAX BENEFITS FOR THOSE WHO ARE MARRIED

Billy Connolly, one of my favourite comedians, famously said: 'Marriage is a wonderful invention, but, then again, so is a bicycle repair kit.' However, unlike a bicycle repair kit, marriage has some very tasty tax benefits attaching to it. And in this chapter I will explain how you can take advantage of them.

MARRIAGE BRINGS GREATER FLEXIBILITY

The first big benefit of being married is that you get to choose how you are taxed. The options open to you are:

Joint assessment. This means that you will be taxed as one unit and allowed some tax concessions not used by one spouse to be transferred to the other.

Separate assessment. This is very like joint assessment except that all the available allowances are split evenly between you and your spouse.

Single assessment. This is where you and your spouse decide to be treated as if you were two single people for tax purposes.

Why this flexibility of benefit? Basically, you can choose to be taxed in the way that will produce the greatest possible tax advantage given your personal circumstances.

Under **joint assessment** and **separate assessment**, some **unused allowances** can be passed between husband and wife. This is particularly beneficial in the case of a two-income couple where one spouse earns more than another. Under normal circumstances, the Revenue Commissioners will assume that you wish to be taxed under joint assessment, and will calculate your tax liability accordingly. However, it is worth checking that you are taking full advantage of all the allowances and tax credits open to you, as the Revenue Commissioners may not be fully aware of your financial situation.

The only circumstances under which most people might wish to be taxed under the single assessment system is where they are separated.

What is interesting is that on a combined salary of, say, €55,000 a couple is likely to save over €1,000 by being taxed under the joint assessment system over and above what they would pay under the separate or single assessment system.

OTHER TAX CONCESSIONS MADE TO MARRIED COUPLES

A number of other generous tax concessions are made to married couples, including:

- Assets may be transferred between husband and wife without being subject to capital gains tax.
- Any capital losses made by one spouse may be used by the other spouse to reduce a capital gains tax bill.
- Any gifts or inheritances given by one spouse to another are completely free of capital acquisition tax.
- Any money received by yourself or your spouse from a life assurance policy (providing you or your spouse were the original beneficial owners) will be completely tax free.
- Married couples do not have to pay stamp duty when they transfer assets from one to another.

EVEN BETTER NEWS IF YOU'RE MARRIED AND SELF-EMPLOYED

If you are **self-employed** or run your own business, by employing your spouse, you may be able to save up to €5,250 a year in tax. To make this saving, the total amount of income you and your spouse earn each year must be at least €70,800. It doesn't, by the way, all have to come from your own business. Your spouse can earn up to €25,000 and you can still gain a tax benefit.

The reason why the tax saving can be made is the fact that a two-income family can take advantage of a €70,800 standard rate band as opposed to the €44,400 band available to a single-income family.

The best way to illustrate this is with a real example:

One income			Two incomes		
Income	€75,000		Income		€75,000
€45,400 @ 20%	€9,080		€72,800 @ 20%		€14,560
€29,600 @ 41%	€12,136		€2,200 @ 41%		€902
Total tax before tax credits	€21,216		Total tax before tax credits		€15,462
Tax credits			**Tax credits**		
Married person €3,660			Married person €3,660		
PAYE	€1,830	€5,490	PAYE	€1,830	€5,490
Tax payable	€15,726		Tax payable		€9,972

Tax saving   €15,726 − €9,972 = €5,754

MONEY DOCTOR WEALTH CHECK

Turn your children into a tax advantage

If you're self-employed, and if you have children, you may be able to avoid tax on up to €18,300 per child a year. This is because your children are entitled – like anybody else – to earn up to this sum every year free of tax. Of course, the child must actually be doing the work for which they are paid – and it may be necessary for you to register as an employer for PAYE and PRSI purposes – but given the tax saving this has to be worth it! Also, depending on the sort of business you run, PRSI may not be applicable.

31
TAX FOR THE EX-PAT

TAX PLANNING TIPS IF YOU'RE LIVING AND WORKING ABROAD

What happens to your tax position if you decide to live abroad? Much depends, of course, on where you go, what you do, and how long you're away. If, for instance, you move to a country with much lower rates of tax than we have here in Ireland, you could make a substantial saving. Since there are over 130 different tax jurisdictions in the world, it's obviously beyond the scope of this book to look at all the different possibilities. However, in this chapter I can, at least, explain how your Irish tax situation will be affected by a move overseas.

IT'S ALL ABOUT RESIDENCY AND DOMICILE

Every country in the world has its own rules about whom it taxes and under what circumstances. In some countries it's all about whether you **reside** there for legal purposes. This may have absolutely nothing to do with the amount of time you actually spend in the country. For instance, you can be tax-resident in Malta (thus taking advantage of a very liberal tax regime) but not set foot on the island from one end of the year to the other. Other countries have more complicated rules that are not only linked to your residence but also to your **domicile**, a rather complicated legal concept. Put simply, it is considered to be *the country that you call your natural home*. When you're born you usually have the same domicile as your father. If you marry, or move abroad for a long time, then your domicile may change.

Here in Ireland your tax liability will be determined by *both* your resident status and your domicile. Just to make things more complex, we have two types of residence. You may be **ordinarily resident** or simply **resident**.

You will be viewed as being resident here for tax purposes in the current tax year if:

- You spend 183 days or more in the state.
- The combined number of days you spend here in the current tax year and the number of days you spent here in the last tax year exceeds 280. In

applying this two-year test, a period of less than 30 days spent in Ireland in a tax year will be ignored.

Incidentally, the term 'day' really refers to whether or not you were in the country on the stroke of midnight.

Once you've been in Ireland for **three** consecutive tax years you are considered to have become ordinarily resident. You stop becoming ordinarily resident in Ireland once you've left the country for three consecutive years.

WHAT HAPPENS WHEN YOU MOVE ABROAD?

Assuming that you are resident, ordinarily resident, and domiciled in Ireland – what happens when you decide to move abroad on a permanent or, at least, long-term basis?

The year you leave Ireland you will still be considered resident. However, the year after your departure you will not be considered resident. Since this could lead to a very unfair situation – where you're taxed in two countries simultaneously – the law says that:

- As soon as you depart Ireland you may apply to be granted **emigrant status**, which means that your earnings outside Ireland after that date will be ignored for Irish tax purposes.

If you move to a country that has a **double taxation agreement** with Ireland, then you won't be expected to pay tax on the same money twice.

A MONEY-BACK OFFER: TAX REBATES

If you leave a job in Ireland and move overseas to work, you may well be entitled to a **tax rebate**. In fact, you can claim a rebate going back for up to four years. The reason you get this rebate is that under the PAYE system your various tax credits and allowances are spread out over an entire year. Under these circumstances, if you leave your job and move abroad halfway through the year, you'll only ever see the benefit of half your tax allowances and credits. You won't, however, be given this rebate automatically, though you may apply for it before you've even left the country.

WHAT IS YOUR TAX STATUS?

So, what is your tax status? There are four different possibilities:

1   If you are resident and domiciled in Ireland then you pay Irish tax including income tax on your Irish income and on your worldwide income.

2   If you are resident in Ireland but not domiciled here, and if you haven't lived here for at least three years (in other words you are not ordinarily resident in Ireland), then you pay Irish income tax on your Irish and UK income, and on any foreign income paid to you in Ireland. In other words, foreign income (unless it comes from the UK) that you don't deposit in an Irish bank or spend in Ireland escapes Irish tax.

3   If you are ordinarily resident in Ireland, but not resident here for a particular tax year, then your tax status changes dramatically. In theory you're liable to Irish income tax on your whole worldwide income. However, employment or income which you earn wholly abroad (plus an extra €3,810) will be ignored for tax purposes. Furthermore, you may be able to take advantage of double taxation agreements to further reduce your tax bill.

4   If you are not resident, or ordinarily resident – in other words, if you haven't lived in Ireland for at least three years – then your only liability to Irish tax is on Irish income.

Budget 2010 introduced a **Domicile Levy**. From 1 January 2010 certain individuals who are Irish citizens and Irish domiciled in a tax year will pay a levy of €200,000. Specifically the levy will apply where the individual has:

•   Irish located property greater than €5 million,

•   worldwide income in excess of €1 million, and

•   an Irish income tax liability less than €200,000.

The Finance Bill clarified that Irish property is all property located in Ireland but does not include shares in a trading company or a holding company that derive the greater part of their value from subsidiary trading companies.
The individual's Irish income tax liability for the year will be allowed as a credit in arriving at the amount of the domicile levy for that year. The levy will apply irrespective of where they live or where they are tax resident.

YOUR PERSONAL TAX CREDITS AND RELIEFS

What happens to all your personal tax credits and allowances if you cease to be resident in Ireland? The answer will be determined by the source of your income, and your resident status.

GET PROFESSIONAL HELP!

In the excitement of moving abroad, many people omit to take professional advice on their tax position, and end up with an unexpected tax bill or – just as bad – missing an opportunity to claim back tax they've already paid. The Money Doctor's advice to anybody moving abroad is get professional tax help sooner rather than later.

32
SPECIAL TAX ADVICE FOR FARMERS

We city folk have an idyllic view of farming life – sun-drenched fields, wholesome food, healthy lifestyle, happy people. There is all that, but there is also the everyday issue the farming community face that we all face – tax. Tax is and always has been a thorny issue on both sides of the fence. Some city folk may think that farmers don't pay enough and farmers might say that they should be given special status because of the importance of their role in Irish heritage – not to mention the produce they yield from Irish soil. Being married to a farmer's daughter, I tend to agree with the latter!

If you are a farmer, you need to consider a number of areas:

- income tax
- capital acquisitions tax
- capitals gains tax
- VAT
- stock relief
- compulsory disposal of livestock
- capital allowances
- milk quotas
- stamp duty
- farm consolidation relief
- leasing of farm land.

Let's look at them all in more detail now.

INCOME TAX

The Finance Act allows for a **deferral of tax** on FEOGA income. This is the European Agricultural Guidance and Guarantee Fund, support through funding from the Common Agricultural Policy. (FEOGA are the French initials!) However, you must meet certain conditions:

- You must be a farmer in receipt of payments under the EU single payments scheme for farmers and certain terminated FEOGA scheme payments in 2007.

- You must not be availing of **farm averaging**.

The provision allows payments received under terminated FEOGA schemes to be disregarded for tax purposes in 2007, and instead to be deemed to arise in three equal instalments in 2007, 2008, and 2009. If you cease to farm during this period, any untaxed payments will fall to be taxed in the year the farming stopped. Once agreed to go this route, it cannot be changed.

CAPITAL ACQUISITIONS TAX

A gift/inheritance of land, buildings and other agricultural property (e.g. machinery and livestock) may be reduced by 90% of its market value for gift/inheritance tax when received by a qualifying farmer as long as:

- the farmer is domiciled in Ireland
- 80% of the market value of the property after taking the gift/ inheritance consists of agricultural property.

However, do keep in mind that this relief is lost if the assets are disposed of within a six-year timeframe, without being replaced within one year of sale, or within a period of six years in the case of a sale or compulsory acquisition made on or after 25 March 2002. Make any claims for agricultural relief on Form I.T.41.

Gifts or inheritances of agricultural property qualify for **business relief** (where the relevant criteria are met) in circumstances where it fails to qualify for agricultural relief. This reduces the market value of the gift/inheritance by 90%. Again, business relief will be clawed back if the assets are disposed of within six years, without being replaced.

Before you receive a gift of farm assets, make sure that 80% of your personal assets are agricultural assets after you have received the gift.

CAPITAL GAINS TAX

Retirement relief means that a **disponer** (the person who is giving the legacy, generally the mother or father), can hand over land to a child without capital gains tax liability for that child. However, the conditions are:

- The disponer must be over 55 years of age.

- She or he must have used the business assets for at least ten years prior to handing over to the disponer's child.

You should also note these other key points:

- Periods of ownership of a deceased spouse may also be included.

- 'Child' includes anyone who has worked substantially on a full-time basis for five years before the handover.

- Where proceeds do not exceed €750,000, relief on the disposal can be given to an unconnected person. There is marginal relief exceeding this amount.

In addition, land that has been let for up to five years prior to a compulsory purchase order being made will qualify for retirement relief if it was used for farming for ten years prior to the letting.

Note that a farmer who participates in the EU 'Early retirement from farming scheme' by leasing the land qualifies for the relief. Therefore, while it is called 'retirement relief', you don't actually have to retire to qualify for this relief!

VAT

- A flat rate of 5.2% applies to supplies of agricultural goods or services.

- If you engage in any other services and your turnover exceeds €37,500 in a calendar year, normal VAT rates will apply – this includes the farming itself.

- Keep in mind that if you are a flat rate (5.2%) farmer, you can also reclaim this VAT on any expenditure incurred in the construction or improvement of farm buildings, farm structures, fencing, drainage and land reclamation.

- VAT on farm vehicles (vans, pick-up trucks but not passenger vehicles) can also be reclaimed.

- VAT on diesel is also reclaimable.

STOCK RELIEF

Stock relief is a basic relief for first-time farmers (who meet certain required criteria) whereby they can reduce their taxable trading profit by 100% of the increase in their farming stock at the end of their trading year over their farming stock at the beginning of that year. The 2009 Budget extended this relief to 31 December 2010. The existing 25% general stock relief for farmers was also extended to this date.

COMPULSORY DISPOSAL OF LIVESTOCK

There is a special relief for farmers (individuals and companies) in respect of profits resulting from the **disposal of livestock** due to statutory disease-eradication measures.

You can have tax on profits spread over four consecutive annual instalments *after* the year in which the profits arise or spread equally over the four years including the year in which the profits arise.

This relief extends to all animals and poultry.

CAPITAL ALLOWANCES

Relief is available for farmers who have:

- incurred expenditure on necessary pollution-control measures
- who have a **Farm Nutrient Management** plan in place.

The maximum allowed is €63,500. This scheme has been extended to 31 December 2010 with the Finance Act 2005 shortening the write-off period to three years in respect to expenditure incurred after 1 January 2005.

MILK QUOTAS

Capital allowances are available to farmers incurred in purchasing a milk quota. The period for write-off is seven years – 15% for the first six years and 10% for the seventh year. **Do note that capital allowances may be claimed by a farmer who leases a milk quota from a relative and who later purchases that quota.**

STAMP DUTY

Essentially a tax on buying or transferring property or land, this duty payable is restricted to half for related bequests (e.g. giving your son your farm) but to young trained farmers this duty is nil. There are clawbacks whereby within five years of receiving a stamp duty relief, the proceeds of that disposal of the property are not reinvested within one year in other land.

FARM CONSOLIDATION RELIEF

This is another type of stamp duty relief for exchanging farm land between two farmers to consolidate each other's holding. There are a number of conditions attached to this relief and you should consult your accountant for more advice on this.

LEASING OF FARM LAND

If you are over 40 and you lease your farm land, you are eligible for income tax exemption subject to certain thresholds – bear in mind the lease income of the husband and wife are treated separately for the purpose of the relief, whether jointly assessed or not.

In January 2007, a new exemption of €20,000 per annum was introduced for leases of 10 years or more duration. This measure was subjected to clearance with the European Commission under state-aid rules.

PART 9

WHEN THE LAST THING YOU WANT TO THINK ABOUT IS MONEY

This section of the book offers advice and information relating to four highly sensitive subjects:

- *redundancy*
- *separation*
- *divorce*
- *the death of a loved one.*

In each of these situations, of course, the last thing you'll want to think about is money. And yet, unfortunately, each of these difficult experiences has important financial implications.

33
REDUNDANCY

TOP TIPS, INCLUDING ADVICE ON YOUR RIGHTS SHOULD YOU EXPERIENCE REDUNDANCY

Whether you have opted for redundancy because of the financial benefits it offers you, or whether it was thrust upon you, it is vital that you know your rights and that you can make sure that you come out of it in as strong a financial position as possible. In this chapter I will explain your rights and offer general advice on making the most – from a money perspective – of the situation.

BACKGROUND BRIEFING ON 'REDUNDANCY'

The term 'redundancy' applies to a very specific situation, so the first thing you must do is find out whether or not you are covered by the relevant legislation. Essentially, in order to be eligible for a redundancy payment, you must:

- be aged between 16 and 66
- have been working for at least eight hours a week for your employer
- have at least 104 weeks (in other words, two years) of continuous service for the same employer.

Redundancy can only exist when an employee is dismissed because:

- The employer is no longer undertaking the business activity which necessitated employing you.
- The employer is moving the location of the business.
- The employer has decided to carry on business with fewer employees, or to carry out work in some different manner.

Voluntary redundancy – also known as 'voluntary parting' – is where an employer wants to lose members of staff and asks for volunteers for redundancy. If you do volunteer, you will automatically become entitled to a

statutory lump sum payment. Note that employers must give you at least *two weeks' notice* before making you redundant, and notice must be given using the specific form – **Form RP1** – at that time.

HOW MUCH ARE YOU ENTITLED TO?

The law is very precise about the amount of money an employer must pay you if you are to be made redundant. It is calculated as follows:

- You should receive two weeks' pay for each year of employment continuous and reckonable between the ages of 16 and 66.
- You should also receive an equivalent of one week's normal pay.

However, there *is* an upper limit. No matter what your salary, one week's pay will never be more than €600.

WHAT HAPPENS IF THE EMPLOYER DOESN'T PAY UP?

There are many situations where employers either don't – or can't – make the lump sum redundancy payment. For instance, the employer may be inefficient, insolvent, or even dead. Under these circumstances, it may be possible to receive a payment from the government. To pursue this, contact the:

> Department of Enterprise,
> Trade and Employment
> Davitt House, 65A Adelaide Road
> Dublin 2

or contact your local FÁS office.

WHAT'S THE TAX SITUATION?

Depending on your circumstances, and the amount of money being paid, your redundancy lump sum may or may not be liable to tax. It will be totally exempt from tax if the payment was made:

- under the Redundancy Payments Acts of 1987–1991
- as a result of injury or disability
- from an approved pension scheme.

Even if your lump sum isn't entirely tax free, you may be able to claim an extra tax-free amount. How much you can claim will be the highest of the three different exemptions outlined below. Where you are receiving a larger sum, it is likely to become taxable. Under these circumstances, you can either treat it as income in the year in which you receive it, and have it taxed as such, or else you can take advantage of something called **top slicing relief**, which works by calculating your average rate of tax for the five years prior to the tax year in which you received a lump sum.

Do note that it is often possible to reduce your tax bill on a redundancy lump sum by using it to make an additional voluntary contribution to a pension scheme (see Chapter 20).

CLAIMING TAX RELIEF ON A REDUNDANCY PAYMENT

You can claim tax relief under one of these three exemptions:

Basic exemption. You can receive up to €10,160 as a lump sum together with an additional €765 for each complete year of service without paying a cent of tax.

Increased exemption. The tax-free sum you are entitled to receive may be increased by €10,000 to a maximum of €20,160 (plus the additional €765 for each complete year of service) if you haven't made a claim for an increased exemption amount in the previous ten years, nor received a tax-free lump sum under an approved pension scheme.

Standard capital superannuation benefit (SCSB). This is a way for those with a long service record to receive a higher tax-free sum. The SCSB formula involves taking your average salary over the past three years, multiplying it by the number of years of service, dividing it by 15, and deducting any tax-free lump sum paid, or due, from a pension scheme.

Let me give you an example:

Peter, aged 65, has given 44 years service to his company. His average salary over the last three years was €47,500. If you multiply this by 44 (the number of years service), you would get a total of €2,090,000. Then divide it by 15, giving you a total of €139,333.33 tax free.

THE MONEY DOCTOR SAYS...

If you have been working for an employer for a sufficiently long period of time to entitle you to a redundancy payment, then there is no doubt in my mind that it's worth seeking professional help to ensure that you not only optimise that payment but that you pay the least possible amount of tax on the benefit.

34
SEPARATION

THE FINANCIAL CONSEQUENCES OF SEPARATION

Sadly, no book dealing with personal finances is complete without chapters covering separation and divorce. First of all, it's worth pointing out that from a legal perspective the breakdown of a marriage actually has three separate stages:

1　When a couple make the decision to **live apart**.

2　When a couple seek a **legal separation**.

3　When a couple seek a **judicial separation**.

In this chapter I will explain the consequences and issues surrounding a separation, and in the next chapter I will explain what happens as a result of a divorce.

The implications of living apart

Living separately from your husband or wife does not in any way alter the legal status of your marriage. For example, you don't automatically lose your Succession Act entitlements (see next page for further details) if you are separated from your spouse. However, do note that if a spouse is found guilty of **desertion** or **bad conduct**, they might well be deemed by a court to have forfeited these rights.

WHAT HAPPENS WHEN YOU 'LIVE APART'?

The financial effects of **living apart** can be summarised as follows:

- In the case of a **temporary** or **short-term** separation, there will be no alteration in the income tax situation and you can still elect for joint, separate or single assessment.

- If the separation is considered to be **permanent**, then the husband and wife will be assessed for income tax under the **single assessment system**. The only situation where this really alters is if there are legally enforceable maintenance payments being made. In some circumstances, these will be tax deductible to the payer, and taxable in the hands of the recipient; in other circumstances, they will be ignored for income tax purposes.

- With regard to capital gains tax, a temporary separation will make no change in either spouse's tax status. In the event of a permanent separation, any transfer of assets that are connected with the separation itself will remain capital gains tax free. However, other transfers will become taxable and unused capital gains tax losses will no longer be permitted.

- Couples who live apart continue to be exempt from capital acquisitions tax on the transfer of assets between each other.

- Life assurance proceeds continue to be tax free – providing the beneficiary was originally named in the policy as such.

Couples who are separated continue to enjoy exemption from stamp duty when transferring property between each other.

WHAT HAPPENS WHEN YOU GET A 'LEGAL SEPARATION'?

A legal separation (often referred to as a 'Deed of Separation') is a voluntary agreement made between a husband and wife who have decided to live apart on a permanent basis. Interestingly, it does not change the *legal* status of a marriage. Its purpose is really to resolve the key financial and, where relevant, child-custody arrangements. Under normal circumstances, a legal separation makes provision regarding two key financial matters:

- any maintenance payments to be made by one spouse for the benefit of the other spouse and/or their children

- any desired change regarding rights under the Succession Act 1965.

With regard to Succession Act rights, these only change if altered legally by the Deed of Separation. However, on becoming legally separated, many people alter their wills to account for the new circumstances.

From an income tax perspective, a legal separation is no different from a married couple simply deciding to live apart. Thus, if the separation is likely to be permanent and legally enforceable maintenance payments have been agreed, most couples decide to opt for separate assessment. If this happens, then maintenance payments are ignored for income tax purposes.

While the income tax situation may be relatively straightforward in the first year of separation, in subsequent years it may become slightly trickier. This is because a number of different factors come into play, including:

- voluntary maintenance payments, whether made to a spouse or for the benefit of a child
- legally enforceable maintenance payments, whether made to a spouse and/or child
- interest relief on mortgage repayments
- single-parent credits.

PRSI and **health levies** may be payable on maintenance payments, depending on whether the separated couple have opted for single or separate assessment.

Keep in mind that – in most circumstances – there is a **tax benefit** to legally enforceable maintenance payments. This is because they are tax deductible for the spouse paying them but will not, necessarily, be large enough for the recipient to have to pay tax on them.

The situation regarding capital gains tax, capital acquisition tax, and stamp duty do not alter if you become legally separated as opposed to simply living apart.

WHAT IS A JUDICIAL SEPARATION?

If a couple cannot agree to a legal separation, one of them may apply to the courts for a **judicial separation**. In this case, instead of a voluntary arrangement regarding the marital assets, maintenance and so on, the court will make a number of **Ancillary Orders**, which are legally enforceable.

From a financial perspective, there is little difference between a legal separation and a judicial separation. There is one area, however, where a judicial separation is more like a divorce, and this is with regard to **pension benefits**. Under the Family Law Act of 1995, if a judicial separation takes place, a spouse's pension benefits will be treated in one of three different ways:

1   **Earmarking** may occur. This means that when a pension becomes payable, a share of it is earmarked for the other spouse.

2 **Pension-splitting** results in the pension benefits being split on a pre-set formula between the two spouses.

3 **Offsetting** whereby the spouse with pension rights may be entitled to keep them in exchange for something else. For instance, the spouse with pension rights might give up all entitlement to a family home.

Keep in mind that a decree of judicial separation does *not* affect the legal status of a marriage – it merely means that a husband and wife no longer have to live together. The key difference between a judicial separation and a divorce is that a judicial separation will not allow either party to re-marry.

THE MONEY DOCTOR SAYS...

Sadly, many separating couples take legal but not financial advice. I strongly recommend a thorough review of your finances both before and after separation.

You should consider every aspect of your finances – life cover, income protection, critical illness cover, borrowings, savings, investments and (especially) pension plans.

Given that after a separation both parties are likely to be managing on a lower income, it is also important to work out a new monthly budget.

35
DIVORCE

THE FINANCIAL CONSEQUENCES OF DIVORCE

Although a great deal has been written about the legal, emotional, religious, moral and logistical aspects of divorce, there are very few sources of reference relating to the *financial* consequences of ending a marriage.

The financial consequences will, of course, vary considerably depending on a variety of factors including:

- each partner's age
- the income of each partner
- whether or not there are any children
- whether or not there is a family home
- other joint and individually held assets
- the pension entitlements for each partner
- the health of each partner
- whether or not any life assurance is in place for one or other partner
- whether or not they both live in Ireland.

Decisions over whether or not the family home should be sold, or concerning maintenance payments are legal rather than financial and, therefore, outside the scope of this book.

If you are divorced, whatever settlement was reached – whether voluntary or decided by the courts – you need to now re-consider and review your financial planning.

In this chapter, then, I look at the key issues facing a newly divorced person, and I make a number of specific suggestions relating to your personal finances.

THE IMPORTANCE OF BUDGETING

There is no doubt that divorce is expensive. Leaving aside the legal costs, both husband and wife are likely to find themselves now having to fund two homes where, previously, they only had to pay for one. By the same token, other assets are likely to be depleted:

- Extra life cover may become necessary.
- All sorts of living expenses will increase.
- You may be required to start or increase retirement savings.

In addition, the emotional strain of divorce is often such that people become somewhat reckless about their spending and borrowing habits. If you do find yourself in this unfortunate position, my advice is that – at the earliest possible moment – you sit down and work out a **new budget**.

If you would like assistance with this, I would refer you to my website (www.moneydoctor.ie) where you will find a free, online monthly budget planner.

HOW YOUR SITUATION WILL HAVE CHANGED

Once you are legally divorced, your financial position in relation to succession, tax, pensions, insurance and social welfare will all have changed:

- Your **succession rights** will automatically be lost. However, if you have made any specific bequests in your will to your former spouse, they will stand unless you change your will or make a new one.

- In terms of **income tax** your position is broadly the same as if you were simply legally separated (see Chapter 34). The main thing to remember is that if there are legally enforceable maintenance payments, then you can usually opt to be taxed either under the single assessment or separate assessment systems. Under the single assessment system, maintenance payments are tax deductible for the person paying them, and taxable for the person receiving them. If you decide to be taxed under the separate assessment system, then maintenance payments will be ignored for income tax purposes.

- Any transfer in assets that is made because of the divorce will be **capital gains tax** free. Do note however that after that point transfers will no longer be exempt from capital gains tax.

    Any transfer of assets or gifts that take place as a result of the divorce settlement are exempt from **capital acquisition tax**. As with capital gains tax, once you are divorced, the spouse exemption for capital acquisitions tax no longer applies.

MAKING PROPER PENSION PROVISION

Pension rights can be a very important part of the financial arrangements resulting from a divorce. Indeed, for many married couples, their pension rights can be as valuable, if not more valuable, than the family home. For this reason, I advise you strongly to take expert advice when you separate.

In fact, the law recognises the vital importance and value of pension rights – as a result, spouses are *not allowed* to arrange a **pension adjustment order** between themselves. Only a court of law has the right to decide what happens to pension rights after a couple separate or divorce.

Deciding on the value of the pension is not easy. It will depend on the beneficiary's salary, type of pension scheme, level of contributions, prescribed benefits, years of service, and scheme performance.

A court will not necessarily make any decision regarding pensions if it believes that the rest of the agreed settlement is fair to both parties. However, there are three things concerning pension benefits that divorcing couples should be aware of:

1   A court can make orders about the pension benefits of either spouse.

2   Normally any decisions about pensions will be made at the time of the divorce, but if this doesn't happen, either spouse can go back to court for a **pension adjustment order** at any time during the lifetime of the pension scheme member.

3   A court can order that part of a pension is paid to either a spouse or to a dependent child.

THE MONEY DOCTOR SAYS...

If you are getting divorced, do not rely solely on the services of a solicitor – call in one or more financial professionals to help with financial planning, tax planning and pension planning. I cannot stress how important it is to do this at the earliest possible opportunity.

36
COPING WITH BEREAVEMENT

WHAT TO DO ABOUT THE MONEY SIDE OF THINGS WHEN SOMEONE CLOSE DIES

When somebody close to you dies, tax and other financial matters are obviously the last thing on your mind. If there are dependants involved, however, it may be necessary to tackle such matters with a degree of urgency. Even if dependants aren't involved, there is a legal obligation for the personal representative to carry out certain responsibilities within a reasonable period of time.

Making and executing a will, especially after purchasing a property, is probably the most important legal task a person should perform. Despite that fact, very few people during their lifetime actually execute a will. Many of us have a psychological or emotional difficulty addressing thoughts of a will, or with meeting a solicitor or other persons to instruct the drafting of a will and then executing it. These aversions are very understandable as nothing can be as stressful or as morbid as planning for one's own death. However, as anybody who has been touched by bereavement knows, creating a will during one's lifetime will in fact minimise the grief and distress felt by surviving relatives.

A will also guarantees that the affairs of a deceased person will be dispensed with and distributed far more urgently than someone who dies either without having made a will (intestate) or with an invalid will, thereby minimising stress for surviving loved ones.

A SHORT LIST OF DEFINITIONS

Below you'll find a plain English definition of the different legal terms and expressions that are used to sort out the affairs of someone who has died.

The administrator. Where the deceased hasn't appointed a personal representative (in his or her will), the person looking after the financial situation is known as an administrator.

The beneficiary. A beneficiary is someone who inherits either part or the whole of the deceased's estate.

The deceased. The 'deceased' refers to the person who has died.

The estate. The 'estate', or the 'deceased's estate' is made up of all the assets that the deceased person owned. This includes bank accounts, property, jewellery, stocks and shares, furniture, and so on.

The executor. If the deceased has written a will, he or she will have appointed an executor to ensure that his or her wishes are carried out. Many people appoint several executors, and it is normal for the personal representative to be one of them.

Intestate. If the deceased did not write a will, they are said to have died 'intestate'. The word 'intestacy' refers to the situation where no will exists. What happens to the assets where there is no will is set out in the 1965 Succession Act.

The personal representative. The personal representative is the person ultimately responsible for sorting out and finalising the deceased's affairs.

The Succession Act. This piece of legislation sets down the requirements for a valid will. Under Irish law, a spouse and children are legally entitled to a certain share in the property of a deceased parent or spouse – whether a will has been made or not. As it currently stands, if there are children then the spouse's share, by legal right, is at least one-third of the estate. Where there are no children, the spouse is entitled to at least one-half of the estate.

The trustee. If there is some reason why some or all of the deceased's assets cannot be distributed immediately to the beneficiaries, then the will may provide for certain assets or property to be held 'in trust'. This situation might arise, for example, if the deceased was leaving something to someone who was under the age of 18. The person whose responsibility it is to look after such property or assets is called the trustee. Many people appoint more than one trustee in their will.

The will. This is the legal document in which the deceased set out his or her wishes regarding his or her assets.

WHEN THERE IS A WILL

If there is a valid will, the following rules apply:

- On the death of a **married person with no children**, their surviving spouse is entitled to one-half of the deceased's estate.
- On the death of a **married person with children**, their surviving spouse is entitled to a one-third of the deceased's estate.
- The spouse is legally entitled to the appropriate share, regardless of the actual terms of the will. The fact that the parties may have lived apart for many years does not of itself affect their entitlements under the Act.

WHEN THERE IS NO WILL OR NO VALID WILL

In these circumstances, under the Succession Act 1965, the following rules apply:

- On the death of a **married person with no children**, the surviving spouse is entitled to the entire of the deceased's estate.
- On the death of a **married person with children**, their surviving spouse is entitled to two-thirds of the deceased's estate and their children are entitled to the remaining one-third.
- If a **single person or widowed person passes away** without having made a valid will, their next of kin will be entitled to inherit their estate as outlined in the Succession Act 1965.

THE RIGHT OF THE SPOUSE TO INHERIT

A spouse, i.e. somebody who is legally married to another person, is entitled to share in the estate of that person on death regardless of the will made by that person prior to their death.

If a person has made a will and passes away, regardless of what is mentioned in that will (e.g. entire estate left to a third party), the spouse is entitled to one-half of the deceased's estate if there are no children.

If a person has died having made a will with a spouse and children, the spouse is entitled to one-third of the deceased's estate.

The spouse is also entitled to a portion for their own benefit of the family home, namely the place where the husband and wife normally resided prior to the death of a spouse.

However, note that the right to apportion the family home should not exceed the legal right share (i.e., one-half if there are no children; one-third if there are children of the spouse to share in the estate of the deceased).

In order to explain this element of the law more clearly, it may be useful to give an example:

> Mr and Mrs Murphy are legally married. Mr Murphy makes a will. They have no children and live in a house which is registered in Mr Murphy's sole name.
>
> Mr Murphy dies and when his will is read it appears that under his will he has left everything to charity.
>
> The value of Mr Murphy's estate is €2million. Regardless of the will of Mr Murphy, his spouse is entitled to:

- The family home *and*
- One-half of the share of Mr Murphy's estate to include the family home.

If in this example, Mr and Mrs Murphy had children, but the facts were exactly the same, Mrs Murphy would be entitled to only one-third of the value of the estate (to include the family home).

STATUS OF CHILDREN UNDER A WILL

If a party dies leaving children and no surviving spouse, these children will be deemed to be the next of kin of the deceased and entitled to share in the estate of the deceased.

However, they are only entitled to share in the estate of the deceased because they are the next of kin of the deceased for legal purposes.

It is a common misconception that an individual has an obligation to their children to leave a portion of their estate to them. Unlike a wife or husband (spouse), children over the age of eighteen have no right to share in the estate of their parents and rank as a beneficiary to the estate of a parent purely in their position as next of kin.

A child (again over the age of 18) of a deceased person who has been disinherited in a will may challenge this will in the courts on very strict legal grounds to the extent that the parent **failed during their lifetime to make proper provision for the child.**

Just because a child has a right to challenge the will of a parent, this does not mean that the parent has an obligation under law to leave anything to that child in their will. Irish children beware!

Confusion often arises because spouses have certain rights in the estate of a deceased person by virtue of the fact that they were married to the deceased, plus the fact that children often share in the estates of deceased persons not because they are children, but because they are legally the next of kin of the deceased. In other words, a party may make a will during their lifetime wherein they endeavour to disinherit their spouse and children. Once he or she has passed away, the spouse has an automatic right to share in the estate despite what is in the will but the children do not have such automatic right. However, if a party dies without making a will, the children may share in the estate of the deceased person by virtue of the fact that they are the next of kin.

NON-MARITAL CHILDREN

The status of children born to an individual outside marriage is exactly the same as children born inside marriage.

For example, a couple may have never married but have three children. If one of them does not make a will and passes away, the partner will not be entitled to any share in the estate of the deceased, but rather the children as next of kin will be entitled to a share. In this example, if the deceased had made a will leaving everything to the surviving partner and the children over the age of eighteen, the children have no right to share in the estate of the parent who has passed away.

The matter becomes even more complicated in the following example:

> A married couple have three children. One party to the marriage has a fourth child outside of the marriage with another party. This parent passes away without making a will: all four children as next of kin are entitled to a proportionate share in the estate of the deceased parent.

NON-MARITAL RELATIONSHIPS

Non-marital partners have no right to share in the estate of a deceased partner. For example, a man and woman may have lived together all their lives as husband and wife (often referred to as a common-law husband or wife) and the male partner passes away without having made a will.

The surviving partner has no right to share in the estate of the deceased and the estate will be inherited by the next of kin of the deceased person, e.g. parents, brother or perhaps even children.

Accordingly, one can envisage the situation whereby a man and woman live together as husband and wife for thirty years and have three children but never marry. One party to the relationship passes away without having made a will and the surviving party is entitled to no benefit in the estate of the deceased. Instead, the estate passes to the children of the couple as the next of kin, legally speaking, of the deceased person.

THE ROLE OF THE PERSONAL REPRESENTATIVE

When someone dies, it usually becomes clear fairly quickly whether he or she has left a will. If they have, then this will list one or more executors, one of whom will be appointed as the **personal representative** of the deceased.

If a personal representative has not been appointed in the will, or no valid will is in existence, then the courts will appoint an administrator to act as a personal representative (usually the next of kin).

It is the personal representative's or administrator's responsibility to finalise the deceased's affairs. The administrator or executor is usually referred to as the personal representative. The personal representative should within a reasonable period of time collect the deceased's assets, pay any debts and distribute the remaining assets to the beneficiaries.

Obtaining the Grant of Representation

The primary obligation of the personal representative is to obtain a **Grant of Representation**. If somebody has died with a will, they will be entitled to a **Grant of Probate**, and if somebody has died intestate (without a will), they will be granted a **Grant of Representation**.

The grant is made by the Probate Office, which is an office of the High Court. If the application is made for the grant in Dublin, one applies to the Probate Office in the Four Courts. Outside of Dublin, every County Hall or Registrar will have a Probate Office. Only somebody with a valid will may apply for probate. If somebody has died with an invalid will or no will, the personal representative applies for administration rights called **Letters of Administration**.

Commonly, regardless of the status of the will and the estate of the deceased person, somebody is said *to apply for Probate* even if they are applying for a **Grant of Administration.**

The Grant of Representation (i.e., Grant of Probate or Letters of Administration) is an Order from the High Court which allows the party to whom the grant is issued to deal with the affairs of the deceased person. It is effectively a Court Order or an authority from the Court for this person to step into the shoes of the deceased person and carry out the wishes of the deceased person if there is a will or alternatively, deal with the estate as per the law of the land if there is no will.

A Grant of Representation allows the personal representative to execute documents for the sale of property, the lease of property and the remortgage of same, for the transfer of property to other members of the family who may inherit under the will or the law, to close bank accounts, transfer money and discharge debts.

In order to obtain the grant, clearance must be sought from the Revenue Commissioners.

The importance of notifying the tax office

Prior to obtaining the Grant of Representation from the Probate Office, the Personal Representative must settle the deceased's **tax affairs.** Furthermore, before financial institutions can release money, the personal representative must apply to the Capital Taxes Office of the Revenue Commissioners for something called a **Letter of Clearance** – effectively stating that all taxes have been paid to date or are in the process of being paid. Without this Letter of Clearance from the Revenue Commissioners, banks, building societies, credit unions, insurance companies and other financial institutions are prohibited by law from releasing any monies other than those:

- held in a current account lodged or
- deposited in the joint names of the deceased and another person or persons.

The only exception to this is money that is being held in the joint names of the deceased and his or her surviving spouse.

Furthermore, the application to the Revenue Commissioners will also contain details of the beneficiaries to the estate of the deceased person.

A Personal Representative must obtain a Grant from the Probate Office to deal with the affairs of the deceased person. The Probate Office will not release such a Grant until such time as the **Tax Clearance Certificate** or **Letter** of Clearance from the Revenue Commissioners has been delivered which does not just address the tax affairs of the deceased but also the tax affairs of the beneficiaries to the estate.

What the personal representative could be liable for

If the personal representative makes payments or passes assets to the beneficiaries of the estate without paying any outstanding tax liabilities, he or she will be liable to pay the tax out of his or her own pocket. By the same token if, as personal representative, you fail to claim a tax rebate due to the deceased, then the beneficiaries will be entitled to come after you for this money.

If the deceased was an employee, there may be a PAYE tax rebate due. This can be arranged by asking the deceased's employer to send a Form P45 to the tax office. If, on the other hand, the deceased was self-employed, you will need to file an outstanding income tax return and business accounts to the deceased's tax office. Don't forget that you may also need to deal with outstanding VAT and PRSI matters.

Before the Probate Office can process the application for the Grant of Representation, they will require a certified Revenue Affidavit from the Capital Taxes Office. It is the responsibility of the personal representative to provide the Revenue Commissioners with a Revenue Affidavit. The Revenue Affidavit requires the personal representative to supply:

- full details of the deceased's assets and liabilities
- information about assets passing outside of the will
- details of the beneficiaries and the value of the benefits taken.

How the assets are passed on

The deceased's assets will be passed on to the beneficiaries in one of three different ways:

1 Assets left by will pass to the beneficiaries in accordance with the terms of the will.

2 If there is no will, assets that would otherwise have passed by will instead pass by special laws laid down by law.

3 Assets may also pass outside of the will or intestacy.

The benefits of Joint Ownership

Regardless of the law in relationship to intestacy or the will drafted by an individual, the **Rule of Joint Ownership** is extremely important. Joint Ownership effectively takes precedence over either the law or the will.

Under law, two parties or more can own property in two ways. They can own it as **Tenants in Common** or by **Joint Tenancy**. I do not propose to set out in depth details of the differences between Joint Tenancy and Tenants in Common as this is a very particular legal issue, but it is important that the concept be understood – particularly in relation to any post-death planning.

When two parties or more are said to own property as Tenants in Common, they are said to own shares in that property. For example:

> Mr Murphy and Mr Smith buy a house as **Tenants in Common**. They own a half share each. On the death of either person, their share is passed on to that person's devisees or heirs, either by will or by intestate succession.

If in our example given above, Mr Murphy and Mr Smith buy a property and own the same as **joint tenants**, they do not own shares in the property but rather they own the property jointly.

If Mr Smith were to die, Mr Murphy would be the surviving/remaining owner of the property and would be deemed to automatically inherit the property. If, for example, Mr Murphy, Mr Smith and Mr Jones were to purchase a property as **joint owners** and Mr Smith were to pass away, Mr Murphy and Mr Jones would be the surviving joint owners. If Mr Jones were then to pass away Mr Murphy would be the remaining owner of the property.

The relevance of Joint Ownership is extremely pertinent, particularly in relation to family financial planning. If a husband and wife have bank accounts in joint names, they do not own shares in this bank account but rather they own the bank account jointly. If the husband or wife pass away, the surviving spouse is said to be the surviving or remaining owner of the property, i.e., the bank account.

The same concept applies to all property, including the family home. If a family home is held in joint names, neither the husband nor wife own a share of the property but rather own the property jointly. If one party passes away the other is deemed to be the surviving owner of the property.

Regardless of the law or any will made, if property is held jointly it cannot be severed.

HOW IS IT THAT ASSETS CAN PASS OUTSIDE OF THE WILL OR INTESTACY?

This is best explained by an example. The deceased may have taken out a life insurance policy or pension scheme where the beneficiaries have been named. Under these circumstances, the insurance or pension company would pay the beneficiaries directly without any reference to the will or estate.

THE MONEY DOCTOR SAYS...

- Sorting out the financial dealings of someone who has passed on is an emotional business. Help whoever will be looking after your affairs by making a proper will and keeping a file somewhere containing all your financial documents.

- Many parties believe that there is no necessity to make a will as they are happy to allow their spouse or their next of kin inherit as per the Succession Act Rules. However, a will should *always* be made – this means that the estate is distributed more quickly and also distributed in accordance with your wishes – there may be relatives, next of kin or bequests you may want to acknowledge. Remember it is also a simple process – you will need two independent witnesses (who cannot gain from the will) and a nominated person to execute your wishes (executor/executrix), then date the will and sign it.

- It is extremely important if you are involved in a non-marital relationship to ensure that you have proper wills drafted to ensure inheritance for your surviving partner and your or their children.

- It is also important to take professional and perhaps legal advice in relation to the drafting and execution of a will especially where there are complications. Many homemade wills can be ineffective and can often lead to further confusion after death. Remember: the bulk of wealth in Ireland is in property – to convey the transfer of ownership, a solicitor will be required to effect same.

- One other reason for making a will is you can direct who is your Personal Representative and who is charged with the responsibility of dealing with your affairs after your death. This way, you will avoid any application to the Courts to appoint somebody who is inappropriate for that purpose.

- Many people apply to the Revenue Commissioners and the Probate Office to be appointed as the Personal Representative of the deceased themselves. Both the Revenue Commissioners and the Probate Office are extremely co-operative when dealing with members of the public. Again, depending on the complexity of the estate, legal accounting and financial advice should be sought prior to contact with these offices.

- Ensure that all family and marital property is held jointly, including the family home – it is better for all concerned.

- If involved in a non-marital relationship, both partners should ensure that all property is held *jointly* as the death of one partner will ensure the other partner inherits, which is denied under law or via the will.

APPENDIX 1
LEARN TO SPEAK THE LANGUAGE

A QUICK GUIDE TO THE MOST IMPORTANT 'PERSONAL FINANCE' TERMINOLOGY

One of the first things about finance that puts people off is the language. The moment an expert starts to bandy around terms like 'dividend', 'yield', 'compound interest' and 'net present value' it can all start to sound very intimidating.

Like every other area of life, finance has a specialised language. It has its own jargon. Jargon is actually very useful – we need precise terms that are clearly defined so that there is no confusion about what is being said. On the other hand, if you don't understand what the jargon means, you are automatically at a disadvantage. This is something which I believe many financial institutions use to confuse their customers. After all, customers who don't understand something are hardly in a position to ask awkward questions – or to compare value for money.

In this appendix then we will look at four important terms used in personal finance. Never again will you be dependent on someone else to explain any of the following to you:

1   Percentages.
2   The difference between **capital** and **income**.
3   **Compound interest**.
4   **Gearing**.

Please note that other terminology you may find useful is explained in the 'Jargon Buster' section on www.moneydoctor.ie.

PERCENTAGES MADE EASY

You are not alone

If you aren't entirely comfortable with percentages you are not alone. In a survey designed to test graduates on their knowledge of percentages, only 8% could calculate a percentage accurately, and only 19% actually understood what a percentage was. In other words, more than eight out of ten people with a third-level education were completely at sea when it came to one of the key mathematical concepts used in personal finance. Under the circumstances, is it any wonder that the majority of people struggle to sort out their money matters?

What is a percentage?

The word 'percentage' literally means 'parts per 100' – *cent* being the Latin word for 100. Because percentages always deal with parts per hundred, they allow you to compare things that would be very difficult to compare otherwise. They are particularly useful when it comes to choosing a loan or deciding on the relative worth of different investment opportunities.

How to work out percentages

You calculate the percentage by turning your numbers into a fraction, dividing it out and then multiplying by 100.

Imagine that you have three apple trees and you want to know which one of the trees produces the highest number of good – as opposed to rotten – apples. When you harvest the apples from each tree you keep a note of the total number of apples picked and the number of apples that have to be thrown away. Your note looks like this:

Tree	Apples on tree	Apples spoiled
A	750	150
B	550	88
C	670	101

Clearly, from the above figures, it isn't easy to gauge which is your best tree. However, if you express the figures in percentage terms it will immediately become obvious.

On Tree A, 150 out of the 750 were rotten. So your calculation would look like this:

$$\frac{150}{750} \times 100 = 20 \text{ percent}$$

If you were using a calculator you would key it in like this:

150 ÷ 750 = 0.2 x 100 = (answer 20)

For Tree B, 88 apples out of the 550 were rotten, so the calculation would be like this:

$$\frac{88}{550} \times 100 = 16 \text{ percent}$$

For Tree C, 101 apples out of the 670 were rotten, so the calculation would be like this:

$$\frac{101}{670} \times 100 = 15 \text{ percent}$$

Converting the numbers to percentages allows us to make a fair comparison between the 'performance' of the apple trees. So, 20% of the apples on Tree A were rotten; 16% of the apples on Tree B were rotten; but just 15% of the apples on Tree C were rotten – making it the best-performing apple tree in the orchard!

It is hard enough comparing apple trees with apple trees – but even harder to compare apple trees with – say – orange trees. This is where percentages come in so useful. By giving everything a base of 100, we can compare things which aren't alike in other ways.

Now let's put percentages into context – you are told the yield in a property you wish to buy is 6% while the internal rate of return (IRR) is 11%. The first element, the yield, is the return or rental income in proportion to the cost of the property excluding stamp duty and costs.

For example, an investment property costing €300,000 with a rental income of €18,000 per annum will give you an initial rental yield of 6% per annum. Capital growth on the property is expected over the next few years and just taking the first five years of ownership together with the yield, the combination is called the Internal Rate of Return (IRR) and is generally in excess of the initial yield. If in five years' time the property is worth €450,000 the returns would be:

- Growth = 50% (five years)
- Annual rental yield = 6%
- IRR = 16% per annum (on an un-geared investment and before tax).

> ### MONEY DOCTOR WEALTH WARNING
>
> ### *Don't trust your calculator!*
>
> Don't always believe the answer the calculator gives you. Why not? Because the tiniest slip of your finger could give you a completely wrong answer without you being aware of it. Here are five things you can do to avoid calculator error:
>
> 1 Estimate your answer before you begin a calculation.
>
> 2 Do every calculation twice.
>
> 3 Know your calculator.
>
> 4 Don't be overawed by your calculator.
>
> 5 Hang on to common sense and what you know.

THE VITAL DIFFERENCE BETWEEN CAPITAL AND INCOME

All money is not equal

One of the most important financial concepts to understand is the difference between capital and income. Capital is something – it could be money, a property, shares or some other investment – that generates an income for whoever owns it. A good way to remember the difference is to think of a fruit tree. The tree itself is the 'capital'. The fruit it produces is the 'income'. You continue to own the tree (capital) and it continues to bear fruit (income) every year. Your wage or salary is the income which comes from the capital of your labour – hence, the expression 'human capital'. Money is not just money – it is either capital or income.

And then there is 'interest'

When you own capital and it produces an income you have a number of choices:

- You can hold on to the capital and spend the income.
- You can hold on to the capital, add the income to it, and generate even more income.
- You can dispose of some or all of the capital and thus reduce the income you receive.

Let's use the example of chickens and eggs! You have some hens (capital) which lay eggs (income). You can do one of three things:

1   You can hold on to the chickens (capital) and eat the eggs (income).

2   You can hold on to the chickens (capital) and leave the eggs to hatch into more chickens (more capital) that in turn will produce even more eggs (income) for you.

3   You can eat your chickens (thus eating into your capital) and thus reduce the total amount of eggs (income) you receive.

There are lots of different names for the income produced by capital. In the case of property, for instance, it is called 'rental income'. In the case of a cash deposit in a bank it is called 'interest'.

THE MIRACLE OF COMPOUND INTEREST

A financial concept that can make or break you

When you are earning it, it has the power to make you very rich. When you are paying it, it has the power to make you very poor. Albert Einstein described it as 'the greatest mathematical discovery of all time'. It is the reason why banks, building societies, credit card companies and other financial institutions make so much profit from lending money. And it is the reason why ordinary investors can make themselves rich simply by doing nothing. It is the fiendishly simple concept of 'compound interest'.

Compound interest in one easy lesson

Perhaps the easiest way to understand compound interest is to look at a hypothetical example. Imagine that you have €1,000 and that you invest it in a savings account which pays interest at a rate of 10% per year. At the end of one year you will be entitled to €100 interest. If you withdraw this interest but leave your capital, at the end of the second year you will be entitled to another €100 interest. Supposing, however, that you don't withdraw the interest but leave it to 'compound'. At the end of your first year your €1,000 is worth €1,100. At the end of your second year you will have earned €110 interest, meaning that your original €1,000 is worth €1,210. Put another way your interest is earning you more interest.

You will sometimes see the initials **CAR** in relation to interest. This is the **compound annual rate**… in other words it is the amount of interest you will receive if you keep adding your interest to your capital in the way I have just described.

Now let's look at a real example:

According to research, the Irish stock market has produced an annual average return of 14% since 1989. At this rate, if you invested €1,000 today it would be worth €3,700 in less than ten years.

Still not impressed? How much do you think your money would grow by if, at the age of 25, you had started saving €100 a month (that's €25 a week) for just 10 years at the same return? €15,000? €18,000? You are not close. At the age of 35 your money would be worth €25,000. Better still, at the age 65 your money would be worth €1.5 million!

No wonder lenders love you

When you **borrow** money, compound interest is working against you. Supposing, for instance, you borrow €5,000 on a credit card at an interest rate of 15% – which isn't high by today's standards. The credit card company allow you to make a minimum payment of 1.5% each month. After two years, you will still owe approx. €4,700, having made repayments of €1,750, of which €1,450 has been swallowed up in interest. Work out for yourself how long it will take you to pay off the full debt!

Compound interest is your greatest enemy and your greatest ally. When you are in debt, it works against you. But when you have money to invest you can make compound interest really work for you.

GEARING

Allowing other people to make you rich

Using borrowed money to buy an asset is called **gearing**. If you can make it work in your favour, gearing can dramatically boost your profits. For instance:

Supposing you buy a €200,000 apartment using a €40,000 deposit and a €160,000 mortgage. After one year the apartment is worth €240,000. It isn't just that you have made a €40,000 profit – you've actually doubled the €40,000 you originally invested. In other words, you've achieved a 100% gain in just 12 months.

Even if you deduct the mortgage interest you've had to pay for the year you've owned your apartment – you have still done very well. However, what goes up can also come down. In the UK between 1987 and 1989 house prices fell by around one-third. If this happened to someone selling an apartment they bought for €100,000 using an €80,000 mortgage they would not only have seen their €20,000 deposit wiped out they would owe an additional €13,333 (the difference between the mortgage of €80,000 and the €66,666 you would get for the apartment). When this happens it is called being in '**negative equity**'.

> Gearing is the easiest and most effective way of increasing the potential profit from any investment. It is also the most effective way of increasing the potential loss, something every investor contemplating gearing would be well advised to remember.

There is a commonly held view that owning property is a one-way bet. But in the recent history of many European countries there have been periods when residential property prices fell. In fact, over the long term the Irish stock market has outperformed Irish property. Furthermore, it is vitally important to diversify your investments – thus spreading your risk.

> Many people re-mortgage their homes in order to have a deposit with which to buy a second investment property. This can be very sensible. However, if you have an existing mortgage on your home it might make more sense to pay that off first and then to invest in another area – such as the stock market. It very much depends on your circumstances.

Without gearing, most of us would never be able to own our own homes. It also allows us to make other, highly lucrative investments. Nevertheless, you should think carefully before you embark on any investment that requires you to borrow money. You want to make sure that the investment is going to earn you more than the loan is going to cost you.

THE MONEY DOCTOR SAYS...

- It is well worth your while to practise calculating percentages as these are the most common way of comparing both investment and lending products.

- If you are trying to remember the difference between capital and income think of an apple tree. The tree is your capital and its annual crop of fruit is your income.

- Compound interest can make you rich and it can make you poor, too. In the case of an investment it is the process whereby the interest you earn from something is added to the capital to produce even more interest. In the case of a loan it is the process whereby the interest you owe is added to the capital making it harder to get out of debt.

- Gearing allows you to buy an asset with borrowed money. There is no better way to achieve dramatic investment returns but, remember, it can work the other way, too.

- You'll find a full explanation of all the most commonly used financial expressions and terms in the 'Jargon Buster' at www.moneydoctor.ie.

APPENDIX 2
DECISION TREES

What to do about your pension arrangements if you are self-employed

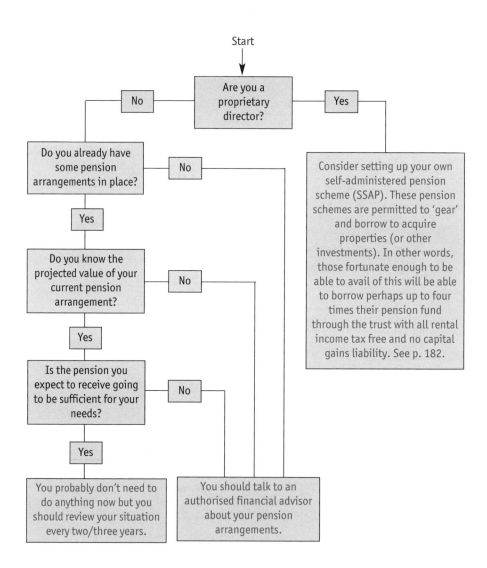

What to do about your pension arrangements if you are an employee

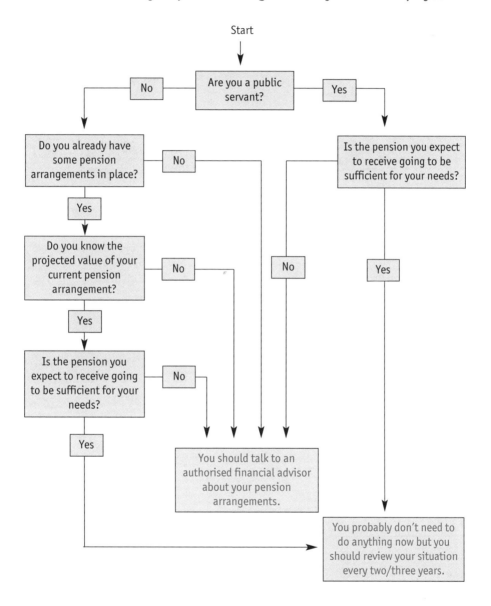

How to generate a regular income from a lump sum

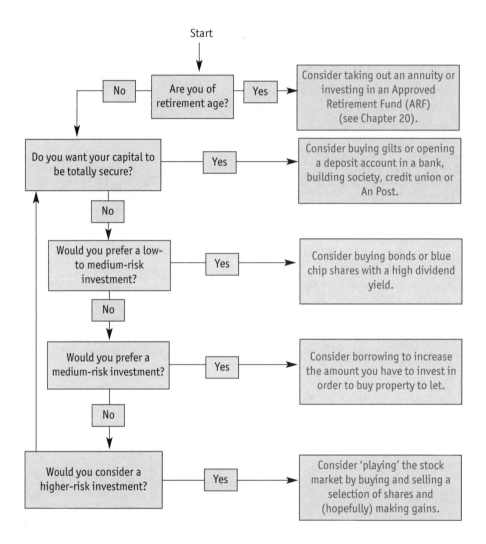

Investment options at retirement for the self-employed

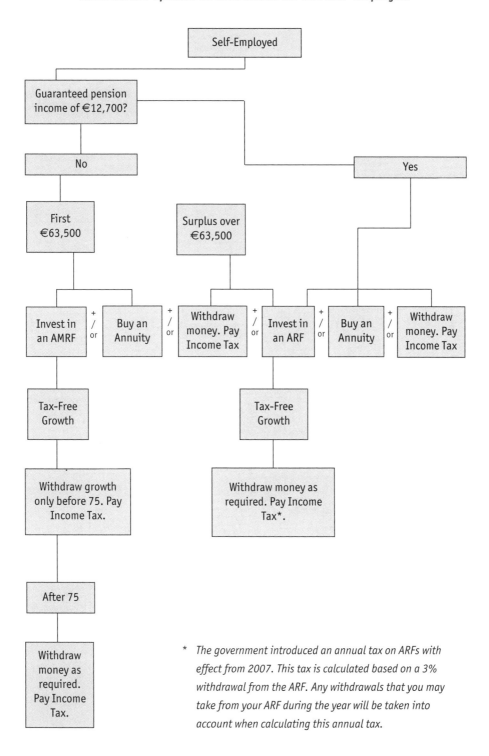

* The government introduced an annual tax on ARFs with effect from 2007. This tax is calculated based on a 3% withdrawal from the ARF. Any withdrawals that you may take from your ARF during the year will be taken into account when calculating this annual tax.

How to create a financial plan

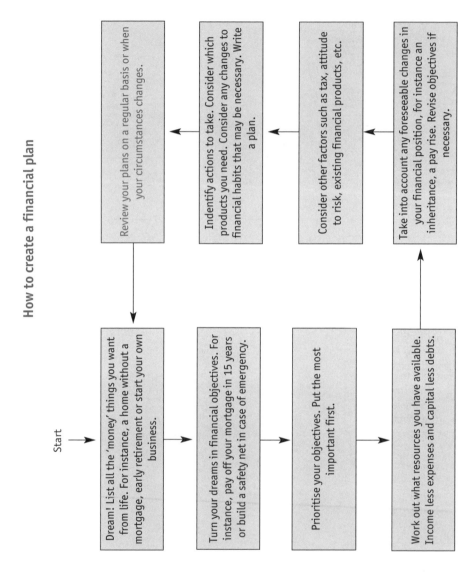

Start

Dream! List all the 'money' things you want from life. For instance, a home without a mortgage, early retirement or start your own business.

Turn your dreams in financial objectives. For instance, pay off your mortgage in 15 years or build a safety net in case of emergency.

Prioritise your objectives. Put the most important first.

Work out what resources you have available. Income less expenses and capital less debts.

Take into account any foreseeable changes in your financial position, for instance an inheritance, a pay rise. Revise objectives if necessary.

Consider other factors such as tax, attitude to risk, existing financial products, etc.

Indentify actions to take. Consider which products you need. Consider any changes to financial habits that may be necessary. Write a plan.

Review your plans on a regular basis or when your circumstances changes.

Do you need life cover?

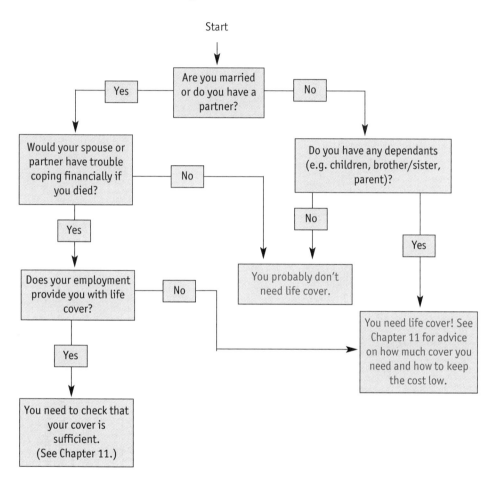

Do you need income protection insurance?

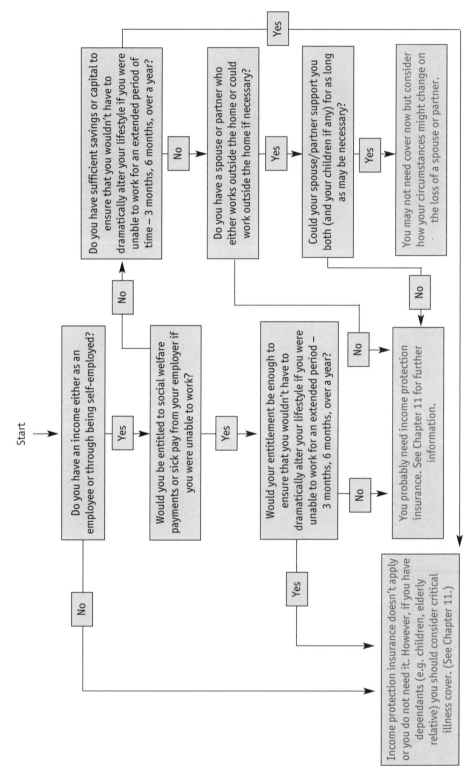

Start

Do you have an income either as an employee or through being self-employed?

Yes → Would you be entitled to social welfare payments or sick pay from your employer if you were unable to work?

No → Income protection insurance doesn't apply or you do not need it. However, if you have dependants (e.g. children, elderly relative) you should consider critical illness cover. (See Chapter 11.)

Yes → Would your entitlement be enough to ensure that you wouldn't have to dramatically alter your lifestyle if you were unable to work for an extended period – 3 months, 6 months, over a year?

Yes → Income protection insurance doesn't apply or you do not need it. However, if you have dependants (e.g. children, elderly relative) you should consider critical illness cover. (See Chapter 11.)

No → You probably need income protection insurance. See Chapter 11 for further information.

No (from social welfare question) → Do you have sufficient savings or capital to ensure that you wouldn't have to dramatically alter your lifestyle if you were unable to work for an extended period of time – 3 months, 6 months, over a year?

No → You probably need income protection insurance. See Chapter 11 for further information.

Yes → Do you have a spouse or partner who either works outside the home or could work outside the home if necessary?

Yes → Could your spouse/partner support you both (and your children if any) for as long as may be necessary?

No → You probably need income protection insurance. See Chapter 11 for further information.

Yes → You may not need cover now but consider how your circumstances might change on the loss of a spouse or partner.

Yes → (loops back to start/top)

Do you need private medical insurance?

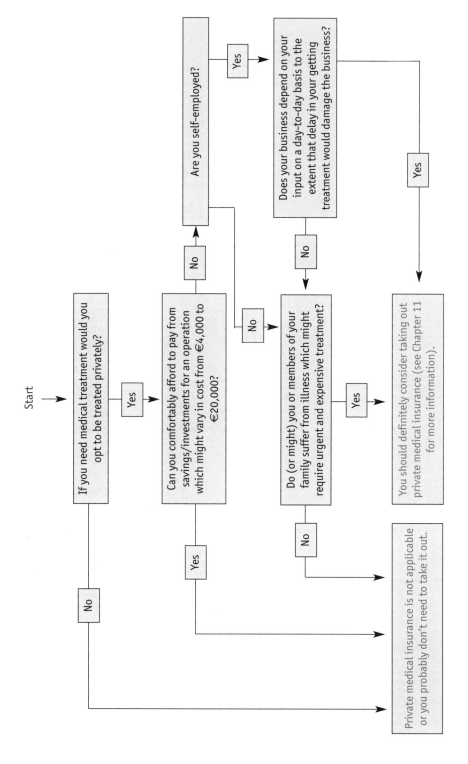

How to maximise the value of regular saving

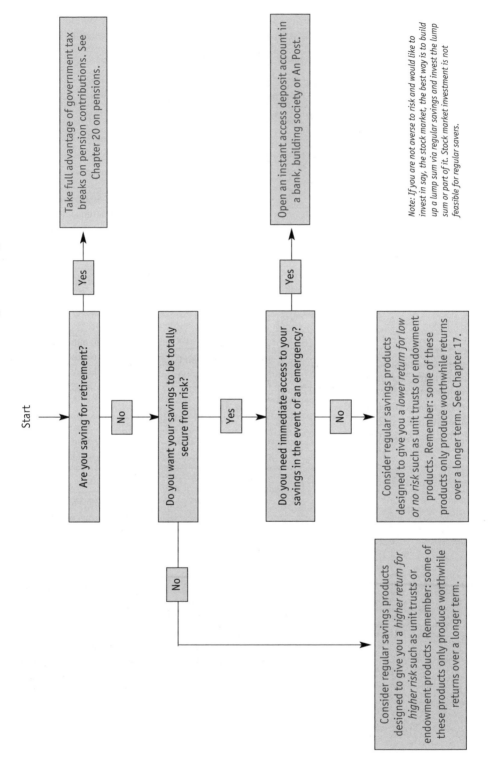

Start

Are you saving for retirement?

Yes → Take full advantage of government tax breaks on pension contributions. See Chapter 20 on pensions.

No

Do you want your savings to be totally secure from risk?

Yes → Do you need immediate access to your savings in the event of an emergency?

Yes → Open an instant access deposit account in a bank, building society or An Post.

No → Consider regular savings products designed to give you a *lower return for low or no risk* such as unit trusts or endowment products. Remember: some of these products only produce worthwhile returns over a longer term. See Chapter 17.

No → Consider regular savings products designed to give you a *higher return for higher risk* such as unit trusts or endowment products. Remember: some of these products only produce worthwhile returns over a longer term.

Note: If you are not averse to risk and would like to invest in say, the stock market, the best way is to build up a lump sum via regular savings and invest the lump sum or part of it. Stock market investment is not feasible for regular savers.

Inheritance on intestacy (no will in existence)

The diagram below outlines how your assets will be distributed under the Terms of the 1965 Succession Act, should you die without a valid will.

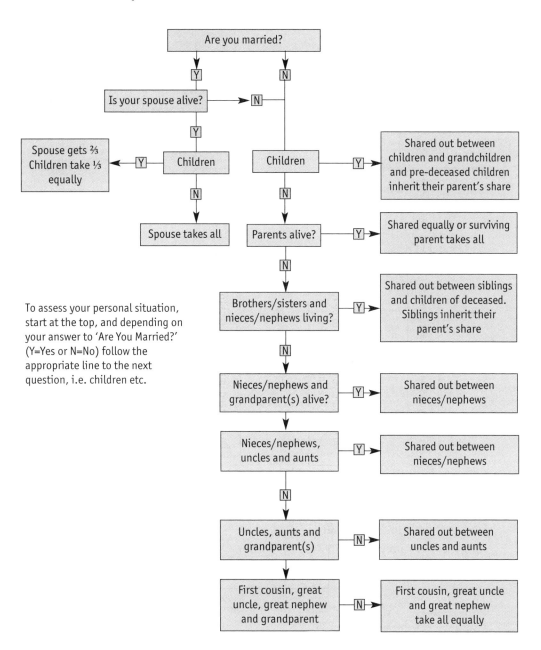

To assess your personal situation, start at the top, and depending on your answer to 'Are You Married?' (Y=Yes or N=No) follow the appropriate line to the next question, i.e. children etc.

APPENDIX 3
TAX RATES AND CREDITS

	BUDGET	
Tax Credits @ 20%	2011	2010
Personal Tax Credits	€	€
Single Person	1,650	1,830
Married (assessed jointly)	3,300	3,660
Widowed Person in year of bereavement	3,300	3,660
Widowed Person – no children	2,190	2,430
Additional allowances for widowed persons in the years after bereavement		
Year 1	3,600	4,000
Year 2	3,150	3,500
Year 3	2,700	3,000
Year 4	2,250	2,500
Year 5	1,800	2,000
One-Parent Family	1,650	1,830
Home Carer's Credit (max.)	810	900
PAYE Tax Credit	1,650	1,830
Age Tax Credit		
(a) Single/Widowed	245	325
(b) Married	490	650
Incapacitated Child Tax Credit	3,300	3,660
Blind Person's Tax Credit (one spouse blind)	1,650	1,830
(both spouses blind)	3,300	3,660

Bin charges – if eligible, the maximum allowance claimable is still €400 per annum on a prior year basis.

Tax allowances @ marginal rate		
Additional Allowance for Guide Dog	825	825

Incapacitated Person –
Allowance for Employing a Carer (max.)   50,000   50,000

Exemption Limits	**2011**	**2010**
(being abolished over a four-year period from 2011)	€	€
Single/widowed 65 years of age or over	18,000	20,000
Married 65 years of age or over	36,000	40,000

Additional for Dependent Children		
1st and 2nd child (each)	575	575
Each subsequent child	830	830
Marginal Relief Tax Rate	40%	40%

Tax Rates and Tax Bands Personal Circumstances	**2011** €	**2010** €
Single/Widowed without dependent children	€32,800 @ 20% Balance @ 41%	€36,400 @ 20% Balance @ 41%
Single/Widowed qualifying for One-Parent Family tax credit	€36,800 @ 20% Balance @ 41%	€40,400 @ 20% Balance @ 41%
Married couple (one spouse with income)	€41,800 @ 20% Balance @ 41%	€45,400 @ 20% Balance @ 41%
Married couple (both spouses with income)	€41,800 @ 20% (with an increase of €23,800 max.) Balance @ 41%	€45,400 @ 20% (with an increase of €27,400 max.) Balance @ 41%

Note: The increase in the standard rate tax band is restricted to the lower of €23,800 or the amount of the income of the spouse with the lower income. The increase is not transferable between spouses.

UNIVERSAL SOCIAL CHARGE (USC)

Income €0 to €4,004 per annum	0%
€4,005 to €10,036 per annum	2%
€10,037 to €16,016 per annum	4%
In excess of €16,016 per annum	7%

APPENDIX 4
TAX COMPUTATION TEMPLATE

	Example		Enter your figures	
Taxable Income	€	€	€	€
Gross income		40,000		
Add: Benefit in kind		1,000 +		+
		41,000		
Deduct: Pension contributions		(2,000) −		−
Total taxable income	A	*39,000*		
Tax payable				
Tax				
32,800 (41,800 married) @ 20%		6,560		
39,000−32,800=6,200 @ 41%		2,542		
Tax before tax credits		*9,102*		
Deduct: Tax credits				
Personal credit				
(3,300 married)	1,650			
PAYE credit				
(each PAYE employee)	1,650	(3,300) −		−
Total tax after credits	B	*5,802*		
Income after tax	A−B	**33,198**		
Deduct: Universal Social Charge				
7% of gross income		(2,800) −		−
Deduct: PRSI				
4% of gross income		(1,600) −		−
Net income after tax, social charge and PRSI		**28,798**		

APPENDIX 5
THE MONEY DOCTOR'S ANNUAL BUDGET ACCOUNT*

Description	Monthly/quarterly	Total
Electricity		€
Home heating (oil/gas)		€
Telecoms (land/mobile/broadband)		€
TV licence/cable TV		€
Household insurance (contents)		€
Car insurance/tax/service/fuel		€
Food/drink/eating out/cinema/concerts		€
School fees/uniform and sportswear; extracurricular school costs		€
Alarm/security		€
Repairs/cleaning/waste/garden		€
Health insurance/medical expenses (incl. dentistry)		€
Christmas and birthday expenses		€
Mini breaks/holidays		€
Clothes/footwear		€
Club subscriptions/donations		€
Other		€
Totals		

* Does not include mortgage and loan repayments, life assurance or pension costs.

When you have totalled your expenditure, divide by 12 and that is the amount you have to provide monthly. All other costs (e.g. capital expenditure, new washing machine, TV, etc.) must be found outside of this budget.

THE MONEY DOCTOR'S STUDENT MONTHLY BUDGET

Category	Totals	
	Weekly	Monthly
Rent		€
Home heating (oil/gas)		€
Mobile		€
Books		€
Course materials		€
Printing/Photocopying		€
Commuter expenses (Bus/Train/DART/Luas)		€
Food		€
Household items/toiletries		€
Medical expenses/dentistry		€
Clothes		€
Gym/club subscriptions		€
Movies/theatre/concerts		€
Other (pubs, clubs & incidentals)		€
Loans		€
Total		

When you have totalled your expenditure, multiply by 12 and that is the money you have to provide annually. All other costs (e.g. holidays, buying iPods, etc.) must be found outside of this budget.

APPENDIX 6
MONEY DOCTOR SERVICES

Money Doctor, the trading name of **Providence Finance Services Limited**, was founded on 1 December 1999 with an intention to *tell* and not *sell*. The company, an **Authorised Advisor** fully regulated by the *Central Bank of Ireland*, has built up an enviable reputation for offering solid, independent and transparent advice with no bias to any one financial supplier, delivered through a first-class service and administrative support.

This is the **company mission statement**:

> *As an independent financial advisory company for debt management, insurance, savings and investments, Money Doctor aspires to give to clients the best financial advice, service and aftercare in the most transparent, honest and professional manner. We are always at your service.*

Now you can experience for yourself a number of services from *Money Doctor*.

MONEY DOCTOR PERSONAL DFINANCE CONSULTANTS

There are THREE types of personal finance consultations:

In-depth – a one-hour consultation, face to face, during which all financial and personal information is extrapolated and considered. A ten- to 12-page comprehensive report is then produced and sent out within five working days. There is at least four to six hours' work covered in these in-depth consultations, at €250 an hour, so we are offering a special €500 all-in deal for this consultation type. Some clients, though, want this service irrespective of the cost as they want to be led by the hand through the maze of financial obstacles and hurdles. See details of this consultation below.

Prescriptive – instead of a *Money Doctor adviser* spending time filling out your personal and financial information onto a form, the client receives the form by email and fills it out. Once completed, the client then sends back that form and arranges for a 20-minute consultation. At this meeting, a *consultation prescription* is written with recommendations, action plans along with financial aids and templates. The cost of this is the same as you would pay for a medical GP – €65. Why so cheap? Because by not having to complete the initial personal details form and the time-sapping comprehensive report, pure unbiased, impartial and experienced advice can be given and noted on a *consultation prescription* page in those 20 minutes. Time is therefore greatly reduced and accordingly the fee to the client is also greatly reduced.

Prescriptive 2 – as above, but the *consultation prescription* is done through email or over the phone.

Each further visit or contact will elicit a fee of €65 for additional financial advice, again, similar in price to a GP visit.

Paying for advice

When you look for independent and authorised financial advice and do not pay a fee, you should ask two questions –

1 How does the adviser earn income?

2 And, when you realise the **ONLY** way the adviser can earn income is to sell a product, the second question has to be 'is there a vested interest in that product?'

One of the reasons that financial advice can be costly is **TIME**.

- *Time* to complete a fact-find – filling out a form covering all the personal and financial details of the client while following compliance regulations.
- *Time* to evaluate the client's financial situation and write up a comprehensive ten- to 12-page report.
- *Time* to review with the client once the client has digested that report.

When you go to your doctor with a particular ailment, the doctor will prescribe there and then, or suggest further investigation by referring you to a specialist. Once you receive the advice you pay the consultation fee. **Money Doctor** treats clients with **financial AILments (A** for apathy, **I** for ignorance and **L** for lack of time) and that is why the company has now come up with this novel solution to remedy those financial ailments but at a similar cost to what you would pay your local GP.

The benefits

Unbiased, impartial advice together with a wealth of financial experience is what you are paying for – **Money Doctor** *tells* NOT *sells* — where the best or safest deposit and mortgage rates are, whether to fix or not, investment advice, how to deal with maxed-out credit cards, negative equity, debt management, pensions, redundancy, insurance, tax credits and allowances.

MONEY DOCTOR PERSONAL FINANCIAL REVIEW (IN-DEPTH)

This is a fee-based full wealth check on every aspect of your finances. We do for your wealth what a good doctor would normally do for your health. There is no point in a piecemeal approach to your finances as you will only find the symptoms of problems, not the causes. We analyse the A to Z of your finances and then recommend and implement any actions required. The **Wheel of Services** includes:

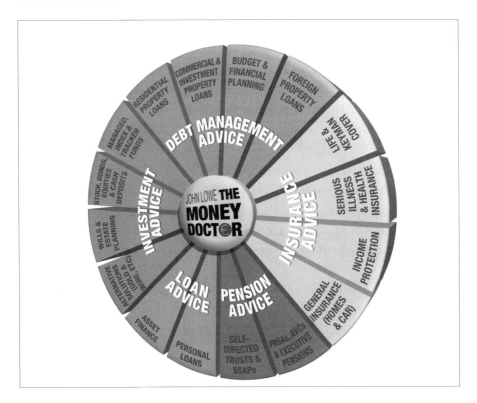

As you can see, all areas of your personal finances are covered, and you WILL save and make money. The consultation takes between one and one-and-a-half hours, followed by a comprehensive report on every aspect of your finances.

The whole point of these reviews is to give you **independent financial advice**. It is for this reason *we charge an hourly fee*. That way you can be certain we aren't being influenced by any commission we might earn from *selling* you a product.

WHAT ACTUALLY HAPPENS?

Stage one

We discuss your financial situation and identify your objectives as per your email, letter or telephone conversation. We make sure that you need to have a financial review in the first place and look broadly at what we might be able to do for you. This is analysed at this stage and there is no charge or obligation for this response. You may of course simply request an **execution-only product** (e.g. life cover on the arrival of the first child) for which there is **NO charge**.

Stage two

We meet. The idea is to go through all of your finances in some detail so that we can put together a step-by-step plan for you. We will make some tentative suggestions on the day to get your feedback and we will also be able to answer any questions you may have. Ideally you will bring to this meeting all the documents relating to your finances.

Stage three

We then write up your new financial plan covering everything we have discussed (saving money, investments, loans, insurance, pensions, etc.). This plan will include detailed advice, tips and useful information.

Stage four

You give us your feedback. We make any adjustments. Then, if required, we can handle anything you want us to act on. For instance, if you decide you want us to arrange a lower-cost mortgage or to move your investments, we will handle all the paperwork. Indeed, one thing we pride ourselves on is always making sure that clients have as little paperwork to plough through as possible.

Therefore, if you do need a **personal one-to-one financial review,** someone to help you navigate through your financial storms and give you solid independent advice and prescriptive remedies if required without bias to any one supplier, then consider the advantages of a consultation with a **Money Doctor adviser**. This is not a one-off consultation but a *relationship for life* and with a company you can rely on whatever your financial issues during the coming years.

MONEY DOCTOR EMPLOYER – EMPLOYEE SEMINARS

'Surviving the Recession – Simple Steps to Transform your Finances' seminar

Last year, The Money Doctor launched an employer-sponsored seminar for the benefit of hard-pressed employees, empowering them to structure and budget their own finances, slash living costs, reduce and manage their debt while also maximising their savings and investments.

How the Money Doctor can help

John Lowe, author of *The Money Doctor* guides and one of Ireland's best known personal finance gurus, is offering employers the opportunity to support and improve the financial education of their employees and, in so doing, to contribute to the bottom line of their own company with greater employee loyalty and productivity.

The Employee seminar package

- One-off seminar or series of seminars covering all aspects of personal finance and planning – 1½-hour duration to include a Q & A session *at any time* to suit employer/employee.
- One-to-one financial counselling also available if required.
- Free work pack including fact sheets and action guides given to all employees.
- Latest *Money Doctor Finance Annual* guide offered to all employees at discount.
- Presented in person by *John Lowe* and his team.
- Complete turn-key, cost-effective package.

Benefits to the employer

Research suggests that a well-executed financial education programme in the workplace is likely to reap great rewards as it is:

- a practical and inexpensive way to help staff with one of their greatest worries: their personal finances
- a cost-effective way of boosting staff loyalty
- highly topical and demonstrates employers understand what is important to employees
- the cornerstone of family-friendly employment policy
- helping to reduce absenteeism (€793 million lost per annum, 3.5% or 8 working days per year – that's 12 million days every year: source Small Firms Association 2008; this study found that back pain/injury and stress were the principal reasons for being absent
- helping to reduce employee turnover rates (this can be calculated in monetary terms)
- increasing employee productivity and competitiveness
- increasing contributions to the company pension scheme.

Benefits to the employees

With the recession having shown its teeth, helping staff to better manage their money and look forward to the future is a major driver to attend this presentation, funded by the employer. This is what they will learn:

- How to plan, set budgets and financial goals.
- Coping with and managing debt quickly and easily.
- Cutting down your banking bills.
- Savings and investments – where the best deals are and maximising the returns.
- Life and health cover – what you should have and what you should drop.
- Pensions – all you ever wanted to know but didn't have the time to ask.
- Insuring your possessions – the right way.
- Fact sheets on:
  - Top 15 Tips – Cars, fuel & electricity
  - Top 20 Tips – Lifestyle & miscellaneous
  - Top 20 Tips – Food drink & household items
  - 10 entrepreneurial ideas to make extra cash

There is a Q & A after each seminar, with the Money Doctor team on hand to answer any immediate queries employees may have.

These seminars will help to change employee behaviour patterns that negatively affect job performance, while, at the same time, build their assets and reduce their debt. They will also far better appreciate the employer-provided benefits, and it may even increase their ability to retire early or at least on time.

Everyone knows the real challenges that businesses are experiencing in the current economy and most employees are willing to work with employers to ensure the survival of the business.

In every aspect of the current workplace environment, including job satisfaction, motivation, morale, perceived stress levels or job security, it is important for employers in survival mode to recognise the value of a fully focused workforce to the eventual recovery of their business.

Reduced incomes, levies, increased living expenses, servicing immediate household debt and concerns about the future value of pensions and savings are causing sleepless nights for a large portion of the population. We are experiencing a huge increase in enquiries from stressed, anxious and worried people seeking help from the *Money Doctor* because they feel they have lost control of their lives as the economic recession grinds on, as unemployment numbers rise and as financial security appears to be evaporating. What employees need is sound, independent, impartial financial advice in plain English from someone they feel they can trust to bring financial stability and options to their lives.

While most surveys have been carried out in America and the UK, it would be fair to say that Ireland's employees would be even more affected than our overseas brethren:

> 'Workers' financial stress may hurt productivity' (*USA Today*)

> 'Poor personal financial planning behaviours breed productivity-inhibiting stress for roughly 15 percent of US workers' (Dr E. Thomas Garman)

> 'Job stress leads to increased absenteeism, tardiness and desire to quit' (*Journal of Occupational and Environmental Medicine*)

'One in four of American workers are seriously financially distressed, causing negative impacts to individuals, families and employers' (Dr E. Thomas Garman)

'Employee financial education is a critical component of employee-wellness programmes' (Dr E. Thomas Garman)

The cost of each seminar is minimum €500 depending on numbers, and includes advice on dealing with debt, managing credit cards, slashing costs, mortgages, savings, investing, insurance and retirement. To ensure that each seminar is focused on employees' areas of interest, the *Money Doctor* also provides a secure **on-line survey service** where employees can indicate their main concerns and worries in confidence so that the seminars that follow can be focused and tailored accordingly.

Each employee also receives personal finance fact sheets, handouts and the opportunity to purchase the bestselling perennial *The Money Doctor Finance Annual*, described by Gay Byrne as *'a terrific book that you can dip in and out of – and written in a very user-friendly way'*, at a special discount price.

For further information and fee structures on both these services, please contact Administration Manager Stephanie Cahill (scahill@moneydoctor.ie, or mobile +353 86 6080284 or email consultation@moneydoctor.ie) to organise an appointment with the *Money Doctor* or your own preferred Money Doctor adviser.

Providence House
Lower Kilmacud Road
Stillorgan
Co Dublin IRELAND

Tel +353 1 278 5555
Fax +353 1 278 5556

Email
consultation@moneydoctor.ie
Web   www.moneydoctor.ie

MONEY DOCTOR WEALTH CHECK

We are currently recruiting experienced self-employed financial professionals. If you have the experience and qualifications, not to mention the desire, enthusiasm and energy to join our Money Doctor adviser team, please call or email recruitment@moneydoctor.ie with your background details.

APPENDIX 7
USEFUL ADDRESSES

THE REVENUE COMMISSIONERS

Check www.revenue.ie for contact details for your local Revenue office numbers, addresses and email addresses.

You can also avail of the Revenue On-line Service at: www.ros.ie or at:

Revenue On-line Service Helpdesk
Revenue On-line Service
2nd Floor, Trident House
Blackrock, Co. Dublin

The opening hours of the ROS Helpdesk (1890 20 11 06) or for callers outside the Republic of Ireland (+ 353 1 7023021) are: Monday to Thursday – 8.30a.m. to 8.30p.m. and Friday – 8.30a.m. to 6.00p.m.

COMPANIES REGISTRATION OFFICE

Email info@cro.ie
Tel. (01) 8045200 LoCall 1890 220 226
Fax: (01) 8045222
DX No. 145001

Companies Registration Office
Parnell House
14 Parnell Square
Dublin 1

THE FINANCIAL REGULATOR (NOW OPERATING AS PART OF THE CENTRAL BANK OF IRELAND)

www.itsyourmoney.ie
  P.O. Box 9138
  College Green
  Dublin 2
  Tel. (01) 2244000
  Fax: (01) 4104900.

THE INSTITUTE OF CHARTERED ACCOUNTANTS IN IRELAND

www.icai.ie
  Burlington House
  Burlington Road
  Dublin 4
  Tel. (01) 6377200
  Fax. (01) 6680842

THE ASSOCIATION OF CHARTERED CERTIFIED ACCOUNTANTS

www.accaglobal.com
  ACCA
  9 Leeson Park
  Dublin 6
  Tel. (01) 4988900
  Fax: (01) 4963615

THE INSTITUTE OF CERTIFIED PUBLIC ACCOUNTANTS IN IRELAND

www.cpaireland.ie
  17 Harcourt Street
  Dublin 2
  Tel. (01) 4251000
  Fax. (01) 4251001

THE IRISH CREDIT BUREAU

www.icb.ie
> ICB House
> Newstead
> Clonskeagh Road
> Dublin 14
> Tel. (01) 2600388
> Fax: (01) 2600390

LAW SOCIETY OF IRELAND

www.lawsociety.ie
> The Law Society of Ireland
> Blackhall Place
> Dublin 7
> Tel. (01) 6724800
> Fax: (01) 6724801

MABS (MONEY ADVICE BUDGETING SERVICES)

www.mabs.ie

Cork MABS

12 Penrose Wharf
Penrose Quay, Cork
Tel. (021) 4552080
Fax: (021) 4552078
Email: cork@mabs.ie

Dublin MABS

70B Patrick Street
Dun Laoghaire
Co. Dublin
Tel. (01) 2302002
Fax: (01) 2300310
Email: dunlaoghaire@mabs.ie

Galway MABS

The Halls (3rd Floor)
Quay Street
Galway Co. Galway
Tel. (091) 569349
Fax: (091) 569478
Email: galway@mabs.ie

Limerick MABS

Unit 9, Tait Business Centre
Dominic Street
Limerick
Tel. (061) 310620
Freephone: 1800 418088
Fax: (061) 404605
Email: limerick@mabs.ie

Waterford MABS

6b Wallace House
Maritana Gate, Canada Street
Waterford
Tel. (051) 857929
Fax: (051) 841264
Email: waterford@mabs.ie

St Vincent de Paul

www.svp.ie
National office
SVP House
91–92 Sean McDermot Street
Dublin 1
Tel. (01) 8386990
Fax. (01) 8387355

The Samaritans

National Helpline 1850 609090
Dublin Branch (01) 872 7700

APPENDIX 8
IMPORTANT TAX DATES

ANNUAL TAX RETURN

> **Form 12** is the short version for those whose main source of income is from an employment or pension (other than a company director for whom there is a separate Form 12) and is therefore taxed under PAYE.

> **Form 11** or **Form 11E** must be completed each year by self-employed persons or those with income not taxed at source.

To download these forms, go directly to www.revenue.ie/forms

The initial instructions for Form 12 are: 'You are hereby required, under Section 879 Taxes Consolidation Act 1997, by the Inspector of Taxes named above to prepare and deliver, on or before 31 October 2010, a tax return on this prescribed form for the year 1 January 2009 to 31 December 2009.'

You must make a return of income on Form 11 if in the year 2008 you:

- opened a foreign bank account
- acquired a material interest in offshore funds in a member state of the EU, EEA, or the OECD with which Ireland has a double taxation agreement and/or
- invested in a Foreign Life Policy issued from a member state of the EU, EEA, or the OECD with which Ireland has a double taxation agreement.

To assist you in completing this return, each section of the form has been colour coded into the different categories of income, tax credits, allowances and reliefs.

All Revenue forms and information leaflets are available from the Revenue Forms and Leaflets Service at LoCall 1890 30 67 06 (ROI only) or from the Revenue's website www.revenue.ie or from any Revenue office.

PENALTIES

The law provides for penalties for failure to make a return, or the making of a false return, or helping to make a false return, or claiming tax credits, allowances or reliefs which are not due. These penalties include fines up to €126,970, up to double the tax in question, and/or imprisonment.

IMPORTANT TAX DATE DEADLINES

October is an important month in the tax calendar as 31 October is the last day by which an individual taxpayer must 'Pay and File' for the tax year ended on the previous 31 October.

The table below uses October as the example because of its importance, and shows what day in October returns and payments become due.

Some returns are required more than once a year (e.g. every month as in the case of PAYE/PRSI) as indicated in Column 2:

Date	Frequency	Category	Description
14	Monthly	Income tax and PAYE/PRSI	Payment of PAYE/PRSI deductions to 30 September.
14	When applicable	Dividend Withholding Tax	Due date for payment and filing of returns of withholding tax on dividends paid by companies in September 2007.
14	Bi-monthly	VAT	Filing of VAT 3 return together with payment of any VAT due.
14	Monthly	VAT	Filing of Intrastat return for September.
21	Annually	Corporation tax	Company year-end 30 November 2007: First instalment due, minimum 72% of total liability for the year.
21	Annually	Corporation tax	Company year-end 30 April 2007: Second instalment due, bringing cumulative payment to 90% of total liability for the year.

21	Annually	Corporation tax	Company year-end 31 January 2007: Payment of balance of corporation tax and filing of corporation tax return and Form 46G.
28	Annually	Company Secretarial	Filing of Annual Returns dated 30 September 2007.
31*	Annually	Corporation tax	Company year-end 30 April 2006: Close companies with undistributed profits may have to make a distribution by this date to avoid surcharge.
31st*	Annually	Company Secretarial	Company year-end 31 January 2007: Final date for holding Annual General Meeting and latest possible Annual Return Date for 2007.
31*	Annually	capital gains tax	Filing of return of capital gains tax for 2006. Payment of capital gains tax on disposals from 1 January 2007 to 30 September 2007.
31st*	Annually		Income tax and Payment of preliminary income PAYE/PRSI tax for 2007. Payment of income tax balance for 2006. Filing of 2006 tax return.
31st*	Annually	Pensions	Payment of retirement annuity premiums, PRSA premiums and personal contributions to occupational pension schemes for tax year 2006 – you must also elect to have these treated as paid in the tax year 2006.
31*	Quarterly	VAT	Filing of VIES return for calendar quarter ending September.

APPENDIX 9
THE QUICK AND EASY WAY TO FIX YOUR FINANCES

Someone once defined economics – or political economy as it should be more properly called – as maximising the usage of scarce resources. Put simply, this mouthful means getting the best use of your money, which in these recessionary times is certainly a scarce commodity.

Over 160 years ago, a certain Mr Micawber quipped, 'Annual income £20, expenditure £19.19s.6p – result happiness. Annual income £20, expenditure £20.0s6p – result misery.' Charles Dickens's great character from *David Copperfield* was spot on all those years ago.

Whether you are a government, business, family or an individual, the philosophy is the same. If expenditure exceeds income, you have *two* choices – earn more or cut costs. For some, earning more is currently a bridge too far and cutting costs is similarly difficult – paring 'til you can pare no more – so whatever your situation is, even if it is bankruptcy, you have to manage your way through it.

Negative equity (when you owe more than the value of your property) only comes into play when assets HAVE to be sold to meet debts. Remember, you were approved on the basis that you had sufficient income (your number one asset) to meet your loan repayments. If you still maintain that income and it is sufficient to meet the agreed payments, then the value of the property is irrelevant, especially if you intend to *stay* and *pay*.

Debt management is not just a simple matter of setting aside a certain sum each month to meet mortgage, loan and other fixed repayments. It requires planning, prudence and a degree of discipline, which many of us may have lost sight of during the boom years. The beginning of a new year is often the time for reflection and now that we've moved into the second decade of the twenty-first century, this could be the time to take control of our lives. There are two keys that will unlock the maze of personal finance: organisation and control. Let us first of all understand some of the issues:

WHAT IS DEBT?

Debt comes in many shapes and forms but can be divided into three simple categories:

1 **Long-term debt.** This consists mainly of mortgages but can also include any other debt with a time span that exceeds seven years.
2 **Short-term debt.** Borrowings that run for fewer than seven years; these can include borrowings for car purchase, furniture, holidays, educational or other family purposes. Increasingly, this also includes conversion of hard-core overdrafts and credit card borrowings.
3 **Running or current debt.** Typically this includes recurring bills that have to be settled every two or three months, i.e. utilities such as electricity, gas, telephone/broadband, etc. Credit cards used for day-to-day expenditure would also be included here.

The explosion in the availability of easy credit from 2002 onwards changed most Irish people's attitudes towards borrowing. The escalating wages/prices spiral led people to believe that borrowings could be comfortably repaid from ever-increasing *disposable* income. Most of us therefore thought nothing of taking on levels of borrowings that would have horrified the previous generation, who had suffered through the lean years of the '80s. We became the *must-have* generation, and although core values and overt religious beliefs have sadly disappeared for many of us, we adopted a 'God will provide' attitude towards coping with debts. Isn't there an old Irish saying, 'God helps those who help themselves'?

The crash of 2007/2008 has meant – for those who have been fortunate enough to hang on to their jobs – sizeable reductions in real income through a combination of pay cuts and income levies. Add to this the interest rate increases for all but holders of tracker or fixed rate mortgages and the pressures on borrowers.

Therefore, for many people the long-term benefits of creating and implementing a financial plan (as described in Chapter 2) must take second place to facing up to the demands of the here and now. For many people the immediate concerns are to:

• bring up their families with decency
• live their day-to-day lives with dignity

- maintain a measure of optimism for the future.

If you are on top of your debts and are able to meet all your repayments, lucky you!

However, nothing is forever, and if your circumstances were to change, my suggestions in this piece could be your saviour.

TAKING STOCK

Where are you now in your financial life and where do you intend to be at the end of this year, or in five years' time? More importantly, where are you now in relation to 12 months ago and what steps have you taken to prevent further drift?

As I said, debt management is more than meeting your loan repayments as they arise. It should be an active rather than a passive exercise and should form part of a strategy of *constant* review. If you are in control of your finances now, it's important to stay there.

Where to start

1   Look at your family's **net monthly income.** While you may not be able to increase your gross earnings, it is important to ensure that you avail of all the tax allowances and credits, etc. For instance, have you claimed your medical expenses, dental costs, bin charges, even your rent or pension relief? *For the last few years*? Well, now there are Irish companies who specialise in **refunding the tax you have paid** from the relief you should have been allowed – and up to four years' worth of refund!

      To find out if you are eligible for any refund on a NO REFUND – NO FEE basis, text **moneydoctor** to **53377** (standard SMS rates apply) and you will be contacted within 48 hours to start the ball rolling. Alternatively, you could contact www.redoaktaxrefunds.ie and by mentioning **moneydoctor** receive a 10% discount on fees for any tax refund obtained through this company.

      Social Welfare and Child Benefit payments, additional jobs and any other forms of income should all be included in your net monthly income.

2   Now consider your **expenditure**. The budget template in Appendix 5 should help you with this. Many of us have no clear idea of our spending

on groceries, travel, entertainment or clothing. On the other hand, we know only too well how much we spend on utilities, heating, insurances, etc. Over a typical two- or three-week period, try to keep a record of all your spending using a diary or notepad. Involve your partner and family so that a full picture of family expenditure can be determined. The initial shock of how much you spend on casual unwanted items will wear off, I promise you! That bar of chocolate you munch every time you fill your car with petrol, the magazine you bought that you don't have time to read ... the list goes on.

3   Go through your bank statements for three months and have a look at **all** standing orders and direct debits. Are you still continuing to pay club subscriptions or making donations to charities which you no longer wish to continue? **Consider each and every financial commitment –** are they all necessary? Remember the Money Doctor mantra: **STOP SPENDING, BUT IF YOU MUST, ENSURE BEST VALUE**

The budget template can then be completed and your expenditure broken into three categories, the **ABC** of expenditure:

A – Fixed outgoings
B – Discretionary spending
C – Savings

Fixed outgoings consist of mortgage/rent, loan repayments, electricity, gas, telephone costs, transport, education, food, essential clothing, insurance, etc.

Discretionary spending covers all non-essentials such as entertainment, holidays, sporting and leisure activities, including alcohol, tobacco, birthdays, anniversaries, christenings and bereavements.

Savings includes the provision of a rainy day fund. Remember that the ideal is to have three to six months' annual income in an accessible account, and pension contributions, educational plans, or other sums set aside to meet future expenditure for you, your partner and/or family.

By now, you should have mapped out your spending on a monthly or weekly basis. You should then look at your fixed outgoings to see if there are cheaper alternatives. Electricity, gas, telephone/broadband and cable television are items that should immediately come to mind, but substantial savings could also be achieved by shopping around for cheaper car and household insurance and by reviewing your life and health insurance. For example, interest rates for both loan and savings products change constantly and what might have been the highest rate for your savings last year could very well be the lowest this year.

Most deposit takers regularly launch a new savings product that has high interest, and after a couple of months slowly drop the rate, hoping the vast majority of initial subscribers will not notice and will allow their apathy to rule, leaving the investment in this product. One deposit taker in 2010 had 41 different deposit accounts advertised on its website.

- 23 of them were not available to new depositors
- Of the 23 existing (and therefore neglected) accounts, 18 attracted 1% or less
- 14 attracted 0.35% or less
- 9 of them attracted 0.1%

I can confirm that these 'customers' were not written to and offered better rates by the deposit taker and I would further confirm that virtually ALL the deposit takers operate in the same manner. Check and recheck your interest rates. Leaving your money in these kinds of accounts will only compound your problem!

Now have a look at your net monthly income and see how it matches up to your outgoings. Remember also that while you would normally reckon on budgeting on a monthly basis, some of your bills such as electricity or gas are payable every two months or quarterly. However, both of these utilities offer budget plans that allow you to make monthly payments which are reviewed regularly based on metred usage.

All of these steps may achieve some savings but essentially they tidy up your finances; something you should do every year, in good times or bad. That is why you need to spend about two hours EVERY month on your finances.

An area where savings can be achieved is in the field of discretionary spending, but this requires discipline. Consider this! You go to the ATM on Friday afternoon and withdraw, say, €80. Check your pocket Monday morning to see how much, if any, remains. How much of this spending can you account for? Or has some of it fallen through a hole in your pocket? This is where the diary will help. Find out what you are spending your money on. Then you will know whether it was frivolous and unnecessary. You may have more important things to do with your money. Prioritise, as the amount of casual and probably valueless spending can be frightening.

I once worked with a newly married couple who had recently bought a house and earned relatively modest salaries. They had their spending mapped out to such an extent that they operated a daily budget and anything more than the cost of a daily newspaper required a council of war. However, they lived comfortably within their means and managed a very good holiday each year.

KNOW YOUR POSITION

By now you will know your financial position and whether meeting your monthly commitments is causing, or is likely to cause, you problems. You should be totally honest with yourself because the early acceptance of difficulties can be crucial. Also bear in mind that life can throw up mini financial crises on a regular basis, so factor some unexpected outgoings into your calculations.

EXAMINE YOUR OPTIONS

Mortgages

Your mortgage repayments are likely to be your biggest commitment but in terms of interest rate they are also the cheapest. If you are fortunate enough to have a *tracker mortgage*, don't be tempted to switch to any other product. Trackers are like gold dust and lenders are using all sorts of means to try and switch you from them. Looking for an extension to your interest-only facility only gives them leverage to discuss that switch. Pay the full capital and interest repayment if needs must.

If, however, you are on a *standard variable rate mortgage*, some of these vary from lender to lender. Check whether your rate is comparative; if it's on the high side you should certainly consider a *fixed rate* with your existing lender, as variable rates are set to continue to rise even though the ECB rate will probably stay at its present level until late 2011. If you are not offered an attractive rate, you could *shop around* to see if you meet the requirements:

- Your home has less than 80% loan-to-value (so no negative equity switches), e.g. your home is worth €400,000 and you owe less than €320,000.

- You have sufficient earning to justify such a switch (generally as a rule of thumb about 4.5 times your annual income for BOTH applicants).

- You are below age 65, though a few lenders will approve a mortgage up to age 70 – this has to be borne in mind if switching.

- You have a good credit history – no missed payments or judgments.

Personal loans

You may also have car loans, furniture or home improvement loans or overdrafts. 'The sniper approach' (as described in Chapter 9, Getting out of debt) should be adopted; this is when you pay off the most expensive debt first if you can. Some personal loans can attract interest rates of over 16%. The greater the risk, the higher the interest rate.

Overdrafts

This is a bank mechanism for giving you money up front: a loan on the promise of an eventual lodgment to the account to *regularise the account*, but charging you through the nose for it. It can be misleading and lure you into a false sense of security. Firstly, overdrafts are hugely expensive – personal overdraft interest rates start at *c.* 13%. Secondly, the set-up charges, referral fees, unpaid fees and surcharges (an additional amount of interest, which could be 1% per month, chargeable if you exceed the overdraft limit without permission) are simply not worth it. The requirement for an overdraft is that the account is in credit for 30 days each year. Managing without an overdraft is the ideal.

Credit cards

So you have 'maxed out' your credit card(s) – you have used the full credit limits on your card(s). What are your options? Paying 3% of the balance each month will effectively create a 20-year loan for you based on high credit card interest rates. If your credit rating is good enough, however, and you are still in satisfactory employment, then you could *switch* to one of the seven credit cards that offer 0% on transferring your balance over to them for a period of time. Three of those cards offer 0% for 10 months. The MBNA credit card company are behind all these three cards. For example, your debt is €2,000. Transfer over the debt, stop using the card, pay off €200 a month for 10 months, at the end of which you have a debt-free credit card. For those who have not paid off their balance, the interest rate applicable after 10 months is a whopping 14.9%. *It will pay to pay off.*

Remember the Irish Credit Bureau in Newstead, Clonskeagh, Dublin 14, tracks all loans, records every transaction and every missed or late payment and judgment – these missed or late payments stay on record for 5 years, while judgments are recorded for life. Call them on 01 2600388 for details of your credit rating. Safe keep your good name.

Overdrafts and credit cards are by far the most expensive borrowing so it makes no sense to use these to bridge the gap between income and expenditure.

You should establish your priorities in terms of debts and look at all your options. If you have an asset you can dispose of in order to reduce your borrowings, such as a holiday home you rarely use or even a second family car, you should be prepared to swallow your pride and take the hard decision. However, it may not be wise to sell, because you cannot attain the right price, or it may not even be possible to sell. Your option here is to negotiate with the lender in the first instance. Deferring any further borrowings until your finances are back on an even keel is of course essential.

If you are sitting on any substantial level of savings it would make sense to use some of them to pay off your most expensive borrowings, particularly credit cards or personal loans. Also, if you are making monthly payments to a savings plan and you have sufficient rainy day funds, you should consider suspending the plan for a period and diverting the payment to reduce your debts.

If you can avail of none of these options then you could consider consolidating all your non-mortgage borrowings against the security of an asset, e.g. your home, or, if allowable, into one unsecured personal loan, if you can show the ability to repay it. Credit unions are still obliging thousands of customers once they have been able to prove repayment capacity.

If your mortgage is sufficiently low and you have good equity in your home, you may be able to convince your mortgage lender to let you top up the mortgage over its remaining term. However, such loans are getting more difficult to obtain, with some of the bank lenders only accepting their own personal loans for limited consolidation.

Consolidation should be regarded as a ONCE-OFF transaction, especially when homes are being used as security. When values were on the rise, loans of this type were easy to approve. We are now living in different times.

ESTABLISHING PRIORITIES

The greatest priority for most of us is to retain the family home. Therefore, maintaining mortgage repayments, no matter how small, is a must. Other lenders can take various legal steps against you and impair your credit rating by registering missed repayments with the Irish Credit Bureau, but your mortgage lender is the only one who can repossess your home. They have a legal charge against it.

BE PROACTIVE

If the warning signs are there in terms of an ever-increasing overdraft or a credit card on which you make the minimum payment each month, now is the time to take action. Don't wait until you've missed payments and the letters start to come through the letterbox. Ignoring warnings helps no one, neither you nor the creditor.

With mortgages, all the lenders have an agreement with the government in terms of how to deal with mortgage arrears and the various time limitations of pursuing legal action, but this only applies when the mortgage holder is already engaged with the lender in relation to those arrears and is actively communicating with them.

Your mortgage lender will already have a dedicated section for dealing solely with borrowers in arrears, or for those who are struggling to keep up their repayments – one such lender's department is euphemistically called Collections and Recoveries. By taking action early, you can head off impending trouble and impress on the lender that you are determined to work your way through any problems.

Even a hopeless situation still has to be managed. Proactivity will certainly be a help.

DEFINE YOUR ENDGAME

Decide what you want to achieve, but also be realistic enough to know what is achievable.

Look at the trend in your finances over the last two years and determine if your current situation is temporary or likely to last for a number of years. Have you got any source of additional income that will come available in the next few years, such as an inheritance, a maturing investment plan or endowment policy, or anything of this nature? Will any of your dependents become self-financing?

Will your partner be able to enter the workforce if s/he is unable to do so at the moment, or will you yourself be able to develop any sources of additional income? Reinvention is fast becoming a buzz word in business circles.

In other words, if you are preparing to approach any of your lenders/creditors to negotiate with them, be sure that you can show them that, as far as possible, you have a plan that is realistic and achievable. Part of this approach will involve cash flows, budgets and any potential dreams and plans for the future that will repay your debts.

First things first

Look at any short-term borrowings for which the repayments are large relative to the size of the loan. If you can manage to extend the terms of these loans without attracting a higher interest rate or any punitive penalties, you should negotiate these first.

If you then decide to renegotiate your mortgage, it's likely that the lender will give you his own version of an income and expenditure worksheet which you can complete from the budget template you've already prepared. Bank current account statements, all loan statements, insurance policies, savings accounts and investments, including pension contributions, will all be required by your lender. Going to the initial requested meeting armed with all these facts and figures will show your lender how serious you are. If time allows, you should also bring along a copy of your most recent Irish Credit Bureau report to corroborate the full extent of your debt.

It is also essential that your spouse/partner, if applicable, accompany you to all meetings to show that you have a joint determination and solidarity in dealing with your problems.

What to expect

Your creditor/lender will have developed a good level of expertise in handling these situations and will have a suite of tailored solutions to cover most scenarios. The most likely financial solutions they will offer include:

- extending the term for mortgages
- interest-only payments for 6 months, 1 year or 2 years
- a moratorium on all repayments – capital and interest – for a number of months

● a top-up mortgage/loan to allow you to consolidate all your other loans.

The first option of **extending the loan term** could be attractive if it alleviates the problem, i.e. eases the cash flow and allows capital and interest payments to be continued. Age may preclude this term extension but you may have offspring who are prepared to join in the loan allowing for such an agreement to extend.

Bear in mind that if you are on a tracker mortgage interest rate, extending your loan may terminate your original loan contract and you may be forced to accept a standard variable or fixed interest rate. Your lender will always send you full details of any switch agreed. You will need to carefully read same.

Interest only for a period will obviously help, as in many cases it can effectively halve your monthly payments. The saying 'You cannot make a silk purse out of a sow's ear' rings true; if you haven't got it, you can't give it. So lenders are forced to grant interest-only extensions for a set time. Obviously this cannot go on forever, but while the property market continues to weaken and sales are flat, currently there is little choice for the lender.

Some of the lenders will not give further interest-only extensions on home loans but will approve payment reductions – this is effectively the same thing.

The third option of **a moratorium on all payments** is purely a very short-term solution and, unless your problem is also short-term e.g. you are due an inheritance, will not really be of any assistance to you.

The final option of the **top-up**, if available, would be the optimum solution where additional funds are approved to consolidate other debts, possibly give you some upfront cash and give you breathing space. In the present climate this is probably the least likely as all lenders have liquidity problems and have enough impairments without potentially taking on more.

In the absence of a top-up, a combination of the first two financial solutions would be most beneficial to you as it would extend the term of the loan and also give you the breathing space of interest-only payments for the initial period.

Give a little

There is give and take in any case of negotiation. Your lenders will expect sacrifices to be made if you are looking to extend facilities with them. Just as in a new enterprise where prudent bankers like to see entrepreneurs invest their own money into the project before agreeing loan facilities, similar is expected of the debtor in these particular circumstances also.

To sum up, if you have debt issues, these are the steps you *have* to take:

1 **Communicate** – do not ignore creditor letters or calls. Placing your head in the sand will only prolong the agony.

2 **Check your income** – are there any other channels of income? If your employment has gone or your business ceased, have you *reinvented* yourself? Financial commitments have to be serviced and income has to be earned. Dust off your CV, prepare that new business plan, create income. Jobseekers' Allowance or Benefit should only be temporary.

3 **Check your expenditure** – do the analysis of your spending; prepare a full budget, which you may need to show your creditors. Show clearly where you have made cuts and sacrifices. *If you haven't got it, you shouldn't spend it.*

4 **Give hope** – if you have lost your job or ceased your business, you must have a plan that will at some stage recreate an income stream and recommence loan payments or fully pay off the debt. Declare your intention and put a time limit on the recovery.

5 **Pay something** – even if your lender does not agree with your proposals, choosing to either ignore demands or pay nothing at all will only escalate repossession or worse, you could end up in prison. If, for example, your interest-only extension request is refused by your lender, you could cancel the lender's direct debit and manually pay the interest each month *on time*. By making these payments, you stand a far better chance of leniency should the lender take you to court.

Finally, take professional advice. Take the example of golf professionals – they still have their coaches.

APPENDIX 10
MONEY – IT'S CHILD'S PLAY

EIGHT WAYS TO TEACH YOUR CHILD ABOUT MONEY

It is never too early to start teaching children how to manage money. Here are a few different, but straightforward ways you can begin:

1 **Start with coins and notes**
   Teach your child to recognise all the coins and notes. This will help them with their arithmetic, as well as their money-management skills.

2 **Make sure they understand what money is**
   The dictionary defines money as a 'medium of exchange', which isn't much help to anyone! Your child should understand that money represents someone's labour; it could be their own, their parents' or even their grandparents'. There is no harm in using a real-life example; you could explain how many hours you have to work in order to pay a typical grocery bill.

3 **Ask them to work for pocket money**
   One of the best ways to ensure that your child understands the value of money is to make them work for their pocket money. You can't, of course, send them down a mine or up a chimney, but even a very small child can clear the table or sweep the floor. Children who never ever got given money tend to value it more as adults and make better financial decisions. Simply handing over money to your child may be one of the worst things you can do for them.

4 **Encourage saving**
   The old-fashioned piggy bank serves an important role. Urge your children to save their money and, as soon as they are old enough, help them to open a bank account. Show them how to save for things they want.
   Teach them about interest, too. Explain how they can put their money to work. Make sure they understand about the rate of return. Older children

may be interested to know that if they earn an average rate of return it should be possible to turn savings of 78 cents a day into €10,000 between the ages of 13 and 30.

5   **Teach them how to shop well**
One of the worst money habits any child can develop is a careless attitude to shopping. Take your children shopping and show them how to search for value. Explain how you make shopping decisions and how it is possible to save substantial sums of money by looking around.

It is a good idea to get them thinking about how much work they have to do to pay for things they want. This is another reason why it is best not to hand over money too easily to them.

6   **Introduce the idea of planning**
Financial planning is the process of deciding what you are going to do with your money, and its principles hold good no matter how young you are. Ask your child the following questions.

* What do you want money for?

* How much do you need?

* When do you need it?

* Where are you going to get it?

* How are you best going to use it to reach your objectives?

A child of ten may want money to buy a particular toy or a birthday present for a beloved parent – if he or she is a kind-hearted child! In showing them how to plan for this you will provide them with a very valuable life skill.

7   **Warn them about borrowing to support a lifestyle**
There are sensible things to borrow for – to buy your own home or to pay for education. What isn't sensible is borrowing for anything that won't outlive the life of the loan – to pay for a holiday, for instance, or to buy new clothes. When you borrow for lifestyle items you can pay two or three times as much for the same thing, thanks to the interest, as someone who pays in cash. Even young children need to be warned.

8   **Show them by example**
Children absorb everything they hear or observe. If you take a positive

attitude towards money and manage it well, then this will be more help to them than anything else you could do.

THE YOUNG MONEY DOCTOR – SMART MONEY FOR SMART KIDS

Lots of top tips to help you make the most of your money – not just for now but for your whole life.

A quick history of money

Q. What do the following items have in common?

A. They are all different forms of money.

Money began with barter –people would 'swap' things. For example, a fisherman might exchange some of his catch for fruit or a hunter might exchange animal skins for spears.

The Pacific Islanders bartered using cowrie shells, the Aztecs cacao beans, the Romans salt or, for bigger items, slaves, but the first people to manufacture coins, and gold coins at that, were the Lydian people in Asia Minor. The most famous Lydian was King Croesus who had so many gold coins people still use the expression 'as rich as Croesus'.

The trouble with barter is that it takes a lot of time and effort. You have to find someone who wants to swap with you and then you have to work out a deal.

Eventually, people invented what the dictionary calls 'a medium of exchange' and what we call **money**. Money is just a way of making it easy to swap things. Most people get money for working and then spend it on what they want or need such as food, clothes, somewhere to live and so on.

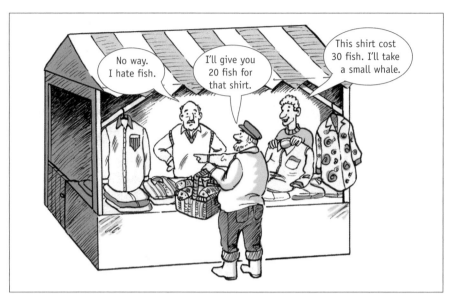

Before money was invented (nothing but trouble!)

After money was invented (everything is easy!)

Well saved! Put your money to work for you

If you get given money for your birthday or at Christmas, or if you earn it (perhaps doing chores), then it is a very good idea to save some or all of it for later.

Why? It will mean that you have some money of your own put aside in case you need it. For example, you may see something you really want in the future, and without savings you won't be able to buy it.

> ***The saving habit is a good one to get into.***

It is important for grown-ups to have money tucked away in case they need to buy something big (like a car) or in an emergency.

Q. Where should you keep your savings?

A. You might keep small amounts in a piggy bank.

But as soon as your savings get to be more than a few euros you should open a bank or credit union account. These 'financial institutions' will pay you money to look after your savings.

The money they pay is called **interest**. Not all banks pay the same amount, so you should shop around to make sure you are getting the highest rate of interest.

Interesting, very interesting. You may be wondering why banks pay interest to look after people's savings. The reason is that they lend this money to other customers who need it and charge them interest. This interest is greater than the interest the bank is paying savers for their money. This is one of the many ways banks make a profit.

The reason why banks pay interest

Animal savings

Animals are savers, too.

- Hedgehogs **save energy** by sleeping all winter.

- Squirrels **save nuts** for when they are hungry.

- Mice **save wool and other warm things** for when they are cold.

- Desert tortoises **save water** for when they are thirsty.

Making your money grow. How €1 a day can become €118,025!

The longer you leave your savings, the more they will grow. It can add up to more than you might imagine because even the 'interest' is earning interest – this is called *compounding*.

For instance, if you start saving €1 a day on your 13th birthday this is what it could be worth in the future:

- At 20 your €1 a day could be worth €3,461

- At 25 your €1 a day could be worth €7,362

- At 30 your €1 a day could be worth €13,093

- At 35 your €1 a day could be worth €21,513

- At 40 your €1 a day could be worth €33,886

How to make a piggy bank

You will need:

- A round balloon

- Sticky tape

- Tube from a kitchen or toilet roll

- Plastic yoghurt pot

- Thin card (from packaging)

- Safety scissors

- PVA glue mix

- Water

- Old newspaper

- Poster paints

- Pipe cleaner

1   Blow up the balloon. Cut up the tube to make four legs (you can use egg carton sections instead) and tape them to the bottom of the balloon.

2   Make the snout from the yoghurt pot (again you could use an egg carton section instead) and tape it to the front of the pig.

3   Using the thin card, cut out triangles for the ears and tape them in place. Mark where the money slot is going to go.

4   Mix the PVA glue with water and stick small strips of newspaper all over the pig's body, legs and ears. Make sure you leave the money slot area free.

5   Once the pig is completely covered and dry (this could take a day or two) pop the balloon through the slot using a pin and paint your pig a colour. Use different coloured paint or felt tip for the eyes, nostrils, eye lashes and trotters.

6   When the paint is dry you can varnish your pig by painting it again with the glue. You can make a tail using the pipe cleaner.

Tip: When you have saved enough in the piggy bank, look for young saver accounts in your local bank, building society, credit union or at An Post. They usually pay much higher rates of interest.

The importance of learning to shop!

There is one simple way that you can make your money go much, much further: **shop well.** Shopping carefully is so important because you can save yourself a lot of money. If you want proof, go into a town centre or shopping centre and compare the price of Coke:

- The price of a 500ml bottle of Coke can range from €1.10 in a supermarket to €1.65 in a corner shop.

- A 2-litre bottle can cost you as little as €1.99. This means that each 500ml amount (there are four 500ml amounts in a 2-litre bottle) is costing you €0.498c each. You can even buy a multi-pack (two 2-litre bottles) for €3.89 – a saving of 4½ cents per bottle if you buy one 2-litre bottle.

- Coke in a restaurant can cost as much as €2.20 per glass – a glass is generally 250ml – four times more expensive than the supermarket price!

In other words, you could save as much as € 0.60c on a 500ml bottle of Coke simply by shopping around.

How to save money when you shop

Here are some of the ways you can save money when you shop:

1   Shop around and compare prices.
2   Don't buy anything without thinking about whether you really want it.
3   If it's something big, see if you can find it on the Internet for less.
4   Ask for some money off! The fact that you are a student may help.
5   See if you can find the same item second-hand for less.
6   Buy more of it! Some things become cheaper the more you buy.
7   Choose something slightly different because it costs less.
8   Buy 'own' brand products, e.g. Tesco cornflakes instead of Kellogg's.
9   Look for special offers and discounts (goods offered for *less* than the recommended price).

Make a money plan

Another great way to make more of your money is to plan ahead. Below is a simple money plan. Why not try to make your own?

Orla's White Mouse Money Plan

My Mum says I can have a white mouse if I pay for everything myself. She doesn't think I can do it ... but I will.

How much do I need? The cage is €15. The exercise wheel is €5. The bedding is €5. The food is €3. The mouse is €2. Mmmm. That comes to €30!

I have €5 in my Money Doctor piggy bank. Well, that's a start. Only €25 to go.

If I do chores around the house I can get paid. If I help Mum and Dad a lot I can probably get them to pay me €5 a week. I still need €25, though. That's five weeks. I can't wait that long.

Mum says I can sell my skateboard. I am *so over* skateboarding. My next door neighbour, Billy, has offered me €10 for it.

Here's my new mouse. I paid for it using my savings of €5, I earned €15 by working for three weeks and I sold my old skateboard for €10.

I believe the only animals that are really scared of mice are elephants. I wonder how much an elephant would cost!

APPENDIX 11: BUDGET 2011 AND THE NATIONAL RECOVERY PLAN

THE NATIONAL RECOVERY PLAN

On 24 November 2010 the government launched its 'National Recovery Plan'. This 140-page document is the blueprint to cover all aspects of Ireland's finances for the next four years ending in 2014, with the intention of achieving a target deficit of 3% of GDP. The figures below from public sector spending over the last few years give an indication of just one of the many reasons why we need to recover:

Increases in public sector spending 2000 to 2008

	2000 €bn	2008 €bn	% change 2000–2008
Social welfare	6,829	17,741	+160%
Education	3,716	8,465	+128%
Health	5,362	15,356	+186%
Capital investment	3,930	9,011	+129%
Total expenditure	25,925	62,395	+141%
Inflation	—	—	+34.8%

Source: The National Recovery Plan, 2011–2014

The plan seeks to reach this target deficit by means of a €15 billion correction over the four-year period, comprising a €10 billion reduction in spending and a €5 billion increase in tax revenues. It is the intention in Budget 2011 to cut spending by €4 billion and increase taxes by €2 billion – a total of €6 billion.

In parallel with this plan, the government has also negotiated an €85 billion rescue plan with the EU/IMF, which was agreed 28 November 2010. This package, known as the bailout, allows the government to extend the four-year plan by an additional year if it becomes apparent that the target deficit cannot be achieved within the originally envisaged timeframe.

Some of the main points of the plan, outside of the major capital expenditure cuts, which will feed through in the next four budgets include:

- Spending on social welfare to be reduced by €2.8 billion.
- Spending on health to be reduced by €1.4 billion.

- Income tax will undergo an overhaul – tax credits and tax bands reduced.
- A significant curtailment of tax relief for personal/employee pension contributions.
- Phased elimination of tax reliefs for over 65s, tax credits on rental and trade union subscriptions.
- Curtailment of artists tax exemption from €250,000 to just €40,000.
- Phased increases in VAT from 21% to 23%.
- Property tax to be introduced in 2012, initially at a rate of €100 per property, pending the development of a new valuation system.
- Increase in the student registration fee.
- Carbon tax to be doubled by 2014.
- New pay scales and pension schemes for new entrants to the public service. Public service numbers will also fall to 2005 levels over the period.
- Water metres to be installed in all properties in 2011 with water charges to be introduced thereafter.

BUDGET 2011

Brian Lenihan, Minister for Finance, delivered his third Budget speech on Tuesday 7 December 2010 and essentially initiated the first elements of the 'National Recovery Plan', described as the harshest ever budget. It also put Mr Lenihan's comment for Budget 2009 into perspective when he said 'The worst is over.'

Bear in mind that Budget 2011 is debated in the Dáil after its delivery and any amendments or clarifications to the measures announced will be incorporated in the Finance Bill 2011, coming into law around early 2011 when we will see the devil is in the detail:

HIGHLIGHTS

- No change to the 12.5% rate of corporation tax, which was reaffirmed as a cornerstone of Irish taxation and economic policy.
- Stamp duty on principal private residences reduced to 1% (but with 2% applicable to any excess over €1million). Abolition of existing residential property reliefs and exemptions, including first-time buyers exemption.
- Removal of €75,036 ceiling for employee PRSI contributions.
- The Income Levy and Health Contribution to be replaced by a single Universal Social Charge (USC).
- PRSI and Universal Social Charge to apply to employee pension contributions.

- 10% reduction to income tax bands and income tax credits.
- Tax-free pension lump sum to be capped at €200,000 and lifetime tax relieved pension pot is reduced to €2.3 million. Tax-free *ex gratia* termination (redundancy) payment is also capped at €200,000.
- Health budget cut by €700 million, social welfare reduced on average by 4%, and Child Benefit cut by €10 for the first two children, €20 for the third child and €10 for each child thereafter.

INCOME TAX

Tax credits and tax bands

- There will be reductions of 10% in both these areas. This will mean, for example, that the personal and PAYE credits will reduce from €1,830 to €1,650 for a single taxpayer. In addition, the tax bands have narrowed, as a result of which the taxpayer will now pay tax at the higher rate of 41% on income in excess of €32,760. This figure was previously €36,400.
- The marginal rate for the self-employed will now come into line with that for PAYE employees.
- The minimum wage will be reduced to €7.65 per hour. However, those on the minimum wage will not be brought into the tax net.

Trade union subscriptions

- The €70 tax credit for trade union subscriptions will now be abolished.

Income and health levies

These will now be merged into a new tax to be known as the **Universal Social Charge** (USC). Up to now the Income Levy did not apply to incomes below €15,028, but rates on the new charge will be:

- 0% on incomes up to €4,004
- 2% on incomes up to €10,036
- 4% on incomes between €10,037 and €16,016
- 7% on incomes above €16,016.

Previously, **medical card holders** aged over 70 and in receipt of private pensions were exempt from health and income levies. In future they will be liable for the USC at a lower rate of 4%.

For the moment, PRSI and USC will remain separate but there are plans to merge them into a single charge at the next Budget.

PRSI

- The PRSI rate for the self-employed will increase from 3% to 4%, the same as employee rates. (The first €127 per week is exempt.)
- The €75,036 ceiling for PRSI is being abolished.

Pensions

- Employee contributions to pension schemes will now be subject to employee PRSI and the new Universal Social Charge.
- Pension tax-free lump sums (TFLS) in excess of €200,000 are to be taxed from 1 January 2011 at the standard rate of income tax (20%).
- Annual earnings limit is being reduced from €150,000 to €115,000.
- Maximum allowable pension fund (known as the Standard Fund Threshold – SFT) is to be reduced from €5.4 million to €2.3 million with effect from Budget day.
- Employers' PRSI saving will go from 10.75% to 5.375% of the employee's contribution.
- Approved Retirement Funds (ARFs) currently require the policyholder to withdraw 3% each year from the fund, known as 'imputed distribution'; this is being increased to 5%. (PRSAs are not currently affected by this.)
- All members of a defined contribution pension arrangement will have access to ARF options on retirement, subject to certain conditions:
  – Members MUST have a minimum guaranteed pension of *c.* €18,000.
  – If there is not a guaranteed pension, and after extraction of the TFLS, then *c.* €120,000 of the pension fund must be placed in an Approved Minimum Retirement Fund (AMRF) – increased from €63,500 – until the pensioner reaches age 75.

Tax breaks

- A total of 25 tax breaks, mainly property related, are being abolished. In particular, Section 23 relief, which applies to properties in certain designated areas, will be severely cut back. Rent Relief will be phased out over eight years. Also, if investors have not claimed their reliefs on certain projects by 2014, these benefits will be withdrawn.
- Approved Share Options Schemes will also be abolished.
- *Ex gratia* termination (redundancy) payments will be subject to tax at the marginal rate on amounts over €200,000.

Deposit Interest Retention Tax

- This tax is being increased by 2% from 25% to 27% on interest earned.
- Long-term investments will also be subject to an additional 2% increase on gains in the investment when exiting. This will now total 30% to include the government tax of 3%.

SOCIAL WELFARE BENEFITS

Child Benefit

- Benefits are being reduced by €10 to €140 per month for the first and second child, by €20 to €167 per month for the third, and by €10 to €177 for the fourth and subsequent children.

Weekly benefits

- The maximum personal rates for all weekly benefits, other than those applicable to those aged 66 or over, are being reduced by €8 per week.
- Payments affected by the reductions will include jobseekers' payments, carer's allowances, disability and widower's pensions.
- Those on fuel allowances are to receive a one-off additional payment of €40 to help them through the recent inclement weather.

Contributory and non-contributory old age pensions

- There is NO change in state pension benefits.

EXCISE DUTIES

Oil and petrol

- From midnight on Budget day, excise duty on petrol and diesel will rise by 4 cent and 2 cent respectively.
- Heating oil will not be affected.

Travel tax

- From March the €10 travel tax will be reduced to €3 as a temporary measure, to be reviewed at the next Budget.

Car scrappage scheme

- This scheme is being extended to 30 June 2011.

VRT

- The VRT refund scheme for hybrid and flexi-fuel vehicles is to be extended to the end of 2012.

Betting tax

- A 1% tax is being introduced for internet punters.

Alcohol and tobacco

- No increases in excise rates on either of these products, mainly to curtail cross-border shopping and cigarette smuggling.

STAMP DUTY

All stamp duty exemptions are now being scrapped. A new simplified system consisting of two rates which will apply to both residential and investment properties will be introduced:

- 1% on properties up to €1m value.
- 2% on properties above €1m value.

The effect of this will be to bring first-time buyers back into the stamp duty net, while the 50% relief for a transfer from parent to child is also abolished.

PUBLIC SECTOR PAY AND PENSIONS

- A salary cap of €250,000 for all public sector and semi-state employees will be introduced and voluntarily embraced by our President Mary McAleese.
- The salaries of the Taoiseach and ministers will be reduced by €14,000 and €10,000 respectively.
- A graded pension reduction will be introduced for existing public service pension recipients.
- A new pension package will be established for future entrants to the public service.
- A car pooling system to be introduced for all ministers and former office holders.
- There will be no further cuts in public service salaries but, under the terms of the Croke Park agreement, employee numbers will reduce by 25,000 by 2014 and further savings to be affected through various efficiencies.

EDUCATION

- Third-level student charges (registration fees) to rise by €500 to €2,000.
- Student grants to be cut by 4%.
- A school transport charge of €50 for primary school pupils to be introduced in September 2011.

OTHER ITEMS

- No changes in corporation tax (currently 12.5%) or VAT rates.
- Business Expansion Scheme to be renamed and revamped; this will require EU approval.
- A flat-rate property tax will be introduced in 2012. In the following years a new valuation system will be used to assess properties on an individual basis.
- Further incentives introduced for local authority tenants to purchase their homes.
- The National Employment Action Plan will be refocused and additional training places will be provided for the unemployed.
- Water charges to be introduced when a metering system has been implemented.
- A new four-year National Solidarity Bond will be introduced in 2011 offering a yearly coupon and a bonus for those who hold the bond to maturity.
- The current tax-free threshold for gift/inheritance tax (Capital Acquisition Tax – CAT) will be reduced by 20% in respect of gifts and inheritances taken on or after 8 December 2010. The new and previous rates for the three different classes are below:

Capital Acquisition Tax thresholds

	2009 (up to 7 April 2009)	2009 (on or after 8 April 2009)	2010	2011
Group A (child)	€542,544	€434,000	€414,799	€331,839
Group B (relative)	€54,254	€43,400	€41,481	€33,185
Group C (other)	€27,127	€21,700	€20,740	€16,592

INDEX

YOUR FINANCIAL NOTES